VOLUME 625   SEPTEMBER 2009

THE ANNALS

of The American Academy of Political
and Social Science

PHYLLIS KANISS, *Executive Editor*

D0080712

The End of Television? Its Impact on The World (So Far)

Special Editors of this Volume

ELIHU KATZ
PADDY SCANNELL

In memory of Michael Gurevitch

Los Angeles | London | New Delhi
Singapore | Washington DC

The American Academy of Political and Social Science

3814 Walnut Street, Fels Institute of Government, University of Pennsylvania,
Philadelphia, PA 19104-6197; (215) 746-6500; (215) 573-3003 (fax); www.aapss.org

Board of Directors
DOUGLAS S. MASSEY, *President*
HEIDI HARTMANN, *Chair*

JULIA ADAMS
FRANCINE D. BLAU
HARRY DeVERTER
FELTON J. EARLS
LEE EPSTEIN
SARA MILLER McCUNE

MARY ANN MEYERS
KLAUS NAUDÉ
KENNETH PREWITT
ROBERT S. SAMPSON
DAVID THORNBURGH

Editors, THE ANNALS
PHYLLIS KANISS, *Executive Editor*   RICHARD D. LAMBERT, *Editor Emeritus*
JULIE ODLAND, *Managing Editor*

Editorial Advisory Board

SCOTT APPLEBY, *University of Notre Dame*
FRANCINE BLAU, *Cornell University*
SIR DAVID COX, *University of Oxford*
LEE EPSTEIN, *Northwestern University*
DEBORAH R. HENSLER, *Stanford University*
DOUGLAS S. MASSEY, *Princeton University*

PAUL DiMAGGIO, *Princeton University*
FELTON EARLS, *Harvard University*
GARY KING, *Harvard University*
ROBERT D. PUTNAM, *Harvard University*
SUSAN S. SILBEY, *Massachusetts Institute of Technology*
MARTA TIENDA, *Princeton University*

Origin and Purpose. The Academy was organized December 14, 1889, to promote the progress of political and social science, especially through publications and meetings. The Academy does not take sides in controverted questions, but seeks to gather and present reliable information to assist the public in forming an intelligent and accurate judgment.

Meetings. The Academy occasionally holds a meeting in the spring extending over two days.

Publications. THE ANNALS of The American Academy of Political and Social Science is the bimonthly publication of the Academy. Each issue contains articles on some prominent social or political problem, written at the invitation of the editors. These volumes constitute important reference works on the topics with which they deal, and they are extensively cited by authorities throughout the United States and abroad.

Membership. Each member of the Academy receives THE ANNALS and may attend the meetings of the Academy. Membership is open only to individuals. Annual dues: $94.00 for the regular paperbound edition (clothbound, $134.00). Members may also purchase single issues of THE ANNALS for $18.00 each (clothbound, $27.00). Student memberships are available for $52.00.

Subscriptions. THE ANNALS of The American Academy of Political and Social Science (ISSN 0002-7162) (J295) is published six times annually—in January, March, May, July, September, and November—by SAGE Publications, 2455 Teller Road, Thousand Oaks, CA 91320. Telephone: (800) 818-SAGE (7243) and (805) 499-0721; Fax/Order line: (805) 375-1700; e-mail: journals@sagepub.com. Copyright © 2009 by The American Academy of Political and Social Science. Institutions may subscribe to THE ANNALS at the annual rate: $714.00 (clothbound, $807.00). Single issues of THE ANNALS may be obtained by individuals who are not members of the Academy for $97.00 each (clothbound, $142.00). Single issues of THE ANNALS have proven to be excellent supplementary texts for classroom use. Direct inquiries regarding adoptions to THE ANNALS c/o SAGE Publications (address below). Periodicals postage paid at Thousand Oaks, California, and at additional mailing offices. POSTMASTER: Send address changes to The Annals of The American Academy of Political and Social Science, c/o SAGE Publications, 2455 Teller Road, Thousand Oaks, CA 91320.

All correspondence concerning membership in the Academy, dues renewals, inquiries about membership status, and/or purchase of single issues of THE ANNALS should be sent to THE ANNALS c/o SAGE Publications, 2455 Teller Road, Thousand Oaks, CA 91320.Telephone: (800) 818-SAGE (7243) and (805) 499-0721; Fax/Order line: (805) 375-1700; e-mail: journals@ sagepub.com. *Please note that orders under $30 must be prepaid.* SAGE affiliates in London and India will assist institutional subscribers abroad with regard to orders, claims, and inquiries for both subscriptions and single issues.

Printed on acid-free paper

THE ANNALS

© 2009 by The American Academy of Political and Social Science

All rights reserved. No part of this volume may be reproduced or utilized in any form or by any means, electronic or mechanical, including photocopying, recording, or by any information storage and retrieval system, without permission in writing from the publisher. All inquiries for reproduction or permission should be sent to SAGE Publications, 2455 Teller Road, Thousand Oaks, CA 91320.

Editorial Office: 3814 Walnut Street, Fels Institute for Government, University of Pennsylvania, Philadelphia, PA 19104-6197.
For information about membership* (individuals only) and subscriptions (institutions), address:
SAGE Publications
2455 Teller Road
Thousand Oaks, CA 91320

For SAGE Publications: Allison Leung (Production) and Sandra Hopps (Marketing)

From India and South Asia, write to:

SAGE PUBLICATIONS INDIA Pvt Ltd
B-42 Panchsheel Enclave, P.O. Box 4109
New Delhi 110 017
INDIA

From Europe, the Middle East, and Africa, write to:

SAGE PUBLICATIONS LTD
1 Oliver's Yard, 55 City Road
London EC1Y 1SP
UNITED KINGDOM

*Please note that members of the Academy receive THE ANNALS with their membership.
International Standard Serial Number ISSN 0002-7162
International Standard Book Number ISBN 978-1-4129-7766-1 (Vol. 625, 2009) paper
International Standard Book Number ISBN 978-1-4129-7767-8 (Vol. 625, 2009) cloth
Manufactured in the United States of America. First printing, September 2009.

For a full list of the databases which articles appearing in *The Annals* can be found at http://www.sagepub.com/journalsProdAbsIdx.nav?prodId=Journal200750.

Information about membership rates, institutional subscriptions, and back issue prices may be found on the facing page.

Advertising. Current rates and specifications may be obtained by writing to The Annals Advertising and Promotion Manager at the Thousand Oaks office (address above). Acceptance of advertising in this journal in no way implies endorsement of the advertised product or service by SAGE or the journal's affiliated society(ies). No endorsement is intended or implied. SAGE reserves the right to reject any advertising it deems as inappropriate for this journal.

Claims. Claims for undelivered copies must be made no later than six months following month of publication. The publisher will supply replacement issues when losses have been sustained in transit and when the reserve stock will permit.

Change of Address. Six weeks' advance notice must be given when notifying of change of address. Please send the old address label along with the new address to the SAGE office address above to ensure proper identification. Please specify name of journal.

THE ANNALS
OF THE AMERICAN ACADEMY OF POLITICAL AND SOCIAL SCIENCE

Volume 625   September 2009

IN THIS ISSUE:

The End of Television? Its Impact on The World (So Far)

Special Editors: ELIHU KATZ
PADDY SCANNELL

FORTHCOMING

The Shape of the New American City
Special Editors: EUGÉNIE L BIRCH and SUSAN M. WACHTER

The End of Television?

By
ELIHU KATZ

For the past few years, a group of experienced media researchers has come together to consider the proposition that the medium of television is approaching its demise and, therefore, that the time has come for looking back to assess its impact and to pronounce its eulogies. This is a report on the progress we have made so far. It divides into two parts. Part One questions the proposition itself. Part Two supplies some (questionable) answers.

Part One: Querying the Proposition

If you will forgive this fundamentalism, let me begin by deconstructing our proposition, which is an attempt to delineate what our group has had to cope with. Let's ask first what television is, or was. Second, let's make sure that it's really ending. Third, we should ask where to look for its impact, or, in other words, what hypotheses there are to guide us in our search for its major effects. And finally, how should we go about verifying those effects?

What, then, is television? The abstract answer is that, like any other medium, it is (1) a technological apparatus (2) embedded in a social institution consisting of rules, roles, and organizations in an environment of other social institutions

Elihu Katz is trustee professor of communication at the Annenberg School of the University of Pennsylvania and professor emeritus of sociology and communication at the Hebrew University of Jerusalem. Recent books include The Export of Meaning: Cross Cultural Readings of Dallas *(with Tamar Liebes, Oxford University Press 1990) and* Media Events: The Live Broadcasting of "History" *(with Daniel Dayan, Harvard University Press 1992). He studied with Paul Lazarsfeld at Columbia University and began his career at the University of Chicago. He holds honorary degrees from the Universities of Ghent, Montreal, Paris, Haifa, and Rome.*

NOTE: I wish to thank Anne-Katrin Arnold for editorial assistance.

DOI: 10.1177/0002716209337796

(3) featuring a repertoire of output (call it content) and (4) characterized by typical "situations of contact" (Freidson 1959) in which it is apprehended. In this sense, "classic TV"—television in its heyday—may be said to have been (1) a technology providing several audiovisual channels of over-the-air broadcasting (2) publicly regulated as a near-monopoly operated by highly trained professionals (3) charged to "inform, educate, and entertain" and (4) characterized by national audiences dispersed in their homes.

Our second question: is television really dying? For the television some of us knew in the 1960s and 1970s, the answer is yes. The television of "sharedness"—of nation-building and family togetherness—is no longer with us, having made room for a television of hundreds of channels, of "niche" broadcasting, of portability, one that is part of a system that integrates with the Internet and the other new media. One might say that television is retracing the footsteps of radio, which, miniaturized and modulated, has now become everyman's personal companion, where, to exaggerate, no two people are attending the same program at the same time. These are changes in (1) technology and (4) contact. They are accompanied by (2) the collapse of public regulation in the maze of technological change and commercial investment along with (3) changes in content reflecting a public opinion that has turned against the professionals who claimed to know, better than we do, what's good for us. This is what we meant by "the end of television."

But our colleagues, or most of them, object. Television, they say, is not dead or dying; it has merely entered a new phase. Thus, says John Ellis (2000), in the initial phase (1950s to 1980s), viewers knew the television of "scarcity," in which choice was limited to a very few over-the-air channels that broadcast to families as if seated around a hearth and to a nation as if assembled around a campfire. Then came the television of "plenty," when satellite and cable and competition reigned, choice was suddenly expanded, and every room in the home had its own TV set. And now, says Ellis, we find ourselves in a situation of infinite choice where we can view what we like; when we like (in real time or in delay); where we like (at home or elsewhere); on a variety of screens, telephones, Web sites, and the rest. Rather than pronounce "the end of television," some of our colleagues prefer to assert that television has moved from a "collectivist" to an "individualist" phase. The family has disappeared into separate rooms, and the nation no longer comes together except for the rare live broadcast of a disaster or a celebration (Katz and Liebes 2007). The internationalization of television has abolished national and even linguistic boundaries, and the once-trusted government spokesperson and the paternal network news anchor have given way to unfamiliar voices (Blondheim and Liebes, this volume) and faces from "nowhere" (Epstein 1973) that arouse suspicion (Ellis, this volume). Dayan (this volume) puts it more starkly, claiming that the "centers" that were created by national broadcasters and media events are being threatened by the local and the global (although he foresees a new symbiosis). Some of us regret this development as undermining the shared bases of democracy and culture (Katz 1996). Others, like Uricchio (this volume), applaud this long-awaited pluralism, claiming that it was denied to us by the centrist control of hegemonic ruling classes, even if the potential was technologically available earlier.

So perhaps it is premature to mourn TV's passing, though I'm not certain. Let us grant that, like its predecessors, print and radio, television has evolved along two axes—content-wise from "same" to "differentiated," and contact-wise from "together" to "alone." In deference to our teammates, let us zoom in on the classic era of "sharedness" that is dead or dying and try to assess its effect. Of course, in doing so, we must also speculate on where the new television is headed, not only on what the old television has wrought.

Next, we turn to the question of where we shall find hypotheses to guide us. Here is the place to note that we are in search of hypotheses not about television's power to influence opinions and attitudes but about the impact that television might have had on society, personality, and culture of the sort that accompanied, say, the widespread diffusion of the automobile (Lynd and Lynd 1929; Ogburn 1946). Indeed, one might have expected an abundance of speculative ideas— hypotheses or not—to usher in the TV era. But while these predictions surely abound somewhere, they are not very evident in the academic annals. Early theorizing by David Sarnoff (1941) and Gilbert Seldes (1941) in this journal are important exceptions. Both these pioneers of the industry foresaw that television's greatest emotional and civic impact could come from viewing the "live" transmission of major civic events; Sarnoff, in particular, went on to predict that the new medium would bring people "home," integrate the nation, and raise cultural standards, while also warning against the potential of political "showmanship," the power of audiovisual advertising, and the danger of ideological propaganda. In the early 1950s, the Ford Foundation commissioned Columbia's Bureau of Applied Social Research to continue along these lines, but the project had hardly begun when it was mysteriously decommissioned (Pooley and Katz 2008). Even if we include more recent discussion, there aren't many *big* ideas. Rudolf Arnheim (1969) was one of the first to speculate that the visualization of reality might affect abstract *thinking*, an idea that was also advanced by McLuhan (1964) and later by Postman (1985). Meyrowitz (1985, this volume) followed with the proposal that the literalness and accessibility of the medium overcame the barriers that traditionally divided the genders and the generations—in short, that in the era of television, there would be no more *secrets*. Another set of ideas revolved around *identity* or modeling. David Riesman's (1950) concept of "other-directedness" was a harbinger, and the concern over imitating aggressiveness soon followed (Baker, Lange, and Ball-Rokeach 1969). Teenage modeling was a pervasive concern (Livingstone, this volume). At the *institutional* level, it was suggested that television would powerfully affect family and children (Himmelweit, Oppenheim, and Vince 1958; Schramm 1961; Newcomb, 1987), while others speculated about how education, religion, and politics might be affected. Thus, Scannell (1989, this volume) believed, and still does, that television fostered inclusiveness and popular enfranchisement, while Gerbner and Gross (1976), and now Putnam (1995), suggest that television disenfranchises.

An unusual problem (conceptual as well as methodological) arises in taking account of critical theorists—such as the Frankfurt School (Horkheimer and Adorno 1977)—who saw the media (not just television) as products of a Culture Industry whose mission is to celebrate the status quo or, in other words, to prevent, or at least to slow, change. Surprisingly, the famous programmatic piece by Lazarsfeld and Merton (1948), functionalists both, attributed much the same effects to the media, arguing that they promoted conformity, reinforced status, and inhibited political participation.

Other places outside of academia deserve the attention of hypothesis-hunters. My favorite is the debates in Israel, lasting into the mid-1960s, over whether to introduce television, that is, whether TV would be good or bad for the Jews. The naysayers, in one committee after another, insisted that the introduction of television would undermine the renaissance of Hebraic language and culture, promote materialism and consumerism that could ill be afforded, personalize politics, lower the status of books and reading, possibly violate the commandment against graven images, and jeopardize the rituals of the family Sabbath (Katz 1971).

However intriguing, even this meager list invites hard work. But the fact is that nobody undertook the job systematically—neither at the stage of formulating hypotheses nor at the stage of examining them.

Finally, how would one go about this? What methods are available—then or now—to "test" these hypotheses and predictions about the impact of television? Ostensibly, the answer should be simple, as thousands of research studies have inquired into its effects. Unfortunately, however, most of these are unsuited to the task we have set ourselves, namely, to identify larger and more enduring effects than those provided by most of the research. Here, we are not interested in whether television is successful in selling products but in whether television has successfully implanted consumerism (Schudson 1984). We are less interested in the popularity of "reality shows" like *American Idol* and more interested in the finding that the Near Eastern version of this show, originating in Lebanon, has succeeded in crossing the traditional boundaries of the other Arab states and advancing pan-Arabism (Kraidy forthcoming). We are less interested in whether Kennedy or Nixon was the more skillful orator in the presidential debates of 1960 than in the fact that this election campaign enabled voters in their living rooms to hear both sides of an argument—something that was quite unusual prior to the introduction of this broadcast format (Katz and Feldman 1963).

Research on this grander—more sociological—scale is not very plentiful. The studies we are seeking are not short-term evaluations of persuasion campaigns but studies of values, ideologies, and institutions, studies of social structure and culture. There are very few of these, and they are mostly think-pieces, mostly speculative. Our experts, each in his or her area of specialization, tried to collect relevant findings, but they have harvested more hypotheses than solid conclusions. It is not only for the paucity of ideas about major effects but also for lack of appropriate methods and, ironically, for lack of planning and resources for longitudinal research. There was plenty of time to prepare for research on the arrival of television broadcasting, but not much was done about it. That we don't have such studies of the effect of, say, the alphabet comes as no surprise, since there were no Departments of Communication in ancient Egypt. But one might have expected to find before-and-after studies of, say, radio—and certainly of television. An exception is the BBC's (1939) study of what families talked about before and after they installed a radio.

We find some partial exceptions, then. The trouble is that they don't include hypotheses about what effects to look for, and why. And, as we shall see, they generate problems of their own. Here are a few examples:

1. Using a before-and-after design, Livingstone (2002) repeated Himmelweit, Oppenheim, and Vince's (1958) pioneering study of children's response to the introduction of television with the aim of seeing what had changed over fifty years. Similarly, Katz, Haas, and Gurevitch (1997) repeated a 1970 survey of the uses of leisure and culture in Israel—taken on the eve of the introduction of television—using an almost identical set of questions in 1990. Even such studies, however, must ask, in each case of an observed change, whether the change is attributable to television. Twenty years later, the Israeli study, for example, had to weigh the possible influence of television against the possible influence of the then-new five-day workweek, the large increase in the number of employed women, and the intervention of two wars! Livingstone's conclusions are also beset by the high likelihood that other social forces, not just television, were working in the same direction.
2. Himmelweit herself (Himmelweit, Oppenheim, and Vince 1958) and Schramm (1961) compared similar towns to which television had come earlier or later. Kottak (1990) used this method to compare culture change in several rural communities in Brazil with varying degrees of television longevity. Reviewing a variety of then-extant methods, Belson (1967) introduced a more sophisticated matching method in a BBC-sponsored study of how the acquisition of a TV set affected family life.
3. More narrowly, but perhaps more reliably, a genre of so-called time-budget studies chronicle the allocation of time over a number of activities. These studies are conducted at frequent intervals in many countries, and allow for comparisons of national and regional differences in the arrival of television, comparison of the activities of families with and without television, and changes in time allocated to other activities with the arrival of television and with an increase or decrease in the number of viewing hours. Here, too, other factors may intervene—if the population has aged, for example, or if large numbers of women have entered the workforce. And, of course, the findings of such work are necessarily limited to a specified set of activities. Examples are Robinson (this volume), Robinson and Godbey (1997), Kahneman et al. (2004), and Kubey and Csikszentmihalyi (1990).
4. An ingenious variant on longitudinal methods is that of Gerbner and Gross (1976) and their colleagues. Using traditional survey methods and content analysis, they compared the worldviews of "heavy" and "light" viewers with the worldview encoded in prime-time television to infer whether heavy viewers are more likely to see the world as television sees it. Thus, using short-term methodologies, they were able to infer long-run effects on values.
5. Yet a different approach—whose focus is more institutional than individual—seeks to link the introduction of a new medium with other social institutions that had undergone a change at the same time or shortly thereafter. This is an inferential method that has its eyes open for indicators of change that might be attributable to the new medium. For example, Putnam (1995) has argued that the weakening of participatory democracy—where people talk politics in informal groups—coincides with the observation that television keeps people from going out.

This institutional method is a favorite of historians and anthropologists. Recall Goody and Watt (1968), for example, who noticed that the diffusion of literacy in ancient Greece coincided with the rise of democracy. They also see the spread of reading and writing as responsible for replacing myths of the past with a historical record and, thus, the earliest histories. Another champion of this method is Eisenstein (1980), who identified institutional changes that coincided with the early days of the printing press in an effort to consider whether print might have been implicated in these changes. As is well known, she proposes that the printed book contributed to the Protestant Reformation by liberating Christian communities from the medieval Church that held a monopoly on the word of God, thus creating an individualism that had theretofore been unknown. Taking note of the rapid advances in astronomy at the same time, Eisenstein further proposed that the printing press had accelerated scientists' ability to keep abreast of each other's findings quickly and accurately. Eisenstein credits the technological attributes of print—speed of reproduction and diffusion, accuracy, and relative permanence— rather than its content. To make similar statements about the effect of television on social institutions, we need comparable hypotheses about the contemporaneous loci of change and ideas about those attributes of television—technology, ownership, content, and situation of contact—that offer causal explanations. Even then, we must ponder the other vectors that influence change, being careful not to assign exclusive credit to television or to any other medium. That holds equally for nonchange as well as change.

Part Two: Some Questionable Answers

How and where, then, shall we look for the impact of television so far? In line with the discussion above, our team members have been searching for the likely targets of impact. Most of their work may be divided between effects on social institutions, on one hand, and on values and everyday behavior, on the other. What follows falls far short of the promise of our search. It is a mélange of findings from various studies as reported in the papers that follow, and in their footnotes and references, but, no less, in the expert opinion of our colleagues. Or, to put it more bluntly, we are only now retreating to the stage of generating hypotheses. Our focus, of course, is on classic TV, but it will make things easier if the findings and speculations we report here are placed in the context of before and after, contrasting the heyday with what came before and what comes next. And, once more, allow me to emphasize that this is a progress report from a group of people thinking together in which others are invited to join.

1. *Institutional change*. We believe that the institutions most likely to have been affected by "classic" television are family and politics, and the two are interrelated. Even before TV, it was radio broadcasting that moved politics inside the home and away from the fervor of the public square. It is possible that this transplantation accounts for the somewhat surprising finding of Wyatt, Kim, and Katz (2000) that home is a major locus of political talk, though there are no pre-TV data with which to compare. Enlisting Schudson (1978), it may even be suggested that informal political talk may be a mimicking of talk on television. Personality has overtaken ideology in the televising of politics, and politicians are busy rehearsing their "sincerity," according to Ellis (2000, this volume). True, television "enfranchised" large numbers of people in its heyday, and implanted a widespread sense of

democracy and belonging, according to Scannell (1989, this volume). The nation certainly seemed more integrated, even if the level of actual participation hardly reflected these changes. Indeed, the evenhandedness of classic television may even have *lessened* political participation, as Diana Mutz (2006) has noted, by creating the kind of ambivalence that Lazarsfeld, Berelson, and Gaudet (1944) called "cross pressures," in which Riesman (1950) discerned evidence of tolerance. Iyengar (1996) suggests that the personalization of victims on television takes pressure off government, while Liebes (1998), in a very different connection, suggests that the televising of disaster puts pressure on government.

A strong case can be made that broadcasting—radio and television—contributed greatly to national integration (Cardiff and Scannell 1987; Katz and Wedell 1977; Dayan and Katz 1992; Katz, Haas, and Gurevitch 1997). The newspaper had a similar effect in creating what Anderson (1983) calls "imagined community." If early broadcasting integrated the nation, the same may be said about the family. According to Livingstone (this volume), the home became a more solidary unit in those days, with parents and children sitting together around the set, watching programs designed for family viewing, on a very few channels, with the *paterfamilias* in charge of the remote. Amanda Lotz (this volume) amends this picture of domesticity somewhat by showing how television programming took careful account of the demographic composition of the household at different times of the day.

For Uricchio (this volume), the remote and the video recorder, along with the introduction of additional channels, produced the beginnings of individualistic escape from the centralized control he decries. For others, individualism is expressed in the move from "together to alone" as television has learned to cater to the increasing diversity of the lifestyles of different family members. As Livingstone (this volume) says, "The goal of individual self-realization overshadows solidarity and stability" (p. 158) in regard not only to family but also to larger political and social concerns. The sense of stability that once radiated from the TV set has been dissipated, say Blondheim and Liebes (this volume). Order, control, comfort have left the living room. To re-create large and heterogeneous audiences, TV journalism is becoming ever more sensational, say Gurevitch, Blumler, and Coleman (this volume).

Indeed, the institution of journalism has changed before our eyes. The live broadcasting of "media events" has extended emotional participation; as the spotlight has moved from more patriotic events to disaster, terror, and war, governments have become more vulnerable to a critical public opinion and to increasing tension between establishment institutions and journalism. "Embedded" military correspondents are only the latest attempt to seek compromise. Even more fundamentally, television news has far eclipsed newspaper news as the main source of daily information, causing the newspapers to respond, as tabloids do, by becoming more like television or, as the elite press does, by becoming *less* like television (at least until lately) through the highlighting of opinion and interpretation.

Foreign affairs have also been affected by television, especially in the global phase in which we now find ourselves. In its classic era, television news was spokesman for the nation, and hegemonic control was never far behind the scenes. With satellites, nations tried to block influence stemming from outside, and the cold war might not have lasted very long, says Monroe Price (this volume), if national borders had not been so impermeable. When satellites plus cable made international transmission routine, broadcasters rose above national commitments and gave both leaders and people new ideas about what was going on in the world. In retrospect, Abba Eban (1983) warns that Woodrow Wilson's doctrine of "openness" can only undermine diplomacy.

Similarly, the live broadcasting of war, and seeing a war from both sides, suggests that the institution of war and the need of government for supportive public opinion have been seriously affected by television. In Vietnam and in Iraq, the media are thought to have stimulated opinion to pressure the United States government to capitulate, though Hallin (1994) is not so sure. On other occasions, an aroused public opinion may have pushed government to initiate action (against its own better judgment), as in reacting to traumatic reportage or even the witnessing of "suffering at a distance." Government attempts to maintain control—to keep cameras out, on one hand, or "embed" them, on the other—do not seem to work.

Sport may be the last refuge of sharedness in the new phase of TV, the only vestige of national and family togetherness (Whannel, this volume). But there is no question that television revolutionized sport in its heyday, not only with respect to habits of consumption, but in the structures of production as well. Sport became increasingly professionalized in the heyday of broadcasting, and a very big business. Certain sports flourished on the small screen, and others retreated. Sporting events designed for TV—such as the American Super Bowl—assemble worldwide audiences and huge amounts of money. The Olympic Games have been similarly transformed. Whannel says of televised sporting events that the aura once reserved for "being there" may now be eclipsed by televised spectatorship.

Many other institutions have been affected by classic television. In the early days, television was not only a national unifier, but a preacher as well. Even from the beginning, says Morrison (this volume), the inherent constraints that led television to portray different habitats and lifestyles led, willy-nilly, to a creeping multiculturalism that undermined the Church and aroused the antipathy of activists such as Mary Whitehouse. In the later phases of television, multiculturalism has continued to flourish, and the idea of postmodern identity choice reigns supreme. While Morrison's argument focuses on Britain, it seems fair to say that the salience of other institutions—such as fashion or health—has been equally affected by TV, not only in Britain but everywhere.

2. *Value change and changes in the everyday.* In considering the long-run effects of television, it is even more tempting to think of value change as a product, primarily, of the content of television. But that is a path full of risks and certainly—as noted above—not the only "causal" attribute of the medium. Moreover, it is a path that calls out for better conceptualization, as we shall see.

It is true that a number of theorists have taken content as their starting point. For example, Ellis (this volume) believes that television viewing breeds suspiciousness because of the incessant diet—in TV fiction and news—of deception and insincerity. More, he believes that emotion pervades (British) television and affects its viewers. This is hypothesizing, of course, based on an analyst's insight and on the assumption that viewers will be similarly affected. But are they? And is this problem of content intrinsic to British television or, perhaps, to the medium more generally; that is, does the medium of television everywhere "naturally" attract this sort of content? Questions such as these warrant empirical investigation, of course, because content analysis alone, however expert, can only serve to produce hypotheses as far as effect on viewers is concerned. Gerbner and Gross (1976) propose a similar hypothesis—that violence on television (in the United States) delivers a message that "the world is a dangerous place." In enacting who may hit whom with impunity, television also instructs us in the status system, identifying the demographics of the heroes and the villains, as also suggested by Dallas Smythe (1954). It is to the credit of Gerbner and Gross that their study tries to establish, empirically, that these messages have actually gotten through to "heavy" viewers, at least to the extent that they believe more than "light" viewers. An even deeper message, according to these authors, is that the establishment wants to keep us out of its way: "they" scare us into staying inside and minding our own business. Andrea Press's argument (this volume) that American television promoted the feminist movement, then put the brakes on, also wants to teach that longitudinal content analysis is one of the ways of approaching the study of nonchange as well as change, but obviously, one cannot do without the reception side.

Consider Schudson's (1984) study of advertising, which suggests that the American media are more effective in selling "consumerism" than in selling specific products. While Schudson's study does not include the values of viewers, our Israeli study (Katz, Haas, and Gurevitch 1997) does find a significant rise in viewer "materialism" during the years following the introduction of television. But, ironically, public TV in Israel—a monopoly, following the BBC model—carried very little advertising. In fact, it appears that television itself—its furniture and its glamour—communicated an interest in consumerism and materialism. It would be worth knowing whether TV viewers in Soviet Russia or in today's China are similarly affected. True or not, other factors also work in the same direction. If so, it would mean that the graven images that are generic to television—a very abstract form of content—may be more influential and that their effect may be universal rather than culture-bound.

Like Ellis, Meyrowitz (this volume) deals with the behind-the-scenes of TV "showmanship." It is not just that we have become aware that everybody is trying to sell us something, especially themselves. Rather, argues Meyrowitz, television has given us a good look at what others are concealing, revealing what we never knew about our most intimate "role sets" (Merton 1957)—for example, husbands and wives, parents and children, and yes, politicians and their constituencies. His emphasis is not only on content but also on the accessibility of television. He thinks we are all media-literate—in other words, that the "situation of contact" for television is altogether different than for print or even film. Meyrowitz goes on to suggest that the pervasiveness of our television habit has paved the way for our acceptance of the normalcy of being watched, that is, of surveillance.

Comparing the experience of viewing a film with the experience of viewing television, Beverle Houston (1984) suggests that the television medium is experienced interactively, the viewer facing the screen, whereas film viewers are voyeurs, peeking into goings-on outside themselves. This is the idea that guides Horton and Wohl's (1956) finding of parasocial interaction—that people "talk back" to television. And it leads to Frosh's proposal (this volume) that the television experience is about learning to read faces. The current "reality" genre, adds Lunt (this volume), is another step toward inviting the viewer to join the other side. Whereas classic TV brought the outside into our living rooms, we are now climbing inside the TV set as performers.

The proposal that a suspicious search for sincerity accompanies our television viewing is repeated by several members of our team. It connects with the often-heard allegation that democratic societies are suffering from a dearth of leadership talent. We are overly familiar with their faces, goes one version of the argument, and suspicious of the extent to which they are like us. Nevertheless, argues Scannell (1989, this volume), the egalitarian access to TV has a highly democratizing effect.

In *The Lonely Crowd*, David Riesman (1950) perceives a relationship between print and "inner-directed" personality type. Riesman's is a technological hypothesis not unlike that of McLuhan (1964), who saw print as a straight and narrow path leading the individual to his goal, unfettered by fashion or other distractions. For McLuhan, television is a medium of dispersal, something like Riesman's "other-directedness." Postman (1985) would agree that television viewing cannot substitute for print as a medium of learning. These thinkers might suggest that postnetwork TV contributes neither to the individualism of inner-direction nor to the groupiness of other-direction but to the uncommitted and uncharted "trying on" of identities.

Prior (2007) seems to be pointing elsewhere. His response to the multiplicity of channels suggests that viewing habits have become more rigid, not more varied, and *less* politically involved. He recalls that "classic" TV made it quite likely that the average viewer would stumble on the national news at least once during an evening's viewing, even if his or her preference was for entertainment. In the postnetwork era of near-infinite choice and time-shifting, Prior shows that viewing habits polarize such that the news-oriented viewer sees more, while the entertainment-oriented viewer (a large majority) manages to evade the news altogether.

In spite of the skepticism they invoke, technological theories seem more suited to hypothesizing long-run effects than the other attributes of the media. For all their differences, Eisenstein, McLuhan, Meyrowitz, Postman, Gerbner, and others are technological determinists in one way or another, although most would concede that it is a "soft" determinism and that society is in charge. Yet, they are interested in the effects of medium more than message. In the radical case of McLuhan, but even Eisenstein, they are interested in how the medium shapes the brain or affects interaction or is incorporated into social institutions. Their "medium" refers to technology, or situation of contact, or ownership, more than it refers to message. Even ostensible messages are less interesting than their latent meanings—as in Schudson's decoding of television advertising as a message of "consumerism" or Ellis's message of insincerity, or Gerbner's message of "stay home." So while it is fair to say that "content" is a causal agent in many of the effects noted here, it is not the surface content of specific TV programs that is responsible, or the persuasive rhetoric of media campaigns, but much more latent or implicit content.

٥   ٥   ٥

This attempt to pull together the many ideas about TV's enduring effects from the research literature and from the proposals of our teammates goes far beyond any reasonable expectation of well-established findings, or even groups of well-integrated hypotheses. If we were to single out the values or institutions that have attracted most of our attention, the top of the list would surely include (1) democracy, in its varied aspects; (2) social integration—nation and family; (3) trust and suspiciousness; (4) materialism; and (5) identity—social and physical. Think of this, then, as a work in progress that invites continued dedication and speculation—not only from the team but also from all who might wish to join us. Or might it be better to wait a few hundred years—as theorists of the effects of print have done—to get a clearer picture?

What follows is the best of what we have accomplished so far, but many more ideas (and many more colleagues) deserve to be included. We begin with an overtime portrait of the diffusion of the medium and the evolution of its audience and its content. Articles by John Robinson, William Uricchio, Amanda Lotz, and David Morrison discuss the early days, joining John Ellis and Daniel Dayan, who take the next steps. Paul Frosh and Peter Lunt take us inside the box and into the viewing experience. Sonia Livingstone, Andrea Press, and Joshua Meyrowitz contextualize the viewing experience within the family, while Gary Whannel gives us a last glimpse of the "everybody" audience that continues to gather for sporting events. Michael Gurevitch, Stephen Coleman, and Jay Blumler consider the changing role of television in politics and vice versa, while Menahem Blondheim and Tamar Liebes focus on the changing character of television journalism. Monroe Price addresses the question of how television has influenced the conduct of foreign policy and the progress of globalism, and Paddy Scannell wraps it up.

References

Anderson, Benedict. 1983. *Imagined communities*. New York: Verso.

Arnheim, Rudolf. 1969. *Visual thinking*. Berkeley: University of California Press.

Baker, Robert K., David Lange, and Sandra Ball-Rokeach. 1969. *Mass media and violence: A report to the National Commission in the Causes and Prevention of Violence*. Washington, DC: Government Printing Office.

Belson, William. 1967. *The Impact of Television*. London: Crosby Lockwood.

Cardiff, David, and Paddy Scannell. 1987. Broadcasting and national unity. In *Impacts and influences*, ed. James Curran, Anthony Smith, and Pauline Wingate, 157-73. London: Methuen.

Dayan, Daniel, and Elihu Katz. 1992. *Media events*. Cambridge, MA: Harvard University Press.

Eban, Abba. 1983. *The new diplomacy*. New York: Random House.

Eisenstein, Elizabeth. 1980. The emergence of print culture in the West. *Journal of Communication* 30: 90-105.

Ellis, John. 2000. *Seeing things*. London: Cambridge University Press.

Epstein, E. J. 1973. *News from nowhere*. New York: Viking.

Freidson, Elliot. 1953. The relation of the social situation of contact to the media of mass communication. *Public Opinion Quarterly* 17:230-38.

Gerbner, George, and Larry Gross. 1976. Living with television: The violence profile. *Journal of Communication* 26:173-99.

Goody, Jack, and Ian Watt. 1968. The consequences of literacy. In *Literacy in traditional societies*, ed. Jack Goody. Cambridge: Cambridge University Press.

Hallin, David. 1994. *We keep America on top of the world: Television journalism and the public sphere*. London: Routledge.

Himmelweit, Hilde, A. N. Oppenheim, and P. Vince. 1958. *Television and the child*. London: Oxford University Press.

Horkheimer, M., and T. W. Adorno. 1977. The culture industry: Enlightenment as mass deception. In *Mass communication and society*, ed. J. Curran, M. Gurevitch, and J. Woollacott, 349-83. Beverley Hills, CA: Sage.

Horton, Donald, and Richard Wohl. 1956. Mass communication and para-social interaction. *Psychiatry* 19 (3): 188-211.

Houston, Beverle. 1984. Viewing television: The metapsychology of endless consumption. *Quarterly Review of Film Studies* 9:183-95.

Iyengar, Shanto. 1996. Framing responsibility for political issues. *The Annals of the American Academy of Political and Social Science* 546:59-70.

Kahneman, Daniel, Alan B. Krueger, David A. Schkade, Norbert Schwarz, and Arthur A. Stone. 2004. A survey method for characterizing daily life experience: The day reconstruction method. *Science* 306: 1776-80.

Katz, Elihu. 1971. Television comes to the people of the book. In *The use and abuse of social science*, ed. Irving Louis Horowitz. New Brunswick, NJ: Transaction Books.

———. 1996. And deliver us from segmentation. *The Annals of the American Academy of Political and Social Science* 564:22-33.

Katz, Elihu, and Jacob J. Feldman. 1963. The debates in the light of research and vice versa. In *The great debates*, ed. Sidney Kraus. Bloomington: Indiana University Press.

Katz, Elihu, Hadassah Haas, and Michael Gurevitch. 1997. Twenty years of television in Israel: Are there long-run effects on values, social connectedness and cultural practices? *Journal of Communication* 47:3-20.

Katz, Elihu, and Tamar Liebes. 2007. "No more peace": How terror, disaster and war have upstaged media events. *International Journal of Communication* 1:157-66.

Katz, Elihu, and George Wedell. 1977. *Broadcasting in the third world*. Cambridge, MA: Harvard University Press.

Kottak, Conrad. 1990. *Prime-time society: An anthropological analysis of television and culture*. Belmont, CA: Wadsworth.

Kraidy, Marwan. Forthcoming. *Reality television and Arab politics*. Cambridge: Cambridge University Press.

Kubey, Robert, and Mihaly Csikszentmihalyi. 1990. *Television and the quality of life: How viewing shapes everyday experience*. Hillsdale, NJ: Lawrence Erlbaum.

Lazarsfeld, Paul F., Bernard Berelson, and Hazel Gaudet. 1944. *The people's choice*. New York: Duell, Sloan and Pearce.

Lazarsfeld, Paul F., and Robert K. Merton. 1948. Mass communication, popular taste, and organized social action. In *The communication of ideas*, ed. Lyman Bryson, 95-118. New York: Harper.

Liebes, Tamar. 1998. Television's disaster marathons: A danger for the democratic process? In *Media, ritual and identity*, ed. Tamar Liebes and James Curran, 71-84. New York: Routledge.

Livingstone, Sonia. 2002. *Young people and new media*. London: Sage.

Lynd, Robert S., and Helen M. Lynd. 1929. *Middletown: A study in American culture*. New York: Harcourt, Brace & World.

McLuhan, Marshall. 1964. *Understanding media*. Toronto, Canada: McGraw-Hill.

Merton, Robert K. 1957. *Social theory and social structure*. New York: Free Press.

Meyrowitz, Joshua. 1985. *No sense of place: The impact of electronic media on social behavior*. New York: Oxford University Press.

Mutz, Diana. 2006. *Hearing the other side: Deliberative vs. participatory democracy*. Cambridge: Cambridge University Press.

Newcomb, Horace. 1987. *Television: The critical view*. New York: Oxford University Press.

Ogburn, William F. 1946. Inventions of local transportation and the patterns of cities. *Social Forces* 24:373-79.

Pooley, Jefferson, and Elihu Katz. 2008. Further notes on why American sociology abandoned mass communications research. *Journal of Communication* 58:767-786.

Postman, Neil. 1985. *Amusing ourselves to death*. New York: Penguin.

Prior, Markus. 2007. *Post-broadcast democracy*. New York: Cambridge University Press.

Putnam, Robert. 1995. Tuning in, tuning out: The strange disappearance of social capital in America. *PS: Political Science and Politics* 28 (4): 664-83.

Riesman, David. 1950. *The lonely crowd*. With Reuel Denny and Nathan Glazer. New Haven, CT: Yale University Press.

Robinson, John P., and Geoffrey Godbey. 1997. *Time for life: The surprising ways Americans use their time*. University Park: Pennsylvania State University Press.

Sarnoff, David. 1941. Possible Social Effects of Television. *The Annals of the American Academy of Political and Social Science* 213:145-152.

Scannell, Paddy. 1989. Public service broadcasting and modern public life. *Media Culture and Society* 11 (2): 135-66.

Schramm, Wilbur L. 1961. *Television in the lives of our children*. Stanford, CA: Stanford University Press.

Schudson, Michael. 1978. The ideal of conversation in the study of mass media. *Communication Research* 5:320-29.

———. 1984. *Advertising: The uneasy persuasion*. New York: Basic Books.

———. 1997. Why conversation is not the soul of democracy. *Critical Studies in Mass Communication* 14 (4): 297-309.

Seldes, Gilbert . 1941. The Nature of Television Programs. *The Annals of the American Academy of Political and Social Science* 213:138-144.

Smythe, Dallas W. 1954. Reality as presented by television. *Public Opinion Quarterly* 18 (2): 143-56.

Wyatt, Robert, Joohan Kim, and Elihu Katz. 2000. Bridging the spheres: Political and personal conversation in public and private spaces. *Journal of Communication* 50:71-92.

Sharing and Showing: Television as Monstration

By
DANIEL DAYAN

This article presents a comparison between two models of publicness (one based on a type of television firmly anchored in the center, another depending on media that blur all distinctions between centers and peripheries) and asks what sort of *sharedness* do these two models allow? The article also explores the notion of "monstration." Through what sorts of *displays* do contending media call on public attention? Can one speak of "acts of showing" the way one speaks of speech acts? What is the impact of such acts on a sociology of collective attention? Third, the article examines the coexistence between television of the center and new digital media. Is their relation agonistic or, paradoxically, cooperative? The present situation may echo many earlier cases in which old media learned to coexist with new media by starting unexpected dialogues and practicing a division of labor. Today's situation might be a (reluctant) partnership in a multitiered public sphere.

Keywords: television; center; periphery; sharedness; attention; monstration

If not altogether on the wane, a certain model of publicness is no longer exclusive and has lost some of its power while another model of publicness seems to be gaining ground.

Daniel Dayan is a professor of media sociology at the Marcel Mauss Institute (CNRS/Ecole des hautes Etudes en Sciences Sociales). He is currently a visiting professor at the New School for Social Research in New York. He is coauthor of Media Events: The Live Broadcasting of History *(with Elihu Katz; Harvard University Press 1992) and* Owning the Olympics *(with Monroe Price; University of Michigan Press 2008) and author of* La Terreur Spectacle: Terrorisme et Télévision *(INA-de boek 2006).*

NOTE: I am grateful to Paddy Scannell and Elihu Katz for their active role in bringing this article into existence and to Jeff Goldfarb for frequent discussions on the theme of "appearing in public." Students of the Annenberg School (University of Pennsylvania) helped me by carefully listening to the first presentation of this text. I must finally thank the graduate students who took my seminar on "visibility" at the New School for Social Research for responding to many points discussed here.

DOI: 10.1177/0002716209338364

Traditional television, as an instrument for connecting centers to peripheries, seems to be fading. It is much too early to pronounce this television dead. Of course, many dimensions of TV as we know it are endangered. But there are perhaps other dimensions of this form of television that are too important not to survive. If such dimensions exist, what are they and under what form will they survive? What about traditional television (the television of the center) is about to disappear or be replaced? And what might be here to stay?

To answer these questions, I propose to focus on two key notions. The first concerns the type of *sharing* that central television in its heyday brought about. Is it still possible? Can it be performed by other media? If not or not entirely, does it constitute that part of television that is bound to survive? The second concerns the activity of *showing*, the practices through which television calls for, organizes, and manages collective attention. The way central television focuses collective attention toward certain events, situations, or individuals is organized through endless instances of showing, pointing, and designating. Of course, many other instances of public display can be found in present and historical contexts (from the rituals of the church to Foucault's ritualized punishments), but rarely have displays of the same situations simultaneously involved so many conflicting versions and so many competing media. The activity of displaying has become a globally sensitive battlefield. What is today at stake is the authority invested in the act of showing, in what I shall call here *monstration*.

Thus, I offer two stories in this article. The first is a story of sharedness, a comparison between two models of publicness. A certain model of publicness is consubstantial with a type of television firmly anchored in the center. Another model of publicness is made possible by media that blur distinctions between centers and peripheries. What sort of sharing do these two models respectively allow? The second story concerns monstration. Through what sorts of monstrations do contending media proceed to manage public attention? Is the relation of media of the center to media of the periphery competitive or, paradoxically, cooperative? Can these media manage to establish and stabilize a modus vivendi, skirmishes and controversies notwithstanding? I suggest that the present situation echoes many earlier cases in which old media learned to coexist with new media by redefining their role, by starting unexpected dialogues, and by practicing a division of labor. Thus, today's situation is perhaps less the story of a dethroned television faced with a new dominant medium than that of a gradual accommodation, a reluctant partnership, a multitiered public sphere.

First Story: Sharedness

Let me propose a comparison between the type of sharedness offered by the *television of the center* and that involved in the *new digital media*. While this comparison is structured like an antithesis, a third partner simultaneously embodies the television of the center in its most extreme form yet already represents a displacement of its power. This genre—the major television broadcasts

that Elihu Katz and I called *media events* (Dayan and Katz 1992)—will often be
present in this discussion, where it will be seen both as a departure from, and a
chance of survival for, the television of the center. The comparison focuses on the
question of attention, considered in terms of geography, temporality, sociology,
and politics. What, in other words, are the flows, rhythms, strategies, and constituencies of shared attention?

Geography of attention

Collective attention may circulate in a geography of solid societies separated
in space: societies with centers, peripheries, and central media connecting the
two; and societies whose central media reinforce actual borders through a daily
reiteration of territorial limits. Collective attention may also circulate within a
porous—if not altogether liquid—model of societies, a model made of networks,
overlapping territories, intersecting peripheries; a model remarkably accounted
for in Appadurai's kaleidoscopic account of multiple "scapes" (ethnoscapes, cre-
doscapes, mediascapes, technoscapes, etc.), each of which is defined by a fundamental heterogeneity (Appadurai 1996). The media of the center, and
television in particular, have an obvious affinity with solid societies. As to the
new media, they have become emblems or metaphors of "liquid" societies. Yet,
changes in the landscape that television as we know it has modeled are far from
entirely due to the existence of new media. They also point to the evolution of
central television itself.

After having been structured for a long time in national terms and dominated
by centralized television organizations, public spheres have extended themselves in a number of directions, most of which involve a postnational dimension. Three such directions are particularly significant. First, mega-television
networks offer world audiences vantage points that are still nationally or region-
ally inflected (Al Jazeera, BBC World Service, TV5 Monde, CNN International,
etc.) but aim at constituencies much larger than nations.[1] In this case, the model
of national television is relativized from above. Second, some television models
cater to immigrant populations and help in constructing or reconstructing spectral
communities, disappeared nations, forgotten empires, and actual diasporas.
These television models broadcast their programs across national communities.
The national model is challenged here by other national models. It is relativized
sideways by the multiplicity of centers catering to the same peripheries. A third
challenge emanates from the new media. Digital public spheres subvert national
space through decentered interactions often described in terms of rhizomes,
networks, or capillarity. In this case, the national model is relativized from
below. The fact that any point in a periphery can be connected (by new media)
to any other point in the periphery puts in question the very notion of "periphery." And the fact that any point in the periphery can be connected by satellite
dish to a number of possible centers questions the very notion of "center." In
both cases, what seems weakened today is a fundamental link between centers
and peripheries: the notion of territory.

Temporalities of attention

In most situations involving news, the facts being shared on central television are not only recent but offered also to a coordinated reception. Recurring schedules organize daily moments of collective attention, of simultaneous viewing. As opposed to this temporal coordination of public attention, the new media offer a radical polyrhythmy, introducing the disjunction of temporalities into the very fabric of conversations. Yet, trends within central television already partake in the disjointed temporality of the new media. Symmetrical, and almost contemporary to the emergence of media events, news channels introduce a disjointed reception; they allow the same events to be seen by different viewers at different times. Programs are no longer in rhythm with the progression of a television day. By being repeatedly broadcast in loops, they become constantly available like airport shuttles (Semprini 2003). A carousel temporality allows each viewer access to news programs whenever he or she wants.

While giving up on certain dimensions of sharedness, televisions of the center are still dealing in converging attention. This might explain why, today, televisions of the center offer three different temporal modalities. *Schedule television* orchestrates the temporality of collective attention on a regular basis. *Carousel television* suspends this coordination. Media events reintroduce it with a vengeance (but on an exceptional basis) and combine it with an additional temporality: liveness.

In the scheduled television of the center, the moment of reception, the moment of learning about what happened, usually does not coincide with its happening. There are many reasons for this delay, in particular economic reasons (simultaneity used to involve high costs) and journalistic reasons (the validation of news takes time). A new dimension of sharing is introduced by media events when the experience of reception and the depicted situation take place simultaneously. This simultaneity—the live format—has become one of central television's major rhetorical possibilities.

But liveness involves two dimensions. The first is technical (simultaneity). The second is social. It is shared attention. Simultaneity without sharedness is not very important (it is routine in surveillance systems). Simultaneity with restricted sharedness is not very important either. The power of live broadcasts lies with the size of audiences invited to share them. New media may occasionally offer live broadcasts. Yet, while *live* is a momentous feature in central television, it becomes much less significant in media that connect peripheries to peripheries. Take the example of an ambitious program that was proposed a few years ago to a number of major European channels. The program offered European viewers the possibility of sharing some time every day with the inhabitants of Nablus or Ramallah. This daily appointment was meant as a ritual. It offered the almost religious experience of witnessing distant sufferings. Palestine would serve as a sort of civil religion, a religion with saints, holy places, and martyrs. When major channels turned the program down, the initiative had to content itself with a Web site. The proposed ritual was still available, but deprived of collective attention, its live dimension seemed pointless. In other words, liveness involves not only coordinating the temporality of an event to that of its reception but also orchestrating this reception itself. To become significant, live requires collective attention. Television of the center is what turns *live* into *deep play*.

Politics of attention

Hannah Arendt describes the public sphere as a table on which a number of items are set (Arendt 1958; Silverstone 2006). These common elements are shared by all participants around the table. There is consensus as to their factuality. Yet, sharing these facts does not entail any political consensus. The shared facts are seen from different vantage points. They are meant to be debated. In other words, the convergent attention offered by central television most often takes place on a background of controversy. Simmel already stressed that controversies entail the paradoxical effect of socializing contending parties to each other (see Lemieux 2008). This is what central televisions allow: a common focusing of attention and the existence of a shared agenda, controversies notwithstanding. Within a few hours, spectators around the world are fed images of the same events with varying degrees of insistence, through varying narratives. For some, certain images accuse or incriminate. For others, the same images call for celebration or sympathy. For all, central televisions serve as an index of the presence of other publics. Spectators around the world know of each other, are aware of the relative sizes of publics, know that their respective responses differ. Political actors direct their actions toward those spectators who form critical masses.

Take the following example, a focal point of many Christmas specials on European television: the midnight mass in Bethlehem. Reports on this mass pointed for many years to the empty seat of Yasser Arafat, who was prevented from attending following a house arrest by the Israelis. But of course Christmas as celebrated by Western Christians marks only one of the possible birthdates of Christ. Christian orthodox and other calendars offer an abundance of alternative dates and corresponding religious celebrations. Was Arafat expected to attend each of them? Probably not. Arafat's presence or absence was not directed at Christians in general, but those Christians who constitute a substantial television public. Similarly, posters brandished in demonstrations all over the world tend to be written in English, no matter where the protest erupts. Any political actor asks himself or herself two questions: Who are the publics to whom given actions will be shown? and What are the major narratives through which such publics will appraise these actions? This leads to privileging certain gestures and to censoring others that might be objectionable to those publics whose mass is deemed critical. There are many ways of bending reality to match a certain type of collective attention.

Political actors are particularly interested in media events because they know these events are stages that offer the highest degree of publicness, the highest available amount of collective attention. For any political actor to step on such a stage is a major victory, knowing that many other actors are doomed to be pushed to the side and altogether eliminated from the attention race. Today's "economy of attention" places those who lack adequate qualifications in a situation of enforced invisibility. Attention seekers may then attempt to capture some of this highly desirable resource by conquering those stages that give access to televisions of the center and their publics. Yet, the stages that attract such attention come equipped with their own dramaturgies. This frustrating situation leads to specific assaults aimed at dissociating stages from dramaturgies. Thus, attention can be *diverted* from any given event through the proliferation of "satellite" events that attempt to "piggyback" the original event and bask in its glory. (Think of Sundance Film festival and of such peripheral events as Slamdance, Slapdance, and Slumdance.) Attention can be *subverted* through the untimely display of an event's back region. (Think of the transformation of the Beijing Olympics into a story of the violation of human rights in Tibet.) Attention can finally be *perverted* or hijacked through the forcible replacement of the planned event by another. (Think of the transformation of the Munich Olympics into a terror event.) Targeted media events divulge the existence of a parallel economy of attention: attention poachers, attention guerillas, attention pirates (Dayan 2008; Wentland 2008).

Sociology of attention

Public attention can be conceived as convergent attention. It can also be organized as divergent attention. Whether a media context is constructed in terms of convergent or divergent attention entails significant consequences. Each conception involves a different type and a different degree of publicity. On the side of divergent attention, new media differ from central television in that they are never directed to the whole galaxies of audiences that form national publics. Sharing exists here, but it involves relatively narrow publics. This restricted sharing results in a significant loss. What is shown on the new media is not truly public. Rather than displaying an authoritative status that once belonged to royal historiographers, images shown on new media tend to circulate along personal networks without ever being ascertained by a gate-keeping institution. Traveling within the periphery, short-circuiting centers, they tend to function like rumors.

On the side of convergent attention, central television represents on the contrary an extended form of sharing, a sharing that involves—to use Paddy Scannell's striking formula—"everyone as someone." This extended form of sharing culminates with media events that are in a way to central television what central television is to new media. The concentration of attention acts like a magnet, attracting further attention and, most of all, inducing performative effects. Shared attention creates reality. W. I. Thomas defines as real whatever "is real in its consequences" (Thomas 1928).[2] For Marcel Duchamp, art becomes whatever is shown in a museum. In the case of televisions of the center, facts become real by being shared on a grand scale.[3]

Central television acts as a vast bulletin board. It largely controls the possibility of appearing in public, the construction of political reality that Hannah Arendt defines as "Polis" (Arendt 1958; Goldfarb 2006; Silverstone 2006). This bulletin board is significant not only for what it retains but also for the connections it makes possible between what it retains. Through these connections the bulletin board turns into a cognitive map. By connecting event to event, by offering a perspective on what is distant and what is close, by organizing the world into megadiscourses (games, reality, fiction), the bulletin board allows an imagination of the collective. This role of television as bulletin board seems endangered today. Will it survive? And will it survive as central television? Can a certain type of collectively focused attention disappear altogether? It seems difficult to imagine a society without some common factuality, without an institution in charge of displaying the selected facts. Will centralized television maintain its role as provider of this common factuality? Will new media inherit television's scepter?[4]

Second Story: Monstration

Consider a TV camera that records the presence of every person who enters a subway station on a given day. At some point, these records will be stored in a computer. At some further point, they will be destroyed. But if an explosion occurs in that station, images of those twenty-four hours will be retrieved and looked at with an intention in mind: reconstituting what happened. Attention has entered the scene.

Television is often presented as an instrument of surveillance. I disagree. Surveillance requires no attention. It is often a purely mechanical operation involving specific instruments, the recorded outputs of which can at some point be mobilized by human beings, but which can also be merely archived, poured from machine to machine without ever being watched. Surveillance is a prosthesis, a substitute for attention. The role of television starts at the moment where images are not only retrieved but also shown. As I have tried to show throughout this article, the role of television is to produce, cater to, and manage public attention.

Showing the subway images—which is really what television is about—can serve to identify who was there, or to express regard for victims, or to condemn the perpetrators. It is never devoid of an expressed purpose, an expressive intention. The art historian Hans Belting proposes that whenever we see an image, there is also, visibly or invisibly, a body that proposes it to our attention. This body can be that of a physical subject or that of an institution. The museum, for example, is an institution devoted to showing. So is television. Television embeds every image in a gesture. That gesture turns the visible into a spectacle that demands attention. That gesture involves not only a scope of attention (attention as quantity) but also a style of attention (attention as quality). In other terms, both attention as quantity and the quality of attention depend on the nature of the performance that shows, points to, designates, underlines. The performance that calls for and modulates attention I call *monstration*.

In theory, the "showing" or monstration involved in television has little to do with a neighboring notion, that of demonstration. A demonstration is a monstration that serves as proof. It is an ostension[5] that serves to close an argument (Rosental 2007). Yet, opposing demonstration to monstration suggests that there are monstrations that make no point, that obey no purpose, that are gratuitous. I believe this is wrong. As is the case for linguistic speech acts, the fact of showing always entails monstrative acts. The only cases when such monstrative acts are elided involve certain forms of contemporary art. Think of the following video by Bill Viola. Laconically titled *Dyptych*, it portrays a young man and a young woman on two parallel screens. The pair does not exactly dance. They move, undulate, flow, as if immersed in water. They are seen together, move at the same rhythm, but they are not together. They do not see each other, do not look at each other, and do not look at us either. All those markers identified by Erving Goffman through which social beings comment on their own appearance and frame their own visibility have been lifted. Something is shown to us. This something is in a museum. But this something eludes nomination or definition. Viola deliberately offers monstrations that evade pragmatics, that involve no equivalent of speech acts; monstrations that oblige the viewer to ask the question, "Why is this being shown at all? Why is this brought to my attention?"

Obviously, this is not the case for television. Think of Boltanski's famous discussion of the rhetorical gestures involved in the witnessing of "distant sufferings." Boltanski (1999) analyzes three major topics that frame the display of suffering. The topic of *sentiment* responds to the sufferer *through* a manifestation of pity; the topic of *denunciation* responds to the perpetrator by issuing a condemnation; the topic of *the sublime* turns the spectacle of suffering into an aesthetic experience, a heightened awareness of the human condition. I would add that the monstration of distant suffering is not a mere prelude to the surfacing of Boltanski's topics. It already incorporates them. Through what I would call "gazing acts" (Dayan 2006), the monstration of suffering involves a performative dimension (Austin 1962). It deploys the "behavitives" of condolence. It calls on the "verdictives" of denunciation.[6] To victims, the monstration of suffering expresses regard. To perpetrators, the same images are a slap in the face. In a word, monstration is an ideal vantage point, both for the discussion of media transformations and for the formulation of a media ethics or morality, both for finding out what a given medium allows to be shown and what the same medium allows by showing.

Monstration and premonstration

Radically different in terms of sharing, television and the new digital media differ also when it comes to monstration. As opposed to the almost continuous flow of monstrations that constitute central television into a constantly updated bulletin board, the types of monstration that the new media provide tend to be discontinuous, fragmentary, almost erratic. Like graffiti, they constitute precarious messages, offer what Deleuze and Guattari (1972) would call "deterritorialized assemblages." But while monstrations provided by the new media are different in status, they cannot be understood without an explicit reference to the monstrations offered by central television. The new media either anticipate the monstrations of central television or respond to them. A curious division of labor has emerged that takes the form of a competitive partnership.

A first version of this partnership concerns situations that have been shown on a Web site and are picked up and shown again by televisions of the center. In the first case, the situation has status as a rumor. In the second case, the situation as shown on televisions of the center is somehow validated, acquires reality, and becomes one of the common facts that are offered to discussion. One could speak of a monstration in two steps. The first step (new media) guarantees only a limited amount of publicness. The second step (central media) ensures full publicness. If the second step is a full monstration and guarantees discussion by society at large, I would define the first step as a *premonstration*.

Consider the photographs taken by U.S. soldier Sabrina Herman in the Iraqi prison of Abu Ghraib (Gourevitch and Morris 2008). Depicting Iraqi prisoners subjected to humiliations, threats, and sometimes torture, these photographs were taken as private mementos. They were not meant to be shown. The absence of any planned public monstration allowed the photos not to be framed as monstrative acts. These photos were neither condoning nor condemning what the prisoners were subjected to. They remained ambiguous, equivocal.[7] A first step toward publicness was taken when the photographs were posted on a Web site. Yet, they became fully public only when they were picked up and circulated by the major media of the center and, in particular, when they were shown on television. At that point, their full monstration no longer allowed any ambiguity. It involved a powerful framing. Showing meant condemning. Besides the late emergence of a monstration act, of a displaying gesture, what is most interesting in the story of these photographs is their step-by-step progression toward the public realm, a progression whose unexpected fluidity challenges the binary opposition between what is public and what is not public. This opposition seems to have lost its strict formality, revealing a continuum of possibilities. There are degrees in publicness, from premonstrations to full-fledged monstrations, from whispers to cries.

Monstration and re-monstration

The second type of interaction between old and new media also involves two steps, but the context is much less consensual. This interaction starts with situations that are shown on major media. Once validated by their large diffusion, once established as real by being shared on a grand scale, such situations are picked up by the new media and submitted to radical critiques or open challenges. Take the example of 9/11. Once shown by the media of the center, shared by most of the inhabitants of the planet, established as the foundation of a new historical reality, images of 9/11 are picked up and shown on sites where their new role is to challenge the central narrative, asserting, for example, that no plane ever crashed into the Pentagon, or that the assault on the twin towers was in fact engineered by the United States, its allies, or its cronies. New media pick up the very images shown by the televisions of the center, but they do so as a challenge. I would define this interaction between old and new media as a *re-monstration*. Re-monstration means showing for the second time. Re-monstration means also showing as a reproach, as a critique. What was made real by central monstration is exposed as fake.

Here is a particularly tense example of re-monstration. On September 30, 2000, the evening news edition of the central TV channel France 2 showed a boy and his father ducking bullets in the Gaza strip. The accompanying narrative made three major points: (1) Muhammed al-Dura, twelve years old, was fatally shot and killed while his father was seriously wounded. (2) The bullets were deliberately targeted by Israeli soldiers and meant to hit the boy and his father. (3) The shooting occurred during an armed confrontation between Israeli soldiers and Palestinian gunmen. The images of the father and son had an immediate impact and acquired a global iconic status (they can be found today on books, stamps, monuments, and photograph exhibits all over the world).

Yet, on the basis of an analysis of the very images broadcast by France 2, each of the three points of the French channel's narrative was challenged. Was there an actual gunfight between opposing Israeli soldiers and Palestinian militants on that day? Did the shots come from an Israeli position? Were the young boy and his father really hit by any bullet at all? A book and a documentary film were made on the subject (Huber 2003; Shapira 2002). Yet, the confrontation involved essentially Internet sites.[8] Criticism of the official France 2 narrative took the form of a *re-monstration*. It was based on the very images shown in the France 2 news bulletin.

Finding out which reading of the al-Dura pictures is correct is certainly important, but no more so than the nature of the controversy that followed, in which France 2 sued one of the bloggers, took him to court, won a first trial, lost the appeal, and circulated a petition condemning the court decision. Ostensibly the controversy was a so-called memory battle. Was the little boy hit or not? Was the whole story a case of martyrdom or an example of media imposture? Less ostensible, but very much present in the public petition, was another preoccupation. It concerned the status of bona fide journalists and the right of outsiders to perform unauthorized (re)monstrations of events. Were such outsiders entitled to discuss the accuracy or truthfulness of central television's monstrations? asked a petition signed by more than a thousand intellectuals and journalists (see "Petition on Behalf of France 2" 2008). Could improvised "monstrators" challenge television journalists' monopoly, or at least their central position in the field? Monstration had become a "field" in Bourdieu's sense: the site of a contest between established players and newcomers. Illegitimate performers had stepped uninvited onto the attention stage. Their performance was dismissed by the established players as a form of *heckling*.

It was indeed the case. Yet certain forms of heckling might signal that a public sphere undergoes profound changes. This is what the historian Jeffrey Ravel (1999) shows in his study of theatergoing public in eighteenth-century France. Ravel focuses on those spectators—usually young men—who, instead of being seated, stand crowded together next to the stage in the theater's cheapest area, an area called the "pit" or "parterre." The parterre represented a constant threat to officially sanctioned performances. Parterre spectators allowed themselves to talk back to the actors on stage, to denounce their performances, to deride their acting style and delivery. The point was not merely to have fun at the expense of actors. Parterre spectators practiced an original form of censorship in the name of the people. The whole institution of official theater was being challenged. Parterre members went so far as to tell the king's appointed actors to forget about the king and conform to their own wishes. They were literally stealing the performance both from its appointed actors and from its appointing patron. This mixture of sarcastic populism and rowdy behavior is shown by many historians to have accompanied the fall of the still-dominant public sphere of "representation." Parterre members were not merely heckling. They were hitting the royal "public sphere of representation" where it was weakest, in those urban theaters where an interface with the public allowed them to do so (Ravel 1999; Darnton 2007).

Certain blogs or Web sites seem to adopt a similar role today, when remonstrating already displayed images. They talk back to major centralized media, to the media of center and periphery, to the media of the imagination of the collective. Monstration has provided them performing possibilities that share at least two dimensions with the performances of parterres. First, like parterre members, the bloggers disrupt a certain order of representation (the role of central television in the imagination of the collective) by daring to challenge the monopoly of established official monstrators. Second, they make clear that members of the public can be performers as well, that members of the public can be the initiators of alternative monstrations. Think of the double death of Saddam Hussein, opposing the official sanitized version of his execution to its infamous cell phone cum Web site version. What characterizes the new public sphere is this proliferation of antagonistic monstrations, a proliferation of discordant images, and, finally, a contrary situation in which images speak to other images of the same events.

Yet, what is interesting about the role adopted by the new media goes beyond the conflicting relationship between an active, vociferous public and the prior performance it talks back to. It is the simple fact that a division of labor has been established between performances that come first and performances that respond to them. In regard to the media of the center, the role that the new media have invented for themselves consists in settling for the space of reception, the space of response. In other words, the new media seem to have adopted a role that is that of publics. Of course, such publics are not merely providers of attention; they are performers in their own right. Of course, they can be a violently critical public. They are nevertheless a public, an entity that attends and responds to earlier and fundamental monstrations. The new remodeled public sphere still has a divide between centers and peripheries. But there are media on each side.

Notes

1. A look at media events shows that even though they reinforce central television's link to nation, their reach constantly spreads over, goes beyond nation and delineates wider peripheries. The major cities where media events take place do not hesitate at upstaging the corresponding countries. In the volume published by the city of Turin in anticipation of its hosting the Winter Olympics, the word *Italy* never appears. Media events can suggest larger forms of community, pointing to a peripheral geography that often encompasses whole ensembles of nations.

2. For a discussion of the Thomas theorem that "if men define situations as real, they are real in their consequences," see Robert K. Merton (1995).

3. This power of defining reality tends to affect the experience of journalists themselves. A French TV team manages to go to Pakistan to get an interview with Benazir Bhutto in an affluent area of Karachi. The situation is tense (seven hundred policemen surround the mansion, ostensibly to protect those inside). Bhutto patiently submits herself to the recording session, waits for the lighting to be fixed, offers her best profile, and so on. Soon after the recording session, Bhutto leaves the mansion and is assassinated. A cassette of the interview is flown to Paris, edited, and aired on a major French central television channel. By now, images have acquired a new status. They have become historical reality. When watching their own images, journalists share the public perception of these images: they are watching the last recorded words of Benazir Bhutto. Their actual encounter with Bhutto is not altogether erased, but it has receded into the background. A perception shared by millions of spectators has become a higher reality than the journalists' own experience. The latter has merely become a plus, a source of distinction or aura.

4. Of course, one can forget about society altogether, replacing sociology by an associology, a study of association. This is Latour's radical position, based on his reading of Tarde through the eyes of Deleuze and Guattari. But one can perhaps oppose Latour's Tarde to Katz's Tarde, who is equally interested in the rejection of grand theoretical simplifications yet less deliberately iconoclastic. Perhaps the divergence has to do with the contradictions in Tarde himself and with the fact that his commentators have based their readings on different essays (Latour 2002; Katz 1993, 2006).

5. Derived from the Latin *ostensio*, the term *ostension* belongs to the liturgical vocabulary where it designates the ritual display of religious objects such as holy relics.

6. In J. L. Austin's (1962) theory of speech acts, "behabitives" are statements (speech acts) uttered in reaction to other people's behavior (past or imminent conduct) and to other people's fortunes (good or bad occurrences). Examples include commending, praising, cursing, congratulating, and offering condolences. "Verdictives" are typically uttered by juries, judges, arbitrators, or umpires to pass judgment (a "verdict") or, at least, propose an appraisal. Examples are condemning, acquitting, convicting, or assessing, ranking, grading.

7. The ambiguous, equivocal nature of Sabrina Herman's photographs must be distinguished from the self-presentation of American soldiers pictured on these photographs. The soldiers do not look like "subjects who do not want their actions to be recorded." Most often, their behavior ("smiling and giving the thumbs-up sign") calls for an audience, implying a will to "share the situation with others" (Smith et al. in Lokeilani 2008).

8. The main Web sites were Augean Stables (www.theaugeanstables.com/); Mena News (www.menapress.com/) Israel; Media-Ratings (www.m-r.fr/) France; and an American Web site devoted to exploring "problems and issues that plague modern journalism" and appropriately called Second Draft (www.seconddraft.org/).

References

Appadurai, Arjun. 1996. *Modernity at large: Cultural dimensions of globalization*. Minneapolis: University of Minnesota Press.

Arendt, Hannah. 1958. *The human condition*. Chicago: Chicago University Press.

Austin, J. L. 1962. *How to do things with words*. Cambridge, MA: Harvard University Press.

Belting, Hans. 2004. "Medium, Image corps", & "le lieu des images". in *Pour une anthropologie des images*. (Paris: Gallimard)

Boltanski, Luc. 1999. The question of the spectator, 3-55; and The topics of suffering, 57-131. In *Distant sufferings*. Cambridge: Cambridge University Press.

Darnton, Robert. 2007. The art and politics of libel in 18th century France. Lecture, Harvard University, November 1, Cambridge, MA.

Dayan, Daniel. 2006. Quand voir c'est faire. In Daniel Dayan, *La terreur-spectacle. Terrorisme et Télévision*. Paris: INA-de boek.

———. 2008. Beyond media events (postface). In Monroe Price and Daniel Dayan, *Owning the Olympics*. Ann Arbor: University of Michigan Press.

Dayan, Daniel, and Elihu Katz. 1992. *Media events, the live broadcasting of history*. Cambridge, MA: Harvard University Press.

Deleuze, Gilles, and Felix Guattari. 1972. *l'anti–oedipe. Capitalisme et Schizophrenie*. Paris: Minuit.

Goffman, Erving. 1959. The Presentation of self in everyday life . N Y: Anchor Books. Reprint, London: Penguin. 1990

Goldfarb, Jeff. 2006. *The politics of small things*. Chicago: University of Chicago Press.

Gourevitch, Philip, and Errol Morris. 2008. Annals of war: Exposure—The woman behind the camera at Abu Ghraib. *The New Yorker*, March 21.

Huber, G. 2003. *Contr'expertise d'une mise en scéne*. Paris: Raphael.

Katz, Elihu. 1993. L'heritage de Gabriel Tarde. In *Hermès*, 11-12. Paris: Presses du CNRS.

———. 2006. Rediscovering Gabriel Tarde. *Political Communication* 23:403.

Latour, Bruno. 2002. Gabriel Tarde and the end of the social. In *The social in question. New bearings in history and the social sciences*, ed. Patrick Joyce, 17-132. London: Routledge.

Lemieux, Cyril. 2007. A quoi sert l'analyse des controverses? *Mille neuf cent, Revued'histoire Intellectuelle*, 25.

Lokeilani, K. 2008. American evil. Graduate seminar paper, Department of Politics, New School for Social Research, New York.

Merton, Robert K. 1995. The Thomas theorem and the Matthew effect. *Social Forces* 74 (2): 379-424.

Petition on behalf of *France II*. 2008. Paid ad, sponsored by *Le Nouvel Observateur, Marianne*. *Le Monde*, June 8-9.

Ravel, Jeff S. 1999. *The contested parterre, public theater and French political culture*. Ithaca, NY: Cornell University Press.

Rosental, Claude. 2007. Demo-cracy in Europe. Démonstration et sociologie des sciences. CEMS-EHESS seminar, Paris.

Scannell, Paddy. 2000. For anyone as someone structures. *Media Culture and Society* 22:5-24.

Semprini, Andrea. 2003. *La société de flux. Formes du sens et identité dans les sociétés contemporaines*. Paris: L'Harmattan, and Habilitation Thesis, I E P University of Lyon III.

Shapira, E. 2002. *Das Rote Quadrat. Drei kugeln und ein totes kind*. Documentary film. ARD, March 18.

Silverstone, Roger. 2006. *Media and morality*. Cambridge, UK: Polity.

Thomas , W. I., and Thomas, D. S. 1928. *The Child in America, Behaviours, Problems and Programs*. P. 571. NY: Knopf.

Wentland, A. 2008. Digital media, morality and the Himalaya. Graduate seminar paper, Department of Politics, New School of Social Research, New York.

We Liked to Watch: Television as Progenitor of the Surveillance Society

By
JOSHUA MEYROWITZ

The rise of mass television allowed hundreds of millions of people to closely watch other people and places on a regular basis, anonymously and from afar. Television watching altered the balance of what different types of people knew about each other and relative to each other, blurred the dividing line between public and private behaviors, and weakened the link between physical location and access to social experience. In these ways, television contributed to the reshuffling of previously taken-for-granted reciprocal social roles, including those related to age, gender, and authority. In cultivating its viewers into the normalcy of the acts of watching and of being watched, television experience also stimulated the widespread use of more recent interactive visual media, including the displays of self on social networking sites. Moreover, familiarity with television as a watching machine has fostered the otherwise surprising level of tolerance for increasingly pervasive government, corporate, and populace surveillance.

Keywords: television; surveillance; medium theory; childhood; socialization; gender; political image; televation

By changing the channel he could change himself. He could go through phases, as garden plants went through phases, but he could change as rapidly as he wished by twisting the dial backward and forward. . . . By turning the dial, Chance could bring others inside his eyelids. Thus he came to believe that it was he, Chance, and no one else, who made himself be.

—Kosinski (1970, 5-6)

Others and Elsewheres

In Jerzy Kosinki's *Being There* (1970), the central character, Chance, is a fool who comes to be mistaken for a genius. He reaches adulthood without ever having left the walled home and garden of his protector, the Old Man. He can neither read nor write. His education is limited to experiences of images and sounds

DOI: 10.1177/0002716209339576

and clichéd phrases acquired from years of television viewing. When he is forced out of the house after the Old Man's death, the world outside is oddly familiar to him. "The street, the cars, the buildings, the people, the faint sounds were images already burned into his memory. . . . He had the feeling that he had seen it all" (pp. 28-29). And yet, Chance is comically ignorant of social life; he knows nothing of real importance. He does not even know how to feed himself. A minor accident— his leg is bruised when he is hit by a limousine—fortuitously brings him into the spheres of the wealthy and the powerful. There, Chance's surface familiarity with reality—combined with his mimicry of the calm and clear tones of a television character's voice—allows him to "pass" for a wise observer of the political, social, and economic realms. Chance is unable to resist watching television at every opportunity, even while being seduced by his new mentor's young wife. He prefers looking to touching or being touched. "Seeing encompassed all at once; a touch was limited to one spot at a time" (p. 113). In any case, one doesn't touch a TV screen. "I like to watch," Chance says repeatedly, and yet he reveals no real under-standing of what he sees on the screen or in front of him. Nevertheless, his advice is sought by economic leaders, talk show hosts, journalists, and even the president of the United States. In the movie adaptation of the book, based on Kosinski's own screenplay, Chance comes to be seen as a promising candidate for the nation's highest office, and the film ends with him walking on water.

Kosinski's charming, yet frightening, fable conveys some not-so-subtle messages about television: that the medium gives us merely an illusion of experience and knowledge, that we sacrifice too much in trading face time for screen time, and that everything of personal and social value is at risk as a result. In this tale about media-informed idiocy, Kosinski captures well the early attitude toward televi-sion among the literati who dismissed TV as an "idiot box" and refused to own a TV set (or hid theirs in a closet). Television clearly represented a threat to literate culture. Even more than radio and the movies, TV challenged the print medium's once strong hold over the pathways to nonlocal experience. Television, through its ubiquity and its open and simple displays of image and voice, offered views and sounds of others and elsewheres on the cheap. One did not have to travel anywhere in particular to discover its scenes. Little imagination or other mental effort was needed to make basic sense of its content. What was on television,

---

Joshua Meyrowitz is a professor of media studies in the Department of Communication at the University of New Hampshire, where he has won the Lindberg Award for Outstanding Scholar-Teacher in the College of Liberal Arts. He teaches courses in mass media, critical analysis of news, media research, and communication theory. He is the author of the award-winning book No Sense of Place: The Impact of Electronic Media on Social Behavior, *published by Oxford University Press (1985). His articles on media and society have appeared in numerous scholarly journals and anthologies, as well as in general-interest magazines and newspapers. His writings have been translated into twelve languages.*

NOTE: The author thanks Renée H. Carpenter, Peter Schmidt, and Josh Lauer for their help-ful suggestions and Elihu Katz for his wisdom, gentleness, patience, and persistence. © 2009 Joshua Meyrowitz

unlike what was in most books, was equally accessible to young and old, poor and rich, illiterate and highly educated, those in one place and those almost everywhere else. Moreover, television threatened to debase "culture," in that most of what was on TV was of low quality and bounded by the desires of advertisers, media owners, and political elites.

Yet, in reacting with disdain to television's threat to literate values, Kosinski also provides some unintended hints that the rise of television may have reshaped social realms in ways that are not simply good or bad and that cannot be reduced merely to questions about what types of content are (or are not) conveyed by the medium. For if Chance—with minimal mental capacity, no formal education, and no live experience beyond an enclosed garden—could wander into the outside world and "recognize" it and somehow find his way in it, then what a powerful force television must be in expanding vicarious experience for children and adults of normal background and intelligence.

Television, Televation, and More Permeable Social Boundaries

The rapid adoption of television provides evidence of how much Americans, like Kosinski's Chance, became fascinated by, and perhaps addicted to, the act of closely watching others from a distance. Now that we are more than a half century into the era of television and other electronic audiovisual media, many members of the population find it increasingly difficult to imagine (or remember) what social life was like before the near-universal availability of such means of almost constant watching of, and listening to, others. Yet, before TV, most Americans and members of other industrialized societies lived in a world where children had limited experience of all-adult situations (or even of the activities of children a few years older than themselves); where male and female spheres of activity could be segregated by physical separation of home from work; and where candidates for, and holders of, national office (as well as leaders in other domains, such as religion) were rarely seen close-up by average members of the population.

Television turned an ages-old assumptive world on its head. Whereas the reality for most of the millennia of human existence was the basic invisibility of most of the world and its inhabitants, we now expect to be able to see a vast array of other types of people and places on a regular basis. Indeed, we tend to be suspicious or fearful of those people and places that remain largely unexposed and inaccessible to the television camera. Moreover, we now typically reverse the process that once granted those of high status the ability to remain relatively inaccessible and out of sight. As average citizens, we tend to believe that we should be able to maintain large measures of privacy and be in general control of our public displays, even if, as I discuss later, we increasingly relish self-exposure. In contrast, we expect to be able to see "celebrities" and "stars," broadly defined, in a variety of personal and professional locations and social contexts. Thus, both pop stars and presidents are now routinely watched by millions of members of the populace in formal performances and in informal "private" settings of vacations, exercise, and "family time." Moreover, most of the accessible images of such celebrated individuals simulate close physical proximity and reveal gestures and facial expressions once visible only to those in personal or intimate relationships with public figures.

The analysis presented here draws on "medium theory," which argues that to understand media influences, one must look beyond the specific messages in the medium to the physical, social, and psychological consequences of using each medium (or each *type* of media) as they can be distinguished from the consequences employing other media (Meyrowitz 1994, 2008). Medium theory does not argue that a medium can have influence without any content; nor does it claim that a medium's characteristics magically "determine" the medium's impact on passive humans. Medium theory does claim, however, that the same or similar content often has different influences in different media and that changes in modes of communication usually lead to new ways of interacting that match the potentialities and constraints of new media. This article looks at some of the ways in which the rise of mass television dramatically altered the boundaries of social experience by allowing hundreds of millions of people to study closely the faces, bodies, words, and vocalizations of other people in other places. In this way, television made the unusual routine. For the first time, average members of the population could watch many different types of behaviors in many different types of settings, including many of those behaviors and settings that were, without television, restricted to most viewers because of their age, gender, social status, time and budgetary constraints, and other limitations. This new form of exposure via television was significant in at least five ways.

First, television's electronic extension of our eyes reshaped the social and psychological meaning of physical location. What humans could experience with their own eyes was once determined by *where* they were physically. A powerful experiential bond existed among those who shared the same locations—homes, neighborhoods, schools, workplaces—with a complementary gulf between the local "us" and the distant "them." Television and other electronic media have diluted shared place-based experiences while creating broader, but shallower, commonalities with people elsewhere who share televisual and other forms of electronic information.

Second, both fictional and nonfictional television altered the balance of "who knows what *about* whom" and "who knows what *compared* to whom." And since the ways in which we view and interact with other people in both mediated and unmediated interaction are dependent in part on what we know—and do not know—about each other and what we know relative to each other, television contributed to the reshuffling of previously taken-for-granted reciprocal social roles, including those related to differences in age, gender, and authority.

Third, television not only exposed many *other* types of people and *other* types of places to viewers, but it also allowed viewers to see how types of people *like themselves* and types of places *like their own* were being viewed from the perspective of other people and places. Children, for example, not only learned about many "adult secrets" via television, but they also learned about the ways in which adults perceived and treated children and how adults viewed child locations, such as schools. Women gained further insight into the ways in which men viewed and treated them and how men viewed "women's places." Average citizens gained further knowledge of the ways in which those in positions of economic and political power conceived of members of the public and their locales. If, as social philosopher George Herbert Mead (1934) argued, we gain a sense of who we are—our "selves"—when we are able to imagine how other people imagine us, then television would logically have shifted viewers' senses of themselves as they have experienced the mediated perspectives of an enlarged set of others. Similarly, TV watchers have gained new senses of their locations through expanded sources for imagining how their places are perceived from other locations (Meyrowitz 2005).

In a fourth dimension of change, our ability to watch others (and to see others' conceptions of people like us) on television, without simultaneously being monitored by those we watch, has freed many viewers from the overpowering and confining web of multisensory face-to-face interaction that long resisted rapid modification. In place of such "conservative," embodied interaction, TV's one-way mirror has allowed many viewers to grasp how others have imagined them *and* to reimagine a different set of roles for themselves in the real world. In this sense, television exposure—rather than encouraging *imitation* of the portrayed age, gender, and average citizen roles—actually gave those of subordinate status new means of *resisting* both their media portrayals and their actual, marginalized social positions. The same was true for those viewers who felt "symbolically annihilated" by their virtual absence from the shared arena of early television: people of color, gays and lesbians, and other minorities. Fictional and nonfictional television have operated together as a type of "global positioning system" in the sense of giving viewers an image of where they fit (or do not fit) in the normalized social order. This mediated view from outside of the matrix of embodied interaction has given those of marginalized status a new mental place from which to position and move levers of social change.

Finally, television in its early decades cultivated its audiences into the "normalcy" of people watching other people closely—yet anonymously and from afar. This initially unidirectional form of observation by the many of the few, I argue, set the stage for the widespread use of more recent interactive visual media, including the displays of self by the many to the many on social networking sites and elsewhere on the Internet. Experience with mass television may also have laid the groundwork for the otherwise surprising level of tolerance among the population of a wide range of forms of government, corporate, and populace "surveillance," including being watched by cameras in many public and institutional settings. Since almost all of us have been avid TV watchers at least at some time in our lives, we understand many of the impulses of all watchers, including the watchers who watch us. Indeed, rather than horrifying us, being monitored by cameras in a culture familiar with decades of television viewing may ironically make some members of the public feel more valued. In a small way at least, we now join media celebrities in being important enough to be watched on television and computer screens. Both through our own digital displays online and through others' monitoring of us in many settings, we may see ourselves as being "televated"— elevated in status by the act of being televised or otherwise mediated.

Children Watching Adults

Diaries and other historical artifacts provide some clues to the lack of knowledge in the pretelevision era of the behind-the-scenes behaviors of others, even of members of one's own family. This lack of knowledge was especially true for children and young adults. Anne Frank's diary, for example, reveals the limits of what even a precocious and incredibly observant young girl knew about adult life—until the boundaries between child and adult spheres became more porous. When Anne, her parents, her sister, and another family were forced into hiding from the Nazis in Amsterdam during World War II, Anne's previous views of adult behavior were shattered. In September 1942, after less than three months in confined quarters with the adults, Anne wrote about her surprise regarding how easily and how much grown-ups quarreled "over the most idiotic things." The thirteen-year-old Anne added, "Up till now I thought that only children squabbled and that that wore off as you grew up. . . . I'm simply amazed again and again over their awful manners . . . and stupidity" (Frank [1947] 1953, 29). Anne no longer could view or treat her parents and other adults in the same manner as before, and the adults—more exposed—could no longer maintain their old roles of authority and self-confidence with respect to their children.

The rise of mass television, in a sense, brought all members of the viewing public into a virtual place akin to Anne Frank's attic, a place where different categories of people are no longer as isolated from each other as they once were, and where, because of enhanced monitoring of each other, traditional reciprocal roles are no longer as easy to stage.

The idea that television could foster such changes is supported by the occurrence of equally powerful shifts in roles with earlier developments in media. A few hundred years before Anne wrote her diary, those adults who were literate discovered that they could use written and printed material to create adult-adult interactions without children and illiterate adults "overhearing," and that they could separate what children of different ages knew by putting different types of social information in books of different reading difficulty. (To this day, many children's books have codes on the back, such as "5:3," which means fifth grade, third month.) To climb the ladder of literacy, a child still has to learn to read simple books before reading more complex books. Yet, one does not have to learn to read to watch television, and one does not have to watch TV programs in a simple-to-complex order equivalent to stages of reading difficulty. Television's images look like reality, and most TV sounds are similar to those of real life. Television speaks in a human voice. Over the years, many programs aimed at adults have been highly popular among children. Although children do not understand everything shown on television (neither do adults, for that matter), children are exposed through television to many dimensions of adult life (adult anger, grief, illness, violence, war, crime, foolishness, and so on) that literate parents, teachers, and other adults spent several centuries trying to hide from children. No children growing up in a television home, for example, could make Anne Frank's mistake of thinking that only children squabbled.

Many of the influences of television, therefore, become invisible when observers focus exclusively on the content of specific television messages or on the questions of whether children and other viewers imitate the portrayed actions or are persuaded by the "lessons" in commercials or other programming. Television's most pervasive influences more likely flow from the ways in which television rearranges relative access to social information. Most children love to watch television because the medium expands their visual mobility far beyond where they could walk, run, or ride bicycles. Television takes children across the city, country, and globe before most parents give them permission to cross the street. Moreover, the ease of changing channels allows children and other viewers to travel with minimal effort through multiple visual and psychological spaces in a matter of seconds. Television also permits children to watch adults in a variety of once adult-only settings. In effect, television encourages children to crash the adult "parties" to which they were explicitly not invited, but with additional twists. Through TV, children can observe adults closely—without being watched by those they are watching and without the adult behavior they are observing being modified to account for their "presence." As a result, TV-era children have become familiar with many dimensions of adult gesture, emotion, behavior, and experience that remained largely hidden from print-era children.

Even a television program designed to help adults decide what to tell and not to tell children usually leads to more, not less, child exposure to adult secrets. This is the opposite of the effect of the same type of content in books. The book as a medium facilitates an interaction in which adults can communicate "privately" with other adults about how to handle children. Children too young to read have no access to this "conversation." Even for older children, the use of small typefaces and complex sentences and the existence of each book as a discrete object that can be hidden from children further protect printed adult interactions from the intrusion of children. Yet, when adults engage in the same type of tactical discussion on television, a paradox arises. Thousands of children are able to watch and listen in on this parenting strategy session. Television, then, not only exposes children to a wide array of secrets, it also exposes children to what may be the biggest adult secret of all—the "secret of secrecy"—the fact that adults, even though often unsure of their parental actions, conspire over what to tell and not to tell children. Through multiple forms of exposure via television, adults have found it increasingly difficult to convincingly portray themselves to children as omniscient.

Some critics of television who mistakenly assume that the medium's impact rests largely on imitation bemoan the loss of 1950s programs portraying innocent children and their replacement with programs in which child characters behave too much like little adults and are cynical about the adults in their lives. Yet such simplistic "child-see, child-do" thinking misses how radical early family programming was for the children on the other side of the screen. Although it is true that the child *characters* on early TV programs such as *Father Knows Best* were innocent and were exposed only to the "onstage" view of adulthood, the child *viewers* of these programs had a "side-stage" view of adulthood. That is, those of us who grew up watching such programs learned that parents behaved one way in front of their children (calm, cool, collected, all-knowing) and another way when away from their children (expressing doubts, fears, and concern over the limits of their wisdom and parenting skill). Such programs revealed to their child viewers that parents manipulated their children and that adults could not always be trusted to tell the truth. Through such programs, we learned that parents *pretended* to know best. The children on these programs were exposed to child viewers as dupes, certainly not as role models to emulate. The generation growing up on such shows, therefore, reached maturity with a concern about the adult "credibility gap" and proclaiming that no one over thirty (from earlier generations at least!) should be trusted. Later programs, which included more cynical and adultlike children, as well as less authoritative adults, were in that sense *less* revolutionary in that they simply adjusted the behavior and understanding of the fictional children to match what the real child viewers of the earlier programs had already learned about parents and other adults.

In short, television—as a new shared arena for child and adult mutual watching and socialization—has encouraged greater overlap in age-related roles, regardless of the specific portrayals of children and adults in the medium. We see more adultlike children and more childlike adults in everyday life. Ironically, this behavioral blurring has occurred even though contemporaneous psychological research into human development has claimed to discover the reality of more and more cognitive distinctions between children and adults and between children of different ages.

Television also tutored its first generation of viewers, and those that have followed, in the rules of watching and being watched. One lesson learned was not to try to maximize privacy (a futile effort in any case) but to accept the exposure and to shape our behaviors to reduce *major* inconsistencies from one setting to another, while also raising our tolerance for (and even pleasure in) public exposure of behavioral idiosyncrasies and variations in behavior over time and from place to place. When developments in technology expanded TV's limited and unidirectional surveillance into broader, multidirectional forms of watching and of behavioral displays, it felt rather natural to accept and even to embrace them.

Men and Women Watching Each Other

In the 1960s and 1970s, feminists rightly criticized the sexist portrayals on television and other popular media. "Television's image of the American woman," Betty Friedan wrote in *TV Guide* in 1964, "is a stupid, unattractive, insecure little household drudge who spends her martyred, mindless, boring days dreaming of love—and plotting nasty revenge against her husband" (1976, p. 48). Yet, the larger claim that often followed the accurate feminist critiques of TV content— that television was an incredibly powerful sexist force that would lead many young female viewers to want to grow up focused exclusively on housework and mothering—has turned out to be false. Indeed, the first generation of women to grow up in television households advanced the feminist movement beyond previous imaginings and demanded gender integration of social spheres. That outcome is rarely attributed to television, except as a medium to be actively resisted. Yet if TV is properly conceived of as a "watching device" and a "secret-exposing machine," rather than as a "message-delivery system" that fosters imitation or persuasion, the subsequent changes in gender politics are more understandable.

When television first spread through U.S. households, the Victorian notion of "separate spheres" for men and women was still strong in middle-class life. The public, male realm was one of competition, work, and accomplishment, of rationality and suppressed emotion. The private, female sphere was mostly centered on the home, a place for cooperation, feelings, emotion, and childrearing. As tutored by separate instructions from parents, teachers, peers, and gender-specific etiquette books, men and women were not supposed to participate fully in the "other's" sphere, or even to know that much about the full dimensions of it. The content of early television also projected this worldview. In mid-1960s television, as Friedan (1976, 48) observed, women were "virtually nonexistent" in the "serious documentary and ordinary reportage and issues and news of the world." And yet the characteristics of the medium undermined the continuity of such gender distinctions among its viewers.

Although most of the *characters* in early TV existed in their separate gender spheres, male and female *viewers* were not separated in terms of what they could see. Women viewers were allowed to watch all-male settings and behaviors, and men viewers were allowed to watch all-female behaviors and settings. TV viewing tutored its audience in the ways of the "other" and in the ways in which the other gender viewed them (and often tried to manipulate them). Television exposed young girls and homebound women to many of the dimensions of the male realm that men used to tell women not to worry their "pretty little heads about"— business, politics, sports, the justice system, battlefields, and so on. On television, the once distant and mystified male realm, and its inhabitants and activities, did not seem worthy of special respect or special entry requirements. Men, as it turned out, often stammered and sweated and spoke ineloquently. Emotions were more evident in the male realm than the gender mythology suggested, and yet "cold male rationality" was also on televisual display in situations when warmer and more caring responses seemed more appropriate to many viewers. Such exposure would be unlikely to encourage female viewers to relish their traditional roles while granting men continued exclusive dominion over the public realm. There are few things as frustrating as being shown activities and places that you are told are too important for you to have access to them. This was especially true for female viewers, who could easily imagine participating in the now-exposed realms just as well as, or better than, the males who were trying to maintain them as their restricted domain. Conversely, television close-ups made it more difficult for male viewers to ignore traditionally female perspectives on the culture, such as the emotional dimensions and consequences of public actions. TV exposed tears welling up in the eyes of leaders and voices cracking with emotion. Television revealed that "glorious victories" and "crushing defeats" both led to scenes of homes reduced to rubble, blood on the ground, and limp bodies of children and adults carried by survivors.

Beyond reconceptualization of individual gender roles, television's new ways of seeing encouraged women to rethink their identity in relation to the men in their lives and to other women in general. As many twentieth-century feminist writers describe, there was a sudden, surprising shift in women's mental images of themselves in the mid-1960s. Gloria Steinem and Sheila Rothman, for example, describe how most individual women once aligned themselves mentally with the status and privileges of the individual men in their lives. Most women, they write, did not usually think of themselves as a political "out-group" that could coalesce on a large scale to bring about social change (Steinem 1980, 11; Rothman 1978, 3-4, 231-32). Yet, what is missing from these otherwise insightful descriptions of women's rising feminist consciousness is the role that television's "view from outside" played in encouraging even isolated homebound wives and mothers, as well as young girls, to see themselves as members of a large, disenfranchised *group*, excluded from the male spheres that television portrayed.

Without mentioning the new household appliance—television—that might have made it possible, Steinem (1980, 107-8) details the manifestation of a "psychic turf" that overrode the lack of a women's shared territory and the "breaking of boundaries between and among women." In a book subtitled "Women Awakening," Elizabeth Janeway (1974, 12) similarly heralds a "sudden enlargement of our world." Barbara Ehrenreich and Deirdre English (1978) offer what sounds like a description of women's self-perception changing as they watch television—but without mentioning the medium:

> Like the men of their generation, they had *seen* beyond the bucolic peacefulness of the suburbs to the war zone at the perimeter—the ghetto rebellions in the cities, the guerilla struggles in the Third World. . . . Inevitably they drew the analogy between women and blacks, between women and all other "oppressed people." (Pp. 283-84, emphasis added)

Television was the medium through which women in suburban homes did, in fact, see into the inner cities and faraway war zones. Indeed, because homebound women were not caught up in the male sphere of work, they ironically often had *more* time than men to watch what was newly exposed on television.

Watching television, as a new source of vicarious experience, can also be seen as the unspoken activity that informs feminist Betty Friedan's ([1963] 1977) description in *The Feminine Mystique* of the "schizophrenic split" that women experienced between the ways in which mainstream media instructed them to act and feel and their new sense of discomfort with those traditional roles. In media content, women were being told that they should relish their social place as wives and mothers protected in the home. Yet, Friedan argued, women were increasingly feeling limited and trapped in those traditional roles and settings. Implicit in Friedan's description of a "split" is the gap between the content of media messages and a new way of seeing a wider world from which women were largely barred. In 1960, writes Friedan, *McCall's* pictured women as "young and frivolous, almost childlike; fluffy and feminine; passive; gaily content in a world of bedroom and kitchen, sex, babies, and home" (p. 30). Yet, in that same year, Friedan notes, "Castro led a revolution in Cuba and men were trained to travel into outer space; the year that the African continent brought forth new nations, and a plane whose speed is greater than the speed of sound broke up a Summit Conference; . . . and Negro youth in Southern schools forced the United States, for the first time since the Civil War, to face a moment of democratic truth" (p. 31). Out of this discrepancy in images, "the problem that has no name burst like a boil through the image of the happy American housewife" (p. 17). Friedan does not identify the source of women's sudden exposure to world events, and yet her list reads like a summary of the top stories on television news. By 1960, TV was in nearly 90 percent of U.S. households, and almost all homebound women were being exposed to the traditionally "male" topics that Friedan outlines. Such new forms of watching, alongside the sexist images in most other media, made women more aware of the spheres and activities from which they were excluded. Two logical outcomes of such awareness were the widespread rejection by women of their portrayal as "frivolous" and the demand to participate equally in the wider world with which they were now much more familiar. In watching television images that blurred public and private dimensions of society, women were encouraged to see the political as personal and the personal as political, a revelation that evolved into a rallying cry for the feminist movement.

Television—as a new form of watching and experiencing—fostered the feminist worldview and an agenda for bypassing patriarchal hierarchies in politics, sports, medicine, academe, and other social spheres. (It also primed women for using the Internet to further those goals and develop ways of accessing previously "male" information as well as sharing female experience that was previously often ignored or devalued by men.) In this sense, television encouraged women to act more like traditional males. Yet, in visually penetrating the shell of male superiority and armored emotions, TV has also fostered a feminization of men by making them more aware of their emotions and behavioral displays. In televised campaigns for political office, for example, even male candidates are now judged as much by "dating criteria" ("What is he like and do I like him?") as by résumé criteria ("What is his training and what has he accomplished?"). Indeed, TV is one of the few arenas in our culture where men routinely wear makeup and are judged as much on their manner and appearance as on their achievements.

Within this view, television—in spite of early sexist content (and perhaps even more so because of it)—has encouraged gender-blending, with more career-oriented women and more family-oriented men. Rather than early TV viewers being relatively passive recipients of gender content for their imitation or persuasion, they actively engaged with the content to make sense of the old gendered society and then to reimagine less bounded gender roles for themselves in it.

Members of the Public Watching Political Leaders

In what was probably the earliest political public relations manual for the era of printing, Niccolò Machiavelli ([1532] 1998) argued that princes should highlight and downplay selective traits to foster the best image. Machiavelli can be seen as guiding leaders to take advantage of the new, disembodied form of communication with their subjects that was being facilitated by print. With print, leaders could communicate more broadly, while also restricting intimate access to themselves as embodied human beings. In this new communication environment, leaders could and should make it *appear* from afar that they possessed certain princely qualities, since only a few people could come close enough to check out the reality. A century later, Balthasar Gracian, rector of the Jesuit College, advised priests to "mix a little mystery with everything" because mystery "arouses veneration" (quoted in Duncan 1962, 218). Political images remained relatively mystified for another three hundred years.

Before the radio era, most Americans had never heard the voice of a U.S. president. Before the television era, only a tiny minority of Americans had been able to see a president closely enough to get a sense of his personal style or his physical limits and idiosyncrasies. To this day, relatively few Americans know that George Washington had ill-fitting false teeth and a pockmarked face; that the freckle-faced Thomas Jefferson was voted the homeliest scholar at William and Mary College and had a speech impediment that led him to try to avoid speaking in public (he never addressed Congress in person); that Abraham Lincoln had difficulty hiding his bouts of severe depression from those around him, used backwoods pronunciation ("git" instead of "get" and "thar" in place of "there," etc.), and spoke in a high, squeaky voice that went up an octave higher when he was nervous; or that William Taft weighed 350 pounds, sweated profusely, and often fell asleep during public events (Bailey 1996; Barton 1930). Although President Franklin Roosevelt was imagined in the minds of many radio-listening Americans as a powerful leader, only a relatively small number of Americans seemed to grasp the extent of his physical disabilities, such as that he had to be carried to and from his limousine or that in the planned presence of a camera he worked diligently to fake the ability to stand and walk with his lifeless legs (Smith 1972).

Presidential images were once very protected. Press-president interactions were relatively private affairs. As late as 1953, at the start of the Eisenhower presidency, journalists were not allowed to quote a president directly without his permission (Cornwell 1965, 187). Teddy Roosevelt had been the first president to meet with reporters in the White House—while he was shaving. Woodrow Wilson held the first regular press conferences. As late as the presidency of Franklin Roosevelt, journalists' questions were to be submitted in advance, the press was not to report on which questions the president refused to answer, presidential press secretaries would often interrupt the president to correct his statements (also unreported by the press), and authorized quotations were routinely "cleaned up" for publication (Cornwell 1965, 61-114; Smith 1972, 76).

Almost immediately, television shattered some of the mystique surrounding the presidency. The availability of new, more sensitive film stock in 1954 allowed movie cameras to shoot indoors without special lighting, which made it more difficult for the White House to justify the exclusion of newsreel cameras. As a result, Ike's press secretary, Jim Hagerty, allowed the first filming of presidential press conferences. Initially, Hagerty demanded the right to review and edit the film before it could be used on television. Later, the film from presidential press conferences was allowed to air without screening and review.

As a result of changes brought on by the televising of press conferences, newspapers began to quote the president without asking permission, and the exchanges between press and president became more public. Among other things, the public was given its first sustained views of a president making numerous speaking and factual errors, using many "ums" and "ahs," and taking long pauses. Through television, the image of the president was being humanized and lowered more to the level of the common person.

Television images, of course, have often been tightly controlled, both in what is made visible and through what is hidden. At the birth of the TV era, advertisers and political consultants began to spend a considerable amount of their energy shaping what the public saw on the screen. And the public has often been fooled by what has been shown and censored. (Relatively few Americans knew—or even know now—that behind the benign image of President Eisenhower at the golf course were a series of "covert operations" that involved overthrowing democratic governments in countries such as Iran and Guatemala, with lasting negative consequences to this day.) At times, however, television seemed to demand so much manipulation that it made the fact of image manipulation more visible— thereby undermining many of the efforts. Television also quickly brought "image" and "image manipulation" to the fore of discussion in our culture, making the public more suspicious of what it is shown.

The new speed of reporting fostered by radio and television also contributed to a less mystified view of the honesty and competence of leaders. In 1960, for example, U.S. news organizations reported that a weather plane had gone off course and was lost. Meanwhile, Soviet Premier Nikita Khrushchev announced that the USSR had shot down a U.S. spy plane that was violating its airspace. Millions of Americans heard the U.S. State Department's press chief, Lincoln White, say that Khrushchev was lying. There had been "absolutely no–N-O–deliberate attempt to violate Soviet air space . . . never has been!" But Khrushchev had a trump card, or rather two trump cards: he had the wreckage of the plane, and he had the live pilot. Embarrassed by the dramatic evidence presented, the president, vice president, and other U.S. government officials scrambled to respond. When juxtaposed through the power of television, however, the very different claims from different sources in the government created an image of an administration that was deceitful and out of control (Barnouw 1970, 138-39). For many U.S. citizens, the U-2 incident was the first time they saw strong evidence that their government lied. It would not be the last (Meyrowitz 2006).

The heightened watching of political leaders through TV has also made it more difficult for leaders to hide dimensions of their lives that are inconsistent with their public images. Or, put differently, political leaders must often now adapt their public image to incorporate those aspects of their behavior that cannot remain hidden. In a pretelevision era, the public never saw much of President Franklin Roosevelt's distant relationship with his wife, close relationship with his mistress, or even his interactions with his political advisors and staff. Therefore, FDR did not need to adjust his public image or public statements to accommodate these fundamental dimensions of his personal and political life.

The close watching of U.S. presidents was intensified after John F. Kennedy's 1963 assassination, partly because that assassination was not captured by professional TV news crews. (The only visual record was an amateur 8-mm film shot by Abraham Zapruder, a clothing manufacturer.) Ever since then, TV news crews have coordinated efforts to "cover the body" of the president at all possible times. Ironically, then, Kennedy's assassination encouraged a degree of close watching that would likely have exposed a number of his many extramarital affairs. Such close watching almost brought down the Clinton presidency and provides strong incentives (albeit ones that are sometimes ignored, as in the case of John Edwards) for more recent presidents and presidential candidates to remain on their "best behavior."

The close watching of political leaders has also altered political style, in that the bombastic rhetoric and delivery of stump speeches are ill suited to the close-up lens and sensitive microphone. (Consider the almost instant collapse of the 2004 presidential candidacy of Howard Dean. When he was unknowingly handed a noise-canceling microphone that muted the background sounds of a roaring crowd of volunteers, the media coined the phrase, "The Dean Scream," replayed it excessively, and condemned him as mentally unstable.)

As a result of a variety of forms of intensified watching, political leaders increasingly try to act more like the "person next door," with low-key style, self-deprecating humor, and (at least feigned) humility. Simultaneously, however, our real neighbors and other average citizens have been demanding more of a say in local, national, and international affairs, as well as in the policy formations of political leaders. The 2008 presidential campaign, for example, was marked by an unprecedented level of grassroots activity for all candidates, largely organized over the Internet. Moreover, in an unusual development, many of the grassroots groups that helped to mobilize support for Barack Obama's election did not disband after their "win." Instead, they vowed to stay active in pushing President Obama toward policies that match his campaign promises (Helman 2008).

Conclusion: Watching Ourselves Being Watched

Pervasive television watching, as I have described in this article, has had a significant impact on the watchers' senses of place and social identity. Television watching has altered the balance of what different types of people know *about* each other and *relative* to each other, blurred the dividing line between public and private behaviors, and weakened the link between physical location and access to social experience. Unlike Kosinki's hapless character, the TV-addicted Chance—who is hesitant to extend his video watching into touch and travel— real TV viewers have actively used what they have learned about other types of people and locations to renegotiate their social positions and extend their real-life activity into new spheres. Such consequences extend far beyond the more commonly researched concerns over the persuasive power or imitative appeal of television content. The greatest impact has been on those whose relatively iso-lated physical locations once severely restricted their access to social information. Children are now included in many discussions and situations from which they were once barred (such as funerals and hospital visits), with a complementary shift in the roles of parents and teachers. Women have successfully integrated most previously all-male spheres, with an associated adjustment in male roles. And average citizens are insisting on greater involvement in political and social decision making, with a related adjustment in the role displays of political and other leaders. Many distinctions in roles remain, of course, and yet the changes have been significant.

As profound as TV's impact has been, however, mass television's boundary penetration was largely unidirectional. Television brought images and sounds from afar into many of the life spaces of most children and adults. In contrast, what most television viewers did in spaces—while speaking, reading, eating, walking, shopping, sleeping, flirting, making love, and even watching television— remained largely place-bound and invisible to others.

In recent decades, however, new technologies and new forms of older tech-nologies have dramatically altered the balance between incoming and outgoing televisual and other electronic information. The wired telephone was once the main medium through which the average person's expressions were communi-cated beyond local space. Now, newer media such as camcorders, webcams, mobile phones, surveillance cameras, social networking Web sites, video posting sites such as YouTube, stand-alone and integrated global positioning systems (GPS), and many other technologies extend the temporal and spatial projection, observation, and impact of individuals' behaviors. "Watching devices" of many kinds have been diminishing in size, decreasing in cost, and becoming simpler to use and more adaptable to different tasks. At the same time, digital technology has made it increasingly easier, faster, and cheaper to distribute the resulting surveillance artifacts across space and preserve them over time. Additionally, the data gathered from different watching technologies are increasingly being net-worked together, especially by government and corporations, but even for the public via the rapid "links" available through the Internet.

Most of those writers who have described the rise of the surveillance society have expressed concern and surprise about the public's general lack of apprehen-sion over the spread of technologies that render us "watchable" in ways that were, until recently, inconceivable. We should be alarmed, these writers point out, by the ways in which new technologies create a "ubiquitous, decentered Panopticon"

(Whitaker 1999, 140); entail "meticulous rituals of power" (Staples 2000, 3); and construct "digital enclosures" (Andrejevic 2007, 2) that limit our real freedoms. Cameras watch members of the public on streets, at work, and in stores. Every credit card purchase creates a data trail. Store courtesy cards monitor purchases and lead to individualized ads and coupons. Online surfing is monitored by spy software and "cookies" planted by Web sites on our own computers. Toll-paying transponders track our location and speed of travel from one toll booth to the next. Some employers use keystroke-monitoring software to keep track of what employees are typing. Many street and highway cams can be monitored by anyone with online access anywhere in the world. Radio frequency identification (RFID) tags (which, unlike bar codes, identify a specific item from hundreds of feet away) are increasingly being embedded in products, books, payment cards, mobile phones, government identity cards (including all new U.S. passports), and even pets and people.

The surprisingly low level of public resistance to increasing modes of surveillance has been attributed to a variety of factors, including ignorance of the trend, naïveté regarding the uses of the resulting data, and seduction by the associated conveniences. Without dismissing the seriousness of the concerns raised by surveillance researchers, many of which deserve our close attention and political action, this article has offered another possible explanation for the public's typical equanimity in the face of increasingly pervasive surveillance: the public is familiar and comfortable with surveillance activity after participating in a form of it themselves. Over the decades of the television era, hundreds of millions of people have engaged in anonymously watching others closely, yet from afar. Indeed, watching others on TV may be the most shared cultural experience on the planet. Moreover, most of those watched on TV have eagerly volunteered their images for display, or at least consented to being televised. After living through a half century of the television era, then, neither the watching of others nor the act of offering oneself up for watching by others can be perceived of as an odd or perverse activity. Moreover, millions of members of the public actively participate in their own surveillance by voluntarily posting profiles and pictures (both still and moving) of themselves online, publicly identifying their "friends" and "relationship status" on networking sites, and posting their off-the-cuff responses to events in weblogs. Such activities now suggest that millions of members of the planet's population not only like to watch others; they also like for others to watch them.

In their influential treatise on the social construction of reality, Peter Berger and Thomas Luckmann (1966) describe how humans, unlike other animals, participate extensively in their own creation. In this article, I have argued that the television era transformed the options and modes of human self-creation. In industrialized societies, few members have resisted the seductive glow of the television screen or been able to escape the new logic of self-actualization that it has encouraged. The unwatched life—and a life without watching many others—now seems less worthy of living. We, like Jerzy Kosinki's TV-watching character, Chance, bring thousands of others inside our eyelids. We now also offer our images—and digital fingerprints and footprints—for consumption by other watchers. And in these ways we, like Chance, find new ways to make ourselves be. We watch and are watched; therefore we are.

References

Andrejevic, M. 2007. *iSpy: Surveillance and power in the interactive era*. Lawrence: University Press of Kansas.

Bailey, T. 1966. *Presidential greatness: The image of the man from George Washington to the present*. New York: Appleton-Century.

Barnouw, E. 1970. *The image empire: A history of broadcasting in the United States from 1953*. New York: Oxford University Press.

Barton, W. E. 1930. *Lincoln at Gettysburg*. Indianapolis, IN: Bobbs-Merrill.

Berger, P. L., and T. Luckmann. 1966. *The social construction of reality: A treatise in the sociology of knowledge*. Garden City, NY: Doubleday.

Duncan, H. D. 1962. *Communication and social order*. New York: Bedminster.

Cornwell, E. E. 1965. *Presidential Leadership of Public Opinion*. Bloomington, IN: Indiana University Press.

Ehrenreich, B., and D. English. 1978. *For her own good: 150 years of the experts' advice to women*. New York: Anchor.

Frank, A. [1947] 1953. *Anne Frank: The diary of a young girl*. Translated by B. M. Mooyaart-Doubleday. New York: Pocket Books.

Friedan, B. [1963] 1977. *The feminine mystique*. Reprint of 1963 edition with new introduction and epilogue. New York: Dell.

———. 1976. *It changed my life: Writings on the women's movement*. New York: Random House.

Helman, S. 2008. Obama backers look for ways to carry out the call for change. *Boston Globe*, December 9, pp. A1, A10.

Janeway, E. 1974. *Between myth and morning: Women awakening*. New York: Morrow.

Kosinski, J. 1970. *Being there*. New York: Harcourt Brace Jovanovich.

Machiavelli, N. [1532] 1998. *The prince*. Translated by H. C. Mansfield. Chicago: University of Chicago Press.

Mead, G. H. 1934. *Mind, self, and society: From the standpoint of a social behaviorist*. Edited by C. Morris. Chicago: University of Chicago Press.

———. 1994. Medium theory. In *Communication theory today*, ed. D. Crowley and D. Mitchell, 50-77. Cambridge, UK: Polity.

———. 2005. The rise of glocality: New senses of place and identity in the global village. In *A sense of place: The global and the local in mobile communication*, ed. K. Nyíri, 21-30. Vienna, Austria: Passagen Verlag. http://www.socialscience.t-mobile.hu/dok/8_Meyrowitz.pdf (accessed March 30, 2009).

———. 2006. American homogenization and fragmentation: The influence of new information systems and disinformation systems. In *Media cultures*, ed. W. Uricchio and S. Kinnebrock, 153-86. Heidelberg, Germany: Universitätsverlag.

———. 2008. Power, pleasure, patterns: Intersecting narratives of media influence. *Journal of Communication* 58:641-63.

Rothman, S. M. 1978. *Women's proper place: A history of changing ideals and practices*. New York: Basic Books.

Smith, T. G., ed. 1972. *Merriman Smith's book of presidents: A White House memoir*. New York: Norton.

Staples, W. G. 2000. *Everyday surveillance: Vigilance and visibility in postmodern life*. Lanham, MD: Rowman & Littlefield.

Steinem, G. 1980. Introduction. In *Decade of women: A Ms. history of the seventies in words and pictures*, ed. S. Levine and H. Lyons, 7, 9, 11, 13, 15, 17, 19, 21, 23, 25. New York: Paragon.

Whitaker, R. 1999. *The end of privacy: How total surveillance is becoming a reality*. New York: New Press.

What Is U.S. Television Now?

AMANDA D. LOTZ

This article explores the institutional adjustments that have altered the operation of the U.S. television industry over the past twenty years. The author first chronicles those industrial norms that characterized television during its "network era" (1952 to mid-1980s) and upon which most ideas about the role of television in society are based. She then explores the ways in which adjustments in technologies, industrial formations, governmental policies, practices of looking, and textual formations have redefined the norms of television in the United States since the mid-1980s. Analysis of the shifts in the institutional and cultural functions of television reveals the articulations between the dominant industrial practices and the forms, texts, and cultural role of the medium. Such a conception of shifts of the medium allows us to understand recent changes as an evolution of this central cultural medium rather than its demise.

Keywords: post-network era; multi-channel transition; television industry

T he two symposiums in Jerusalem and Philadelphia that inspired this special issue of *The Annals* were both concerned with the changing nature and future viability of the entity known as "television." By the late twentieth century, it was clear that this long-taken-for-granted medium was in the midst of profound adjustment. Certainly, the central concerns related to television's changes varied considerably dependent on one's vantage point. Those working in television and its adjacent industries worried about their future employment and devised plans to adjust their businesses to emerging developments. Journalists attempted to represent the concerns of the public and offered

Amanda D. Lotz is an associate professor of communication studies at the University of Michigan. She is the author of The Television Will Be Revolutionized (New York University Press 2007) and Redesigning Women: Television after the Network Era (University of Illinois Press 2006) and editor of Beyond Prime Time: Television Programming in the Post-network Era (Routledge 2009).

DOI: 10.1177/0002716209338366

ANNALS, AAPSS, 625, September 2009   49 "trend" pieces outlining the various technological shifts and how they might affect the ordinary viewer. Scholars of media, communication, and culture, such as the authors in this volume, tried to assess the broader cultural implications of television's evolution, particularly its fading role as a mass medium that addressed whole populations.

Regardless of the varied concerns of workers, the public, and scholars, and despite daily announcements of new revolutionary developments for the future of the medium, all might agree that the key components of "television" were changing and that new versions of television were emerging that differed in crucial ways from its original industrial organization and social role. Lynn Spigel, introducing her coedited anthology *Television after TV: Essays on a Medium in Transition*, writes that "if TV refers to the technologies, industrial formations, governmental policies, and practices of looking that were associated with the medium in its classical public service and three-network age, it appears that we are now entering a new phase of television—the phase that comes after TV" (Spigel 2004, 2). Shifts in these four aspects of the medium, to which I would also add "textual formations," locate broad yet meaningful attributes through which we can trace precisely how television has changed, discover why these changes matter, and establish guideposts for organizing some of the ways current and coming forms of television differ from those of its past.

In what follows, I offer a story of change that is particular to the American experience of television, although in many cases the experience parallels that of other industrialized countries with a similar timeline for the uptake of television.[1] I use the term "post-network era" (from the beginning of the present century) to describe what Spigel (2004) calls the "phase that comes after TV" and contrast it with the "network era" of television (from the early 1950s to the 1980s), the formative period in which the industrial norms of the then-new medium were put in place. I also propose an intervening period of "multi-channel transition" (from the mid-1980s through the nineties) to catch the gradual manner in which the industry incorporated emergent changes into its extant standard operating procedures.

Such a periodization of the industrial history of television is necessary because shifts in norms of operation lead to changes in the textual production of the medium and its role in culture. The attributes of television that Spigel (2004) lays out have shifted so that new technologies enable wholly new uses of television; industrial practices—such as production norms, distribution routes, and financing structures—have become highly varied and consequently enable a greater range of textual possibilities; and governmental policies have lagged behind the rapidly evolving medium and cannot be credited with its evolution (although this may be a particularly American experience). It remains uncertain whether there will ever again be common practices of looking that define television use. Emerging practices are increasingly varied based on factors such as level of technological adoption and generation of the viewer and indicate a substantial array of viewing behaviors. Finally, an expansion in the range of commercially viable television content has occurred, with a decline in content that provides a common cultural experience. The contributors to this volume have not gathered to pronounce the obsequies of television. By evolving into something different than we believed it to be, the medium has revealed the arbitrariness of what we previously thought were characteristics of its essence. Current changes in the institutional and cultural functions of television do not indicate its demise but enable us to see more clearly the dominant industrial practices of the network era and the forms, texts, and cultural role of the medium in that formative period.

What Was Television?

In the network era, we primarily experienced television as a domestic, nonportable medium used to bring the outside world into the home (McCarthy 2001; Spigel 2001). Program options for viewers were limited to the offerings of the three national networks that delivered content on a linear through-the-day schedule—shows were available only at appointed times in a routinized daily sequence of programming. This technological configuration left the viewer with little to do. Minimal choice and control characterized our viewing experience compared with subsequent technological innovations and the modes of engagement they allowed.

The practices of looking that Spigel (2004) acknowledges are shaped both by the technology available at the time and by the industrial norms through which manufacturers, regulators, networks, and stations structure what we get to watch. Conventional practices of looking might be considered to encompass all of the day-to-day behaviors and norms of use that have come to organize our interactions with television. Of course, we rarely think in these formal terms; nor do we often reflect much upon our ritualized behavior with the medium. The dominant practices of looking of the network era were largely defined by the organization of television content in a linear schedule. Viewer activity required little more than turning on and tuning into the "flow" of programs and promotional messages. The three networks regularized the schedule with predictable patterns throughout the day (the same shows on at the same time Monday through Friday) with greater variation in programming on the weekend and in the evening—the most-watched, "prime time" viewing hours. The competing networks also regularized the schedule among themselves—so that all networks began new programs on the hour or half-hour and aired commercial messages at the same regular and predictable intervals.

Another key component of network era practices of looking involved the nature of the set within the household. Introduced as a sizable piece of furniture, network era television was an object around which family life came to be organized as the architecture and organization of domestic space quickly adapted to incorporate this new addition, as Spigel (1992) adeptly recounts. Network-era practices of looking relied upon the construct of family viewing and the family audience. Most homes possessed just one set, and families watched together, which meant negotiations about what to watch—television viewing in the network era was largely a home-based, shared experience. The networks' perception of their target as a family audience led to reliance on content featuring broad and universal themes, and competition pushed them toward homogeneous content likely to be accepted by a heterogeneous audience. Challenging, unconventional, or contentious "edgy" content were planed from programming to avoid alienating family audiences. All three networks generally pursued the same strategy, so despite the appearance of competition, little differentiated the programs airing at any particular time. Throughout this period, the networks could assume that audiences would view programs at the times they transmitted them. In the network era, viewing was, perforce, a shared cultural experience. Television's status as a topic of "water cooler conversation" was based on the reasonable assumption that others had viewed the same programming as oneself the night before. New technologies in the 1980s—the remote control device (RCD), video cassette recorder (VCR), and the beginnings of cable services—all undermined the networks' power to define the viewing situation by giving viewers control over when they would watch and increasing choice in what they might view.

Industrial practices—such as the highly regularized arrangements between studios and networks for procuring and funding shows; the deliberate patterns of selling content through various domestic and international markets; and the division of labor and payment among advertisers, advertising agencies, and networks, to name just a few of the most significant practices—led to standardized production norms and standardized products. The production practices developed in the network era became the norms of the industry and in time assumed hegemonic status. Later innovations, such as the development and adoption of cable distribution, shifts in rules about program and media outlet ownership, and changes in viewer behavior gradually challenged dominant network-era procedures for producing, distributing, and financing shows. Such developments steadily increased the available range and style of program content as the television industry adjusted to change taking place in the 1970s and 1980s.

The medium's regulatory framework was a key factor, and it is perhaps here that the peculiarity of U.S. television is most apparent. The regulatory framework in place as the television industry adapted to new technologies and distribution possibilities in the late twentieth century had been established nearly eighty years earlier for television's precursor, radio. This regulatory framework provided for an industry organized by a commercial mandate with a light regulatory requirement of serving the public interest, convenience, and necessity in exchange for the free use of radio and later television spectrum for signal transmission. Once the television business got going in the 1950s, however, government involvement in its operation became minimal. Occasional incursions—such as the implementation of the Financial Interest and Syndication Rules in the 1970s and the prohibition of cigarette advertising—required some shifts in industrial practices, but for the most part, the logic of commerce provided the regulatory mechanism. The existing, but minimal, governmental expectations obliged the networks to maintain expensive news operations that required costs they would never recoup. The buyouts of the networks in the mid-1980s, however, led to decreased institutional commitment to the democratic, informational role of television as commercial goals increasingly trumped the remaining vestiges of public service.

Post-network-Era Developments

Although the sense of "crisis" that led to frequent headlines regarding the "end" or "death" of television did not become pervasive until the early 2000s, the roots of this crisis began to take hold two decades earlier. The development and deployment of devices that allowed audiences control over viewing were crucial to adjusting the experience of television. The RCD, VCR, and finally digital video recorder (DVR) combined to break the experience of watching television as a continuous flow of program content determined by the networks over which individuals had no control. The new control devices transformed television from a "flow" of content that was available only at a particular moment to individual programs that could be reordered, saved, and re-viewed at will. The nature of the relationship between supply and demand was changing.

It is difficult to assess the comparative significance of the technologies that ultimately have reshaped the cultural experience of television, but of them all, perhaps the most encompassing was digitalization, by which I primarily mean the digital transmission of television signals, but also the adoption of digital production technologies and audience devices. Digitalization introduced many varied changes. It enabled significant efficiencies in transmission that allowed more content to be transmitted and better signals. The efficiency of digital transmission facilitated a vast proliferation of content—endless by some estimates—for a medium long bound first by the scarcity of spectrum availability and later by the bandwidth capacity of cable. Digitalization allowed interoperability between television and the other technologies that came to define the contemporary media world. Convergence between television and computers was a key outcome of interoperability. New ways to digitally distribute television content permitted by convergence were not subject to the same regulations as broadcast and cable, with enormous consequences for production, distribution, and use. Moreover, digital recording facilitated new editing practices and increased portability of production that surpassed the limitations of analog recording. Although digital video files initially proved too large to transmit efficiently over the Internet, advances in compression technologies eventually divorced the transmission of television from broadcast signals, cable wires, and satellite feeds. Digitalization was the key that unlocked new portable, extradomestic uses of television in the post-network era. It also improved the visual and auditory quality of television. The most significant advances in the aesthetic qualities of television in the post-network era, however, came with the adoption of high-definition (HD) standards. The more efficient signal transmission of digital is necessary for HD, but HD should be understood as a technological advance that is broader than digitalization. Those choosing to use HD television in its more traditional "living room" screen application now enjoy an appreciably improved aesthetic experience that has produced ramifications throughout the production process.

Despite the steady stream of innovations—the VCR, remote control, and cable—throughout the multi-channel transition, modifications in the dominant practices for making, financing, and distributing television shows were incremental and subtle. In recent years, however, the extent of changes introduced by new technologies and viewers' response to them has made it increasingly difficult for long-established industrial practices to maintain their grip on the processes of production and the norms of textual output. Recently, a new set of conventions has begun to replace the monolithic norms that dominated industrial operations for much of television history. The coexistence of multiple strategies of advertiser support of content provides one site for considering the increasing variation of practices. Once the dominant norms of television production, distribution, and financing were established in the late 1950s, the industry soon settled into a reliance on "magazine-format" advertising—or the inclusion of fifteen- and thirty-second commercials from a range of advertisers as the dominant means of advertiser financing. This strategy had consequences for the program content the industry produced, just as the shift from single sponsorship had minimized the company voice appeal of the pre-network era. Advertisers began greater experimentation with other advertising strategies as the media field began changing at the close of the twentieth century—particularly spurred on by the various social, financial, and technological possibilities introduced by the Internet and advertisers' growing concern about viewer adoption of devices such as DVRs. In some cases—such as the use of single sponsorship and various forms of product placement and integration—these "new" advertising strategies returned the industry to practices common in a bygone era. The industry also made traditionally peripheral strategies—such as the "infomercial"—more central through the growing use of "branded entertainment" in which the content and advertising message were inextricably linked. Finally, beyond the purview of advertisers, the industry also experimented with various forms of subscription and transaction financing that eliminated advertisers and allowed viewers to pay directly for their desired content. Such means of financing allowed for program content deemed too risky or unacceptable for mainstream audiences in the era of spot advertising and channel scarcity.

Another example of changes in industrial norms can be found in the fracturing of dominant distribution practices. For decades, a bottleneck in the distribution of television limited the supply of program offerings and led to a restricted set of norms regarding how shows were produced, what could be produced, and how and when they might be viewed. The creation and distribution of channels via cable systems began to loosen this bottleneck. Early cable systems offered subscribers a handful of additional channel options that steadily grew into the hundreds by the end of the century. The development of cable channels as additional pipelines for content also refigured the business of content creation, as these more narrowly targeted outlets required cheaper production techniques for original content while also adding to the profitable life of other content by creating a venue through which previously produced programming could be made available again. Today, television operates without any sense of a technological bottleneck—although legal limits protecting copyright and content owners' uncertainty regarding how to profit from their holdings via emergent distribution techniques prevent the free flow of content that is now technologically feasible.

It is in the context of these sizable adjustments in nearly all aspects of the operation and experience of television that the role of regulation, or, rather, the lack thereof, is so stunning. The truly profound adjustments that have already taken place in the United States and that continue to redefine the television industry occurred with minimal governmental intervention or involvement. In fact, if one were to argue for a particular shift in regulatory policies in the recent term, it would have to be in relation to the "regulatory" consequences of deregulatory policies. In the past few decades, the already light touch of government involvement in the television industry has become even lighter, particularly in relation to past policies that limited the consolidation and allowable conglomeration of media industry ownership.

The television networks were nationwide corporations; however, television's early years featured station ownership that was often the provenance of local, independent entrepreneurs. The so-called "mom-and-pop" owners were based in the community in which they owned their station and were limited by government regulations from owning many additional stations (although it must be noted that the networks owned the stations in the largest and most lucrative markets from the beginning of television). Deregulatory policy since the beginning of the 1980s lifted long-standing rules and allowed station ownership groups to steadily amass greater holdings. This led to the consolidation of stations into fewer, less locally based hands, while other policy changes created an environment of significant conglomeration among media industries at the global level. Perhaps the most consequential ownership change resulted from the purchase of each of the three broadcast networks in the mid-1980s, which then became part of global corporate entities involved in many media enterprises. By the 1990s, it was impossible to extricate the companies of the "television" industry (those involved in production or distribution of television shows) from the conglomerated media industry. The deregulatory approach of the government enabled this change in the organization of the television industry and its absorption into a broader media industry realm.

Government intervention was also responsible for the mandated shift to digital signal transmission that began at the end of the twentieth century and remains in process at the time of writing. This particular development illustrates the ineffective and haphazard character of government intervention in the operation of broadcasting. Although Congress mandated the digital transition in the Telecommunications Act of 1996, the process of this change can be described as awkward at best, and the intended outcome of this massive adjustment remains unclear. Members of the broadcasting industry, for whom this change has entailed considerable expense, largely complied with the ordered timetable— albeit with some stragglers. The key failure in the transition process, however, involves viewers whose enforced participation in this technological conversion was scheduled to render useless TV sets in millions of homes in February 2009 (extended to June 2009), thirteen years after Congress legislated the transition. The deregulatory sensibility that has governed U.S. telecommunication policy since the 1980s led this undertaking to be the most modest imaginable. Although

this functional reinvention of television broadcasting—complete with the reallo-
cation of spectrum—presented a prime opportunity to restate or clarify the
responsibilities of broadcasters in exchange for their spectrum use, no new policy
mandates were included. The digital transition was originally sold to citizens as
necessary in order to upgrade to better-quality HD television standards and as a
means for providing more broadcast services through the gains digital signal
transmission afforded. As the decade of transition wore on, broadcasters instead
focused on ways to "monetize" the spectrum through ventures such as home shopping networks or leasing the spectrum to others instead of engaging in endeavors
that might offer greater public service. The Telecommunications Act of 1996 and
subsequent related policy decisions mandated the technological change to digital
transmission but avoided any other engagement with how the industry might differently provide its service of the public interest, convenience, and necessity with
these new technological tools. Indeed, it remains remarkable that the television
industry could experience such considerable change in its norms of industrial
practice without more substantive input and involvement of regulators.

Changes in the Viewing Experience

These technological and industrial changes had many consequences for the
experience of watching television. Crucial developments in the post-network era
involved the new practices of looking that emerged as a result of the breakdown
of the linear daily schedule as a dominant organizing feature of television. The
VCR released content from the network schedules to allow viewing at self-
appointed times while making it more interactive: it was now possible to stop,
rewind, and re-view what one was watching. Such self-determined viewing practices increased as subsequent technologies enabled a greater array of choices in
how and when to view. The "on demand" technologies of the 1990s that allow
viewers to save a range of selected content and create their own schedule represent the most fundamental break from the schedules of the network era and the
constraints on viewing that they imposed.

Once content broke free of the schedule—either because it was available in a
folder of choices for viewers to watch on-demand or because viewers has
recorded it on a DVR—nearly all established ideas about how people watch were
called into question. Much of the institutional purpose for a sequenced flow of
programming was to keep viewers watching the same network. It encouraged
viewers to turn on the set and stay watching in a way that differed from the selective practice of viewing that later recording technologies facilitated. Another
crucial shift in the dominant practices of viewing that developed in the post-
network era resulted from possible extradomestic viewing of television available
once programming was freed from the TV set in the living room. Certainly the
use of television outside of the home is not new—in many ways, group viewing
in locations such as taverns defined one of the earliest viewing experiences common to the medium. The combination of new technologies and new distribution

routes has pushed television outside of its common consumption location in living rooms and bedrooms and into bars, hotel lobbies, airports, and other public spaces.

It is not necessarily "television" in its strictest technological sense that is breaking out of the home; video content long perceived as "television" programming is now being accessed by viewers on computer screens and on portable devices such as iPods. Such devices—and the corresponding economic and distribution practices being negotiated to help content reach these screens—frees television from its fixed point in the home and allows easier attention to it in other locations (such as on office computers) and increasingly wherever the portability of laptops and mobility of cell phones permit. Another practice of looking that corresponds with television's extradomestic circulation involves the increasingly individualized organization of the medium's use. The family viewing experience began to crumble as the cost of TV sets fell, enabling households to own multiple sets. The shrinking screen size of portable television devices allows solo viewing for a reasonable aesthetic experience. The erosion of the family audience reinforced the rise of programming directed to increasingly niche tastes that cable made available. Programming strategies shifted considerably once executives began designing content that would be most valued by individual members of specific demographics instead of programming that would be least objectionable to the aggregate family audience. Again, a combination of developments in technology, economic structures, and distribution possibilities facilitated the creation of new applications and use of the medium.

New programming strategies and new audience expectations became decreasingly salient throughout the multi-channel transition. The rapidly expanding number of cable channels targeted increasingly precise niche audiences and tastes—whether channels aiming at women, children, or African Americans or viewers seeking twenty-four-hour news, music programming, weather, or history. Throughout the 1990s, niche targeting grew ever more specific as channels targeting women multiplied and diversified, as did those offering news. This expansion in viewer choice led to a massive dispersal of the viewing audience across the increasing range of channels, while control devices diminished the mandated immediacy of viewing characteristic of the network era.

The practices of looking related to the extradomestic and individualized use of television have not neatly replaced those common in the previous era. Rather, these new modes of viewing now coexist with those previously dominant, with preferences for one or the other largely determined by age. Older viewers who have spent much of their lifetimes watching network television at home continue to do so, while those who are younger experiment with new ways of viewing that threaten to disrupt the still largely dominant network-era practices should they continue with them as they get older. Yet, more ways of viewing will emerge as the post-network era continues to take shape, and it is likely that the near future will be characterized by a wide array of television viewing behaviors.

The viewing environment today has become so different that the networks are increasingly challenged to abandon their advertising-only economic model tied to programming with broad-based appeal. To try to retain some of their steadily fleeing audience base, network programming has become markedly more edgy— although still avoiding the excesses to be found on many cable networks. The networks have also diversified their programming base to feature some high-budget scripted programming that matches the aesthetic and narrative quality of feature film as well as more affordable unscripted "reality" programming. Likewise, many temporal rhythms that had long governed television production— conventions such as the late-September-through-May television season, seasons composed of twenty-two original episodes, and the integration of new and rerun episodes—eroded as the networks lost their oligopolistic advantage and year-round programming by cable stations undermined their long-established business routines. And just as the shift from single sponsorship to magazine format advertising had altered the guiding imperatives of content at the start of the network era, so an assortment of new (and very old) advertising and viewer payment strategies expanded the range of viable content in the increasingly competitive post-network era.

Consequently, television content now represents a broader array of ideas, forms, and peoples than ever before. This should not be taken simply as whole-sale advance, however, because the simultaneous fragmentation of the audience makes it difficult to assess the cultural consequence of this new diversity. It used to be that simply being "on television" conferred importance because of the medium's broad reach in the network era. This is not the case today, as much of the vast multiplicity of post-network content slips by unnoticed. A newsmagazine may feature a thoughtful profile of a radical thinker, but it may pass into the ether seconds later, unremarked upon and leaving little trace. On the other hand, a politician may make an off-the-cuff comment to a news reporter that is captured and reaired millions of times on twenty-four-hour news networks and on a video distribution outlet such as YouTube. An annual event such as the Super Bowl may bring together that mass audience of the network era, and the country may stand in unison transfixed by breaking news coverage, as we did on the morning of September 11, 2001. Like-minded audiences numbering only a few million—if that—may gather weekly for a comparatively obscure favorite television show, while other shows collect tens of millions of viewers. This variety of circumstance is now common for U.S. television, and—as these scenarios suggest—the cultural role of this single medium consequently can vary profoundly. It is getting harder to assess the role of television today in all its many and varied forms.

While this concise account has been able to offer only the briefest overview of much more complicated practices and norms of television, the developments highlighted here begin to reveal the breadth and scale of change that has begun. Many—in the academy and the industry, as well as popular pundits—have declared that these changes provide evidence of the end of television. Although it should be clear that the medium is experiencing extraordinary adjustments, pronouncements on the passing of the medium are, in my view, exaggerated and overstated. Older media such as radio and magazines have experienced sizable adjustments to their original, dominant norms of practice; their role in daily life;

and their characteristic content in the course of their longer histories. And television is now undergoing just such adjustment. It may evolve into a medium very different from the one we have long thought it to be, but it will indeed continue to exist.

Note

1. I have given a much fuller, detailed account of the transformation of American television in *The Television Will Be Revolutionized* (Lotz 2007), whose basic argument I summarize here.

References

Boddy, W. 1993. *Fifties television: The industry and its critics*. Urbana: University of Illinois Press.

———. 2007. *The television will be revolutionized*. New York: New York University Press.

McCarthy, A. 2001. *Ambient television: Visual culture and public space*. Durham, NC: Duke University Press.

Spigel, L. 1992. *Make room for TV: Television and the family ideal in post-war America*. Chicago: University of Chicago Press.

———. 2001. Portable TV: Studies in domestic space travel. In *Welcome to the dreamhouse: Popular media and postwar suburbs*. Durham, NC: Duke University Press.

———. 2004. "Introduction," in *Television after TV: Essays on a medium in transition*, 1-40. Durham, NC: Duke University Press.

Contextualizing the Broadcast Era: Nation, Commerce, and Constraint

By
WILLIAM URICCHIO

Programming scarcity that characterized the broadcast era, or what this article refers to as *constraint*, served very different goals. Often intertwined, these goals ranged from the formation of an ideologically coherent national public, to the protection of economic self-interest, to the explicit promotion of products and messages. They were deployed rather differently in the commercial American and state/public European spaces of television. The article explores a number of assumptions regarding the institution and medium of television that have persisted from the broadcast era into our own and that might well, given the very different structures of contemporary television, be repositioned. It outlines the contours of that repositioning, sketching the implications for some of our theoretical and methodological defaults.

Keywords: broadcast era; scarcity; commercial and public service television; United States; Germany; audience metrics

The history of television is a history of change. From vacuum tubes, to transistors, to chips; from broadcast, to narrowcast, to on-demand; from cathode ray tube receivers, to plasma flat screens, to projection; from a programmer's vision, to the viewer's choice, to the inner workings of metadata protocols and "smart agents" . . . we have witnessed an ongoing process of transformation in technology, textual organization, regulatory frameworks, and viewing practices. The pace of change has been as dramatic as it has been uneven. Regulation, infrastructure, national interest, and viewer expectation have all at times stimulated development or suppressed it. Overall, the pace of television's change as a set of technologies and practices is

William Uricchio is a professor and director of comparative media studies at MIT and a professor of comparative media history at Utrecht University in the Netherlands. His research considers the processes by which media technologies and cultural practices take form. His most recent books include Media Cultures *(Universitatsverlag Winter 2006) and* We Europeans? Media, Representations, Identities *(Intellect 2008).*

DOI: 10.1177/0002716209339145

striking when compared to the relative stasis of film, radio, and print—all, to be sure, media with their own developmental dynamics.

I write at a moment of accelerated change, a moment when in many nations, analog broadcasting has officially ended, giving way to digital-only television. The change mandates modifications in the receiving apparatus and offers the promise of not only more but also more interactive programming and services. It is a moment accompanied by new display technologies (flat screen, PDAs, high definition), intelligent interfaces (TiVo and other digital video recorder [DVR] systems), and cross-platform production and viewing practices. It is a moment where we can ever more clearly anticipate the end of the thirty-second advertisement, the weakening of once monopolistic broadcasting networks (and their afterlife in cable and satellite distribution) thanks to Internet protocol television (IPTV) and the redefinition of traditional producing and consuming roles through develop-ments such as YouTube. Add to this advances in surveillance video (facial recog-nition); teleconferencing (virtual presence); large-screen simulcast in our stadiums, concert halls, and streets; and easy access to television from almost any producing national culture (mysoju.com), and once invisible forms of television are adding to the noise. It is a moment of confusion, as much for viewers, who seem to have difficulties distinguishing among these new practices, as for the medium's industries, themselves in a state of flux, seeking to secure their market positions while catching the next big thing.

Rather more remarkable, considering the pervasive nature of these transfor-mations, is the oasis of calm that lingers on in our memories in the form of the respectably solid broadcast era. Today's transformations seem all the more radical given this apparently stable past. In this article, I challenge the taken-for-grant-edness of this stability, showing that it was a carefully constructed condition. This is a relevant point not only because it remains referential but also because some of its residues continue on in our fast-changing present as habits that seem dif-ficult to break. Consider the business of audience metrics, for example, which has largely relied upon the same statistical extrapolations that accompanied televi-sion's earliest years as a true "mass" medium. Despite the radical fragmentation of television audiences, and despite the potential availability in digital markets of data streams tracing every twitch of the viewer's thumb, the old methods persist. Like the gold standard, intrinsic notions of value seem less important than wide-spread acceptance of a uniform metric. The academic study of television and its effects, too, remains bound to a number of concepts and paradigms that emerged with the broadcast era. Sometimes, as in the case of the notion of *flow*, the mean-ing of a particular term has modulated to keep pace with shifting distribution and viewing practices, serving as a barometer of change. In other cases, such as notions of media effects, the basic model has been fine-tuned and its deployment technologically enhanced, but like the audience metrics industry, it has largely weathered the storms of change thanks to the supervening demands of institu-tional stasis. Here, the notion of reproduction so central to our academic institu-tions has played an important role, as have the demands of marketers and policy makers for clearly defined notions of agency, impact, and effects (from the efficacy of advertising to the promotion of public discourse). The academic scene has of course responded to the medium's transformation by developing new theories and accreting modes of inquiry, but its traditions—bound, it would seem, to a historically particular configuration of the medium—nevertheless remain remarkably persistent.

I would like briefly to reflect upon this period of stability in the United States and—broadly speaking—Europe. The years between roughly 1950 and 1980, it seems to me, have tended to provide something of a conceptual default to our thinking about television: they have offered stability to an unstable and not always comprehensible medium, they have generated a referent for our notions of medium specificity, they have helped to mask some of the medium's fundamental transformations, and they have continued to shape key assumptions about television's interactions with its audiences, whether on the part of the head-counters or some academics. At its extreme, this period provides a definitional border, beyond which we might well consider certain practices to be beyond television, allowing us to ask whether we are now facing (or have already survived!) the end of television. My contention is that these three decades are but a blip in the larger developmental history of the medium. I readily concede that they are a profoundly important blip, but by slightly repositioning this era and some of its main assumptions about the medium, I hope to show that this constellation of factors and beliefs is as deforming as it was formative, blinding us in some ways to longer-term continuities in the medium's history.

In the spirit of full disclosure, I take television to be a pluriform set of technologies and practices, anticipated and deployed well before the 1950s, and evident in the medium's latest set of transformations. I see the present changes not so much as the end of television as a return to the pluriformity that has long characterized the medium. I will not here rehearse the late-nineteenth-century visions that did so much to establish the medium's technologies and set its horizon of expectations (Uricchio 2008). And I will do little more than reference a segmentation of television's development from 1950 to our present put forward in different ways by Amanda Lotz in her article in this volume, as well as by the likes of John Ellis (2000) and myself (Uricchio 2004), distinguishing among the scarcity of the broadcast era, the relative plenty of the deregulated cable era, and the vast access enabled by the on-demand, Internet-like present. I return to this periodization by the end of the article, but for the moment, I would simply like to underscore television's long-term interpretive flexibility as a way of highlighting the somewhat anomalous status of three decades of stability.

In the pages ahead, I briefly consider the notion of scarcity so characteristic of the broadcast era, arguing that scarcity was constructed and deployed in the service of the period's larger hegemonic goals. Space does not allow for a close consideration of these operations across television's various institutional and cultural settings, so I instead consider two extreme cases as a way of bracketing a relevant range of meanings. The mobilization of scarcity, or what I refer to as *constraint*, served very different goals, from the formation of an ideologically coherent national public, to the protection of economic self-interest, to the explicit promotion of products and messages. Often these goals found themselves intertwined; moreover, they were deployed rather differently in the commercial American and state/public European spaces of television. Implicit in the understanding of how constraint could serve these goals were a number of assumptions that have persisted into our present and that might well, given the very different structures of contemporary television, be repositioned. I close by outlining the contours of that repositioning and sketching the implications for some of our theoretical and methodological defaults.

An Era of Constraint

The apparent stability of the decades in question can be characterized in different ways, and I am sympathetic to John Ellis's use of the term *scarcity* to describe the period's programming (Ellis 2000). Whether we consider the oligopoly of the "big three" networks in the U.S. broadcasting scene or the dominance of public service and state broadcasters in much of Europe, it is evident that relatively little of the broadcast spectrum was deployed for programming purposes. *Scarcity* is an apt—and aptly neutral—descriptor for the little that was available, but I will instead use the more loaded term *constraint* to capture both limited programming availability and the notion of intentionality behind it. Constraint—or the manufactured condition of scarcity—I argue, was carefully and strategically constructed, reflecting neither technological nor economic imperatives. Such an argument is complicated, of course, by the many motives behind television's cautious postwar decades, motives that differed across cultural contexts. But broadly speaking, we can see the constructed nature of scarcity by considering television's homologous relationship with radio, with which it generally shared organizational affiliations (business models, institutional settings, regulatory frameworks). Along with radio, television was shaped by long-standing institutional practices (commercial telegraph and telephone service in the United States, centralized Post, Telegraph and Telephone [PTT] control of the same services in most European contexts) and underlying beliefs regarding the construction of the public (crudely put, the U.S. consumer versus the European citizen). Of course, the particular institutional and professional dynamics that shaped the emergence of television from radio culture (everything from status hierarchies, to the notion of program formats and genres, to the very language used by engineers to describe their practice) also played a crucial role in articulating postwar televisual practice.

Scarcity, it is generally argued, reflects the technological realities of limited spectrum availability, driving in turn the need to control and oversee a limited public resource. The scarcity argument has been used to underpin the notion of the public airways; to justify state, public, and commercial broadcasting monopolies; and to defend the highly constrained status of broadcast speech acts, so dramatically at odds with the protections afforded print and ordinary speech in most developed nations.[1] In this last regard, the ironies of increasing constraint on expression with the appearance of each new technology have been well noted by Ithiel de Sola Pool among others (Pool 1984). As Nicholas Garnham argued several decades ago with regard to public service television (Garnham 1983), "Channels have been limited, whether rightly or wrongly, for social and economic, not technical reasons."[2]

In many national settings, radio entered the world as much a military affair as a grassroots, amateur, two-way medium. The emergence of broadcasting was sometimes related to hardware companies seeking to promote their wares (the United States and United Kingdom) or to a combination of various commercial, public, and state institutions. Yet, in most cases, government regulatory agencies quickly attempted to put the genie back into the bottle, constraining pluriform radio practices by claiming technical and national security reasons. Standardization and regulatory bodies with mandates to control technology, frequency, and program content prevailed. In France, for example, from radio's start in 1922 until the outbreak of the Second World War, fourteen commercial and twelve public radio stations were in operation. Bracketing off the war and occupation as exceptional, what did liberation bring? The imposition of a broadcasting monopoly (by 1965, France 1, 2, and 3), which was maintained until 1981, when private and commercial radio was finally permitted to operate. The story is complicated by the success of extraterritorial radio transmissions (so called *radio périphériques*) from the likes of RTL (Luxembourg) and Europa-1 (Saarbruecken), but these, like the pirate stations that penetrated British and Dutch radio monopolies, were not sanctioned (and were sometimes even the subject of military attacks). In Britain, the BBC began its life as the British Broadcasting Company (1922), a private joint venture backed by Marconi, Western Electric, General Electric, Metropolitan-Vickers, and British Thompson-Houston. By 1927, thanks to a royal charter, it left private hands to become the British Broadcasting Corporation, which in turn maintained a monopoly over radio until 1967. In the Netherlands, the public radio monopoly lasted until 1989, when foreign broadcasts (already available unofficially on the airways) could be officially carried on cable, and 1992 when domestic commercial broadcasts were permitted. In the United States, which lacked precedents for outright state or public ownership, the telegraph and telephone offered organizational models based both on commercial monopolization and the integration of hardware and service. And although the United States gave rise to a relatively robust and even chaotic commercial radio environment, the Federal Radio Commission (1927) and later Federal Communications Commission (1934) imposed order, effectively strengthening the role of the national networks, the most prominent of which, like NBC-RCA and CBS-Columbia, were tied to manufacturers.

Each setting had its tales of signal interference and broadcaster malfeasance. And in each case, national interest was invoked to stabilize the broadcasting environment, albeit with the difference that in the state and public service zones, what was good for the public was good for the nation; while for the Americans, what was good for business and not harmful to the public was good for the nation. In both cases, the medium was understood to be more than a source of information, a site of engagement with the public sphere, or even entertainment: its effects, whether on the construction of nation or the marketplace, were held to be certain, if somewhat unspecified. Let us turn to several exemplary moments of constraint in television service as a way of exploring both the motives for limited programming availability and the sources of some of our persistent notions about the medium.

The Public and the Nation: Lessons from the Third Reich

The March 1935 launch of Germany's daily television service, predicated upon a notion of one *Fuehrer*, one *Volk*, and one sender, would in some ways (leaving out the Fuehrer bit) hyperbolize the shape of things to come in many postwar-era television markets. As such, it offers a clear—if particularly dystopian—site to locate period broadcasting logics and their relation to the nation. Indeed, many other nations would deploy similar tactics but with far more utopian ends in mind. Rooted in the precedent of state monopolies in the postal, telegraph, and radio sectors, television emerged as a concern of Germany's Post Ministry. Its post-1933 appearance gave rise to an important complication: the newly formed Propaganda Ministry asserted control over program content (for radio and the private-sector press and film industries as well) and content-sector hiring practices, leaving the Post Ministry with the task of coordinating hardware manufacturers and controlling broadcasting infrastructure and technological standards. This complication gave rise to considerable theorization about the role and effects of broadcasting, in addition to some distinctive practices. Television, like radio before it, was imagined as an instrument in the service of the nation. The Nazi German example is, of course, extreme—as the conflation of *Volk* and nation, or blood and earth (*Blut und Boden*) in the period's vernacular, might suggest. But the basic structure of state (PTT)–operated infrastructure, user license fee financing, and private-sector hardware development, all in the interest of the nation, was hardly exceptional. More important, the German case offers an extreme instance of the logics that were to define most instantiations of postwar European television (Uricchio 1992).

German broadcast operations were started as much out of a desire to claim technological primacy (they specifically sought to jump the gun on the British) as because of a firmly embedded set of beliefs in the effects potential of the new medium. These latter beliefs were held by Propaganda Ministry specialists with backgrounds in radio and press "persuasion" and were grounded in social science theory that had circulated since the early 1900s (evident, for example, in the first German PhD on the topic of film in 1913[3]). But the notion of effects was by no means limited to the functional interests of the ministry or the advertising industry. One need only consider the work of Rudolf Arnheim, who wrote a remarkable essay on television just as daily broadcasting was about to begin in his native Germany (Arnheim 1935).[4] Looking ahead and making a number of—what seem in retrospect—salient predictions regarding the medium, Arnheim addressed such issues as the medium's superficiality (argued through its ontology, not programming), audience credulity ("seeing is believing"), sensory overload (hyperstimulation), and the threat of social fragmentation (in the sense of television-induced isolation in a mass society), concerns that would all find resonance in the decades of critical thinking and theorization that would accompany the postwar classical notion of television. He feared that the simulated sense of collectivity made possible when viewers connected to events by way of their televisions would ultimately efface embodied collectivity, in the same way that representations of the world would supersede the real thing in importance and impact.

Television, however, was generally too ephemeral a media presence in the prewar years to command its own research profile, and in Germany at any rate, extraordinarily high levels of social control seem to have dampened public critiques of politically supported initiatives. It is nevertheless clear that a cluster of perceived—or desired—television effects motivated Germany's significant investment in the development of the medium and, stated positively, offered something of an inverse confirmation of Arnheim's perceptions. Eugen Hadamovsky, in his launch of the new service, spoke of television's sacred duty to "plant the Fuehrer's image indelibly in every German's heart" (Hadamovsky 1935), and while selling Hitler was not quite the same as selling cars or toothpaste, the Propaganda Ministry's understanding of the medium on the Wilhelmstrasse lined up well with the advertising industry's ideas on Madison Avenue. One can find ample corroborating discourse, both in Germany and the United States, both by professionals (propagandists and advertisers) and academics (both in Germany's *Publizistik* institutes and the U.S.-based Frankfurt School and the Rockefeller-sponsored Radio Project). But German thinking about broadcasting's effects had a far more radical dimension, one, moreover, responsible for a clearly motivated strategy of constraint. Rather than simply relying on radio and television for persuasive images and texts—as they had in the cases of the press and film, theorists in the ministry understood broadcasting as something closer to a neural network, electronically connecting the dispersed population into a coherent *Volkskoerper*. The Reich's campaign to put a radio in every German house, like its plans for national television, sought to forge experiential unity, to extend simultaneous participation in important events to the entire nation, and to set the rhythms of daily life.

In perhaps the clearest expression of these beliefs in the importance of defining the nation through one broadcast network, the Post Ministry—long at odds with its cultural adversary, the upstart Propaganda Ministry—prepared secret plans in 1943 for postvictory European television. The plan called for the construction of a single, live television network, linking greater Germany with occupied territories. Programming, normally the domain of the Propaganda Ministry, would be circumvented because the network would be dedicated to news, historically the domain of the Post (thanks to the deep history of wire news services). This so-called Nazi news network, the Post argued, would do away with the need for the Propaganda Ministry since it would define the nation, its rhythms, and its spirit. The notion of persuasion, trickery, and spin, seen as the domain of the

Propaganda Ministry, would be rendered trivial in comparison to the broadcast-enabled articulation of *Volk*, nation, and reality that the news network promised. While to my knowledge, no postwar nation adopted such rhetoric or was even aware of these secret postvictory German plans, one is tempted in hindsight to read, for example, France's turn from a prewar pluriform commercial-state broadcast model to a postwar state-only monopoly in terms that were equally concerned with the construction of nation and the control of national vision, although framed in utopian terms. And the relatively late date at which deregulation occurred, and commercial broadcasting was introduced into neighboring countries' long-held domains of pure state or public broadcasting, might be seen through the same lens. In the German case, we can see that constraint was explicitly linked to a particular and monolithic vision of nation and media effect—the forging of nation through connectivity and shared experience. Postwar Europe seems to have largely shared the same assumptions regarding the hegemonic effects of a constrained broadcasting regime.

To be clear, despite my use of the German example for its clarity, I do not wish to argue that television in the service of the nation is somehow inherently fascist. The paternalist vision of British broadcasting under the BBC, or the pluriform assumptions behind the Dutch public broadcasting monopoly, for example, suggest very different deployments. Whether used for utopian or dystopian purposes, the question we must ask is why television is treated so differently from the printed word. Have these arguments been grounded in technology? Economics? Representational capacities? Perceived effects particular to television? Nation-building at a unique historical juncture? The radio examples provided earlier suggest that ideologies of control, while diverse, have ultimately been a determiner in setting the regulatory configurations of broadcast media.

A Television Freeze and a Cold War

Let us turn to the United States to consider a different constraint scenario. Despite a highly diversified publishing industry and radio markets (admittedly, with syndicates and a strong network presence), despite a court-mandated breakup of film studio monopolies (the Paramount decrees, which took full effect in the late 1940s), television managed to enter the scene as an oligopoly, albeit fronted by an apparently diverse pattern of station ownership. America's distinctive alignment of hardware and software producers, of television manufacturers and broadcasters, together with the inroads made by the radio networks, helps to explain the curious shape of the television broadcasting environment in a landscape characterized by ritualistic celebrations of its freedoms of speech and press and its limitless opportunities for entrepreneurs. Of course there were mom-and-pop affiliates, complications in spectrum access, sometimes uneasy network-affiliate relations, and transmedia wannabes with promising peripheral applications (cinema television, pay television, subscription television) (Hilmes 1990). These developments have been well charted by scholars such as William Boddy (1990) and offer extremely interesting traces of resistance and negotiation with the dominant industrial practices of the period. But an overriding cultural issue also emerged just as the television freeze began in 1948, and that was full-blown in 1952 when the freeze ended . . . and it was even colder.

The cold war did many things, but one of its lesser-considered results was an acceleration of industrial concentration, particularly in sectors that had experienced the antitrust actions of a more populist government in the 1930s and whose practices were altered by war (Jezer 1982). Military "cost-plus" contracts, limited competition, and massive-scale production all combined quietly to reshape many sectors, the electronics industry central among them. And a postwar redoubling of international expansion further stimulated these sectors, increasing their economic significance and political power. At the same time that key industries were concentrating, a burst of nationwide labor activity and record-breaking participation in strikes took place during 1946 and 1947, as workers sought to make up for the long-term wage losses incurred during the Depression and bracketed off during the war years. The fear of communist subversion was quickly used to stifle any criticism of industry, whether "red" calls for higher wages or "Marxist-inspired" critiques of monopolization and unrestrained industrial growth.

An extreme level of concentration was actively encouraged in the case of postwar television because it was consistent with period industrial trends and with a wartime mentality, particularly for a government deeply concerned with information control and paranoid of communist infiltration of its message system. And it was consistent with the wishes of political powerhouses such as RCA and Columbia, with diverse interests on the hardware and software side and an ability to have things their own way. Concentration was in the economic interests of the hardware and broadcasting industry, of course, but it was also in the government's interest not to unleash television and potentially face the problems of an unruly airway as it did with radio. And as suggested, the more paranoid contingent within the government had an even more compelling set of reasons to have a television industry that was easy to oversee.

Television broadcasting's first formal decades in the United States can thus be read as an amalgam of profit maximization (greed) and message control (paranoia), twin forces leveraging exceptional institutional coherence and control and stimulating political support, if not political collaboration. The result was more than twenty years of constraint, during which time the biggest technological ripple was the conversion to color. Business models, network-affiliate relations, audience rating systems, program format and supply chain, scheduling logics, and even, to some extent, our own disciplinary paradigms as academics were refined and entrenched during this happy time. As a closed system, the operation ran smoothly, with each player knowing its part, each element working synergistically in support of the others. The reign of the "big three" broadcasters, a handful of major advertising agencies, an agreed-upon metric for audience measurement, and a circumscribed body of media theory all combined to reinforce one another and confirm the "rightness" of the configuration. In this closed system, the period's models of mass communication and their effects seemed to operate like a well-oiled machine, each piece fitting precisely with another to drive the whole.

Contextualizing Constraint

The projects of constraint in these two very different cases emblematize certain features that remain basic to our understanding of the medium, despite the very distinct environmental conditions of the present. Constraint was dominant in the German (and European) case, providing the electronic nervous system for the nation—its publics and events—with the unspoken utopian or dystopian hope that all hearts would beat as one. In the American case, constraint was deployed for a hegemonic project that was as much about promoting the economic interests of an industrial class as it was maintaining strict message control. The latter motive, of course, harkened back to the long-standing theories that argued that mass media exposures could sell Hitler or the latest Ford, except that in this case, brand communism was denied advertising space and overwhelmed by the imperative to consume. These heuristic readings are obviously oversimplifications yet help to underscore notions of televisual effect that lurk like defaults in current popular and institutional understandings of the medium. My point is that they, like some of our theories and even our definitions of the medium, are historically specific—and contingent—notions, bound to particular configurations of the television medium and enabled by the particular logics of program scarcity as well as concomitant factors such as television's interface, the form of signal distribution, the nature of the audience, and the understanding of agency.

At least in the U.S. context, the period's television receivers, with their manual dials and fine-tuning requirements, and the dominance of VHF instead of UHF, reinforced the reign of the network programmer and the notion of *flow* put forward by Raymond Williams during his first encounter with the American system. The timing of Williams's trip in the early 1970s enabled him to experience the end of an era (Uricchio 2004). Within a few years, many of the underlying structures of American television changed thanks to satellite and cable deregulation, rapidly growing household penetration of second and third television sets, and the VCR—all symbolized by the remote control device. These conditions combined to allow viewers to take greater control of the medium, whether by taking advantage of expanded program choice; viewing different programs at the same time within a single household setting; or manipulating televisual time and text through zapping, recording, and fast-forwarding. Video collections, enhanced use of television for film viewings, and even creative reworkings of broadcast texts all attested to new uses of television, new consumption practices, and feelings of enhanced agency and even liberation on the part of viewers (Uricchio 2004; Kompare 2005; Lotz 2007).

These developments broke the grip of the big three broadcasters, greatly increasing channel access; they enabled time shifting, enhanced the back-end incentive for independent producers, and provided twenty-four-hour news/ sports/local coverage. As if these threats to the software front were not enough, the quick penetration of the VCR and new television receiver technologies also attested to Asia's attack on the American hardware front. Low-cost electronics, portability, and ubiquity would be the emblems of a new hardware regime; this time, it would not be controlled by the usual U.S. manufacturers. Low-cost production and cheaper means of distribution, in turn, compounded competition on the already traumatized program side. In short, the mid-1970s saw the beginning of the end of America's old hardware and software oligopoly and the rapid increase in new programming sources and the adaptation of new television technologies. This was *not*, to be sure, a technologically determined moment (although the embrace of technological change had dramatic economic effects and political implications in the hardware sector). Europe largely underwent a related set of technological adaptations without, as argued above, undergoing any significant modification of broadcasting organization until a much later date.

The implications of the slide from constraint to plenty to virtually unlimited programming choices are difficult to assess. It is certainly clear that television as an agent of social cohesion encouraged in the era of constraint has given way to television as an accessory, one of many media sources available across widely divergent lifestyles. A lost opportunity? Perhaps, but, as I have tried to argue in this article, only if we normalize the particular configuration forced upon the medium under historically specific circumstances, a configuration at odds not only with every other medium but with television's deep history as well. Viewed from this perspective, television's latest transformation seems consistent with contemporary notions of the individual as "bundled subjectivities," the dominance of taste niches over nation, and proclamations regarding the participatory fruits of cyberculture.

Looking back with historical hindsight, we can underscore the highly contingent nature of television as a technology and array of practices and, in the process, relativize our definitional conceits and reframe some of our theoretical assumptions. The following chart roughly notes some of the changes that have taken place in the U.S. television landscape, illustrating this notion of contingency (in Europe, these technologies and practices aligned in a somewhat different manner). The dates are particularly rough, and these columns need to be understood as accretive—that is, some of the attributes of the broadcast era and remote control era persist into the following eras. In some cases, this persistence is optional—although our TiVos can effectively program an evening's worth of television, we can still abandon ourselves to the vision of a particular channel's programmer. And in other cases, it is stubborn—although audience formations and increasingly the technologies for measuring their activities have shifted dramatically, both undercutting the old metrics regime, we remain affixed to broadcast-era metrics, like the gold standard, for the stability they provide rather than any intrinsic value (or truth).

1950-1975: Dial Television	1975-1999: Remote Control	1999+: From TiVo to YouTube
Transmission	Cable/satellite/VCR	DVR/VOD/IPTV/ . . .
Broadcasting	Narrowcasting	Slivercasting
National	Transnational	Global (including user-produced)
Dial interface	Remote control device	TiVo and its clones
"Real time"	Time shifting	On-demand
Scarcity of content	Plenty of content	Unlimited content
Programmer-dominated	Viewer-controlled	Metadata/filters
Mass audiences	Segmented audiences	Niche audiences
Stable metric regime	Metrics under siege	Complete data sets

We can perhaps add to these period-specific conditions a series of changes in the scientific approaches that have been deployed to understand television and its audiences. For example, the steady shift in interest from media effects on audiences to the uses that audiences make of media maps well onto the shift from the era of programming scarcity and mass audiences to the era of plenty of content and segmented audiences. But as in the domain of audience metrics where the older, mass logics have persisted despite a fundamental change in the nature of the audience, many tenets of the old paradigm remain in place. This persistence might simply be a residual default in our thinking about the medium; or it might be driven by the logics of commercial television, in which advertising is sold because of its implied effects; or it might reflect our eagerness to find simple causes to explain life's complications. Regardless, we can identify a growing tension between certain television concepts and practices that emerged with one configuration of the medium and the very different environment and demands made by a different configuration.

This relativistic or contingent approach to defining the medium is obviously at odds with a more essentialist approach, and essentialists might argue that it leads us down a slippery slope to a point where we will be unable to distinguish between television and our computers. I take this point and embrace it, since my notions of the medium depend neither on the particular screen nor the cable or the network of which television is a part. Previously, I have argued that we must take a long view of the medium, looking at its articulation as a set of clearly defined longings and possibilities that go back to the late nineteenth century. Albert Robida's sharply articulated visions of the *telephonoscope* as a site of news, home entertainment, surveillance, person-to-person communication, and public information—published in 1883, the year before Paul Nipkow filed his crucial television-related patent—established a conceptual framework to which television has remained faithful. Robida and his nineteenth-century contemporaries teased out a vision that was deployed in Germany in the 1930s and 1940s (person-to-person, domestic, public and telepresence models of television) and has been with us since, although we have tended to make fundamental and implicit institutional distinctions between the television worthy of attention and the many televisions (surveillance, teleconferencing, etc.) that fall outside our interest.

Nevertheless, precisely this wide range of historical televisual practices permits us to contextualize and thus relativize the latest transformations of the medium—and with them, the short twenty to thirty years of stability in the broadcast era that have emerged as our conceptual default definition for the medium.

The change and dynamism that so characterizes the present state of the medium is not new. Television, in contrast to its relatively stable sister media, has from the start demonstrated an unusually opportunistic potential with regard to technological platforms. Born with the telephone in the last quarter of the nineteenth century, developed through cinema-style exhibition (theatrical television in the 1930s through 1970s and now evident in the very different developments of home theater and outdoor billboard-type displays), and broadcast to domestic settings in an emulation of radio, television is in the process of another transformation, this time to a computer-based model. These various technological entanglements are by no means determining and, indeed, have been driven by applications that preceded their existence. But they do offer particular affordances, and lend themselves to particular engagements. And as I have suggested above, while they can be shackled to very different hegemonic projects, their particular historical configurations nevertheless bring with them sets of coherent and contingent practices and meanings.

The present in which I write this is very much in transition and, as such, contains residual structures going back to the 1950s as well as new practices antithetical to them. In the United States, the big three networks persist, even though suffering from sliding market share and vastly outnumbered by cable outlets. The old advertising-driven and syndicated broadcast logics exist alongside emerging and emphatically cross-platform and participatory program forms such as *Lost*. And the ongoing struggle between telephone and cable television companies for control of home Internet delivery speaks to the computer's increasing importance as a televisual platform, one, moreover, with global access and a near infinity of programs. The present is very much a period of contradiction, and while the contours of the future are becoming more visible, established media industries are also doing their best to use any means possible (from regulation, to litigation, to outright acquisition) to reposition the new in terms of the old. The end of television? Or simply the latest turn in a long history of assimilated technologies in search of ways to deliver a particular set of experiences? The answer turns on our frame of reference and the strategies we wish to deploy, either to select a particular twenty- to thirty-year period as the embodiment of the medium, or to define a looser set of anticipations and practices as coherent and embrace television as a medium in near-constant transition.

Notes

1. Depending on the national setting, scarcity also reflected such factors as the state of the electronics industry, leisure practices, attitudes toward image-based media, and entertainment infrastructures.

2. Garnham's and my own positions notwithstanding, strong arguments can be made for regulating the broadcast spectrum given its shared use by radio (including emergency, air, military, and marine bands),

wireless telephones, and even cordless microphones. But that early television, like radio, was deployed by cable in many markets, and that most nations preferred limited VHF bands over the more extensive UHF bands that they also controlled, suggest the constructed nature of the argument for constraint.

3. Emile Altenloh's *Zur Soziologie des Kino: Die Kino-Unternehmung und die sozialen Schichten ihrer Besucher*, in large part a study of children's responses to film, was published in 1913. Altenloh was a student of Alfred Weber.

4. Rudolf Arnheim was a perceptual psychologist with a strong interest in media; after moving from Germany to Italy (where the television essay was written) and then the United States, he was appointed professor at Harvard and later Michigan.

References

Arnheim, Rudolf. 1935. Ein Blick in die Ferne. *Intercine* (Rome) 2:71-82.

Boddy, William. 1990. *Fifties television*. Urbana, IL: University of Illinois Press.

Ellis, John. 2000. *Seeing things. Television in the age of uncertainty*. London: I. B. Tauris.

Garnham, Nicholas. 1983. Public service versus the market. *Screen* 1:11.

Hadamovsky, Eugen. 1935. Der erste Fernsehprogrammbetrieb der Welt *Mitteilungen der Reichs-Rundfunk-Gesellschaft* 459: 1.

Hilmes, Michele. 1990. *Hollywood and broadcasting: From radio to cable*. Urbana, IL: University of Illinois Press.

Jezer, Marty. 1982. *The dark ages: Life in the United States, 1945-1960*. Boston: South End Press.

Kompare, Derek. 2005. Acquisitive repetition: Home video and the television heritage. In *Rerun nation: How repeats invented American television*, 197-219. New York: Routledge.

Lotz, Amanda. 2007. *The television will be revolutionized*. New York: New York University Press.

Pool, Ithiel de Sola. 1984. *Technologies of freedom*. New York: Belknap.

Uricchio, William. 1992. Television as history: Representations of German television broadcasting, 1935-1944. In *Framing the past: The historiography of German cinema and television*, ed. Bruce Murray and Christopher Wickham, 167-96. Carbondale, IL: Southern Illinois University Press.

———. 2004. Television's next generation: Technology/interface culture/flow. In *Television after TV: Essays on a medium in transition*, ed. Lynn Spigel and Jan Olsson, 232-61. Durham, NC: Duke University Press.

———. 2008. Television's first seventy-five years: The interpretive flexibility of a medium in transition. In *The Oxford handbook of film and media studies*, ed. Robert Kolker, 286-305. Oxford, UK: Oxford University Press.

Of Time and Television

By
JOHN P. ROBINSON
and
STEVEN MARTIN

Analysis of early time-diary studies suggests that television has had more impact on daily time than any other household technology in the past century. In the United States, viewing time has steadily increased from roughly ten weekly hours in the 1960s to sixteen hours today, encompassing almost half of all "free time" reported in the diaries. A prominent recent TV casualty has been time spent reading the newspaper, providing further support for the functional equivalence argument. This article shows that, so far at least, viewing time seems little affected by the Internet and other recent new technologies. Studies of the public's satisfaction with various activities suggest that viewers find TV to be more enjoyable in the doing rather than in general, even though it may not be particularly challenging or demanding of concentration. Viewing time is also shown to be significantly related to long-term personal unhappiness.

Keywords: TV; mass media impact; time; social change; quality of life; time displacement

"Why didn't anyone have the sense to document the enormous effects TV was having on society?" This oft-heard lament was actually addressed in several empirical studies by scholars and media organizations in the 1950s. Perhaps the most systematic and

John P. Robinson is a professor of sociology at the University of Maryland, College Park, where he directs the Americans' Use of Time Project and the Internet Scholars Program. His areas of research specialization include social science methodology, attitude and behavior measurement, social change, and the impact of information communication and other home technology. He is the senior author of Time for Life *(Penn State Press 1999),* Measures of Political Attitudes *(Academic Press 1998),* The Rhythm of Everyday Life *(Westview 1988), and* How Americans Use Time *(Praeger 1978), the background of his present program of research on uses of time and mass media.*

Steven Martin is assistant professor of sociology at the University of Maryland, College Park. His main areas of research interest are social demography, issues of data quality in social research, and the analysis of various dimensions of social inequality. With Dr. John Robinson, he has written on the income digital divide as well as other studies of time use and quality of life.

DOI: 10.1177/0002716209339275

successful effort, however, was undertaken by researchers in the 1960s as part of the Multinational Time-Budget Research Project organized by Hungarian Professor Alexander Szalai (1972), they had a larger question on their agenda, namely, how people across the globe distribute their time over the full range of everyday activities. The possible effect of the introduction of television on other activities was an obvious by-product of this project.

Of the several social indicators to assess the reach and impact of new technology, the variable of time and how people spend it has many advantages:

1. Time has easily identified and agreed-upon units of measurement.
2. Time is a common currency in everyday life.
3. Time has a "zero-sum" property that allows one to identify the trade-offs in daily life as new technologies (or other events) diffuse through society.

This last feature is particularly appropriate for testing a major hypothesis of activity displacement, namely that of "functional equivalence." According to this hypothesis, a new technology will replace those activities whose functions were served by previous technologies, as when the automobile (or "horseless carriage") replaced the horse, or when radio was thought to have displaced the early phonograph or other forms of home music "production," including playing instruments and singing (Postman 1985).

Changes and Trends in Time Expenditure

Thus, it was expected that time spent with television would displace other platforms of mass entertainment, such as radio, movies, and light fiction. This was the focus of many early empirical studies of TV's impact, such as the long-term studies of "videotown" (New Brunswick, New Jersey). Indeed, these and other similar studies (e.g., Bogart 1956; Coffin 1954; Schramm, Lyle, and Parker 1961), some of which were panel studies, needed to make causal inferences and turned up results quite consistent with the hypothesis (Weiss 1969).

What these media studies were unable to capture with their collection of single measures of activity, however, was the many other daily activities that could be affected, that is, those that were less obviously entertainment equivalents. Much speculation focused—and still does—on how TV might affect social life, particularly visits with friends and neighbors, since one could now be "visiting" with entertainers and other celebrities in one's own home. Putnam (2000) attributes the decline of "social capital" to the inroads that television has made on these and other forms of social contact, such as organizational participation, or simply sitting on one's porch to socialize with whomever came along. It was also thought that TV might affect other major ways of spending time apart from free time, such as work, housework, and personal care.

Analysis of Szalai's (1972) diary studies from 1965 has suggested that television's impact did actually spill over onto these other activities. As evident in Table 1, the

TABLE 1
DIFFERENCES IN ACTIVITIES OF TV OWNERS VERSUS
NONOWNERS (IN MINUTES PER DAY, INTERNATIONAL
DATA BASED ON TWELVE COUNTRIES IN 1965)

	TV Owners	Nonowners	Difference
Non-free-time activities			
1. Main job	254.2	253.2	1.0
2. Second job	3.7	4.1	−0.4
3. At work other	10.6	10.8	−0.2
4. Travel to job	28.2	28.4	−0.2
Total work			0.2
5. Cooking	55	56.7	−1.7
6. Home chores	57.9	58.1	−0.2
7. Laundry	27.9	32.9	−5.0°
8. Marketing	18.1	18.1	0.0
Total housework			−6.9
9. Animal, garden	11.5	17.6	−6.1°
10. Shopping	7.7	6.4	1.3
11. Other house	19.1	20.8	−1.7
12. Child care	29.4	26.9	2.5
Total household care			−4.0
14. Personal care	55	59.5	−4.5°
15. Eating	84.7	84.6	0.1
16. Sleep	479.3	491.8	−12.5°
Total personal needs			−16.9
17. Personal travel	18.4	19	−0.6
18. Leisure travel	16.4	20.5	−4.1°
Total nonwork travel			−4.7
Free-time activities			
19. Study	15.7	18.1	−2.4
20. Religion	3.5	6.2	−2.7°
21. Organizations	5.3	3.6	1.7
Total study and participation			−3.4
22. Radio	5.2	13.2	−8.0°
23. TV (Home)	86.5	7.3	79.2°
24. TV (away)	1.1	4	−2.9
25. Read paper	15.2	15.3	−0.1
26. Read magazine	3.9	5.4	−1.5°
27. Read books	8.3	14.1	−5.8°
28. Movies	3.1	6.5	3.4°
Total mass media			57.7
29. Social (home)	14.6	11.7	2.9
30. Social (away)	22.4	33.9	−11.5°
31. Conversation	14.5	19.5	−5.0°
32. Active sports	2.4	2.6	−0.2
33. Outdoors	15.8	17.5	−1.7

(continued)

TABLE 1   (continued)

	TV Owners	Nonowners	Difference
34. Entertainment	3.9	3.9	0.0
35. Cultural events	1	1.1	−0.1
36. Resting	23.8	24.8	−1
37. Other leisure	16.7	21.9	−5.2°
Total leisure			−21.8
Total minutes per day	1,440	1,440	0.0

SOURCE: Robinson (1972).
Note: Significant differences are noted in italics.
°Differences noted with an asterisk were significant at the .001 level after multivariate controls.

initial twelve-nation survey did show a consistent and pervasive pattern of suggested activity trade-offs to accommodate the new chunk of nearly ninety daily minutes (about ten hours per week) then devoted to TV. As shown in Table 1, TV owners in almost all of the twelve countries reported spending less time on three kinds of activities:

1. "Functionally equivalent" *mass media* activities, such as radio, movies, and light fiction print, as established by the studies noted above (such studies were often conducted for and by the TV networks themselves in the 1950s). Table 1 suggests a 60 percent reduction in radio listening (and a decline in listening as a "secondary activity"), a 53 percent decline in time at the movies, and a 30 percent decline in book and magazine reading. The reduction in newspaper reading to be discussed below was not yet evident. However, this decline in other media accounted for only twenty minutes a day, compared with the nearly eighty-minute differential in TV viewing between owners and nonowners.
2. *Social* activities outside the household (offset somewhat by increases in visiting or social contact inside the household). This may be indicative of an indirect functional equivalent, in the form of "visiting" with the characters on the screen. But this additional roughly twenty-minute decline meant that about half of new viewing time also had to come from other kinds of activities.
3. *Non-free-time* activities, particularly sleep, grooming, gardening, and laundry, accounted for the remaining time. While these are harder to fit under the functional equivalence umbrella, they seem to have a perhaps discretionary character as far as time is concerned. The drop in these activities is largest of all.

This tripartite pattern was found across all twelve individual countries in the Szalai study in spite of the national variance in TV ownership in the 1960s, which ranged from 28 percent in Bulgaria to 80 percent in West Germany to 95 percent in the United States (Szalai 1972). The patterns in Table 1 held after adjustment for education, age, and other strong demographic predictors of viewing in each country using the MCA program developed by Andrews, Morgan and Sonquist (1973). Nonetheless, it should be noted that the data in Table 1 come from single time surveys and not from the kind of panel studies that would be needed to support causal arguments (Table 1 combines the twelve countries of the analysis).

Indeed, these and subsequent diary studies (now expanded to include more than thirty countries) suggest that TV has had more temporal impact on daily life in society than any other single technology in the past century. By contrast, most other "productive" technologies, like automobiles or washing machines, seem more closely linked to increases in *output* (miles driven, for example, or clothes cleaned) than to savings in time. These conclusions are also inferred from the 1965 Szalai study, which compared countries high and low in these technologies (Szalai 1972). Indeed, Eastern European countries in the study had far fewer automobiles and appliances, yet about the same time was spent traveling and doing housework as in countries in the West. The conclusion was further supported by comparing the 1965 study with studies conducted with (nonrepresentative and mainly farm) samples in the United States in the 1920s and 1930s (Walker 1969; Robinson and Converse 1972; Vanek 1974); by other national time surveys (Morgan, Sirageldin, Baerwaldt 1965); and by less careful anecdotal studies that show, for example, that washing dishes with a dishwasher takes people no less time than washing them by hand. Further evidence along this line is reviewed in Robinson and Godbey (1999, 267-70).

At the time, these initial diary findings fit another pattern, namely, one of time constancy. That is, no matter whether the programming was in a capitalist or socialist country, whether the broadcast day was almost full-time or confined to evening "prime-time" hours, viewing time for set owners averaged an hour and a half per day. It appeared as though TV had reached its asymptote in the 1960s, on a per-set per-owner basis (Robinson 1981).

More recent time trends. These initial time transformations, however, have not remained static but have continued since the 1960s, especially in the United States, as documented in subsequent diary studies conducted every decade since 1965. In the United States, Figure 1 and Table 2 show that TV viewing as a primary activity has steadily increased from about ten weekly hours in the 1960s (among those aged eighteen to sixty-four—the results are confined to the working-age population and are not influenced by the increasing numbers of retirees across the years), to almost fifteen hours in 1975 (mainly, it seems, in response to color TV), to fifteen hours in 1985, and to sixteen hours in 1995 and 2005. As shown in Figure 1, the biggest change occurred between 1965 and 1975, when TV time rose by almost five hours a week—which equaled the five-hour increase in free time over that decade. Altogether, time spent viewing TV consumes almost half of the thirty-five to forty hours of free time reported in the time diaries in Figure 1, and more than half of free time, if the five-plus weekly hours of secondary and tertiary viewing time are also included. In modern European countries, average viewing time is closer to twelve hours per week with about the same amount (thirty-five to forty hours) of free time (Gershuny 2000). It may be of interest that free time does not correlate highly with social class in these studies.

For the United States, Table 2a shows these five-hour increases in viewing to be among the most impressive changes since 1965 for all daily activities for both men and women. It is exceeded over the thirty-year period only by the significant effects of the "gender revolution" in the late twentieth century, which resulted in a seven-hour increase in women's paid work, a twelve-hour decrease in women's

FIGURE 1
TRENDS IN TV AND OTHER FREE TIME (AGES
EIGHTEEN TO SIXTY-FOUR, HOURS PER WEEK)

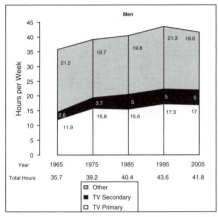 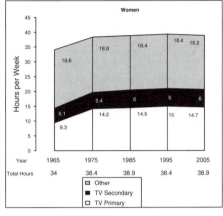

SOURCE: Robinson and Godbey (1999).

housework, an eight-hour decrease in hours of paid work for men, and a four-hour increase in men's housework (Robinson and Godbey 1999). It is larger than the increases in sleep (offset by decreased time spent eating and grooming), the further declines in visiting and conversation among women, and the increases in both fitness activity and resting (Table 1).

Perhaps the most prominent activity trend during this period of increased TV viewing time as shown in Table 2a, however, relates to another mass medium, one seemingly unaffected by TV in Table 1, namely, newspaper reading. The steady and dramatic U.S. newspaper time decline (shown both in Table 2a and more steadily and dramatically in the General Social Survey [GSS] data in Figure 2) provides further support for the functional equivalence argument. This drop is likely related to the rising prominence of TV news in the late 1960s, which may have been abetted by the rise (particularly in the United States) of the so-called "news doctors," industry consultants who recast local TV news content in more appealing formats for local audiences.

While radio listening as a primary activity also declined further since 1965, as shown in Table 2a, it has reinvented itself impressively as a secondary activity (especially while driving). Time spent reading books and magazines (media that have also reinvented themselves), on the other hand, has remained relatively steady or increased slightly, indicating that TV has not led to the death of print. However, it appears that TV (rather than decreased free time) plays a further role in dramatically reducing the reading of newspapers, as evidenced both in the diary data in Table 2a and in the media frequency questions asked in the GSS (Figure 2).

TABLE 2
1965-2005 TRENDS IN U.S. ACTIVITY TIMES
AND ACTIVITY CORRELATIONS WITH DAILY TV TIME

| | (a) Changes in Activity Times (Hours per Week) | | | | | | (b) Correlation between Activity and Daily TV Time | |
| | Women | | | Men | | | | |
Activity	1965	2005	1965-2005[a]	1965	2005	1965-2005[a]	1965	2005
Work	17.5	24.3	**+7**	42.8	35.2	**−8**	−.29	−.23
Commute	1.6	1.7		4.4	2.9	**−2**	−.17	−.13
Housework	26.9	15.4	**−12**	4.7	8.8	**+4**	−.01	−.04
Child care	6.4	6.3		1.7	2.6	**+1**	−.01	−.08
Shopping, services	7.0	7.3		5.1	5.2		−.04	−.08
Sleeping	55.5	58.3	**+3**	55.5	57.2	**+2**	+.11	+.08
Eating	7.8	7.4		8.7	7.9		+.12	−.08
Wash, dress	10.1	7.0	**−3**	7.9	4.6	**−3**	−.13	−.12
Education, study	1.2	1.9		1.5	1.8		−.09	−.11
Total nonfree time	**134.0**	**129.6**	**−4**	**132.3**	**126.2**	**−6**	**−.07**	**−.07**
Church, religion	1.2	1.0		0.8	0.8		−.03	−.02
Other organization	1.1	1.1		1.2	1.1		−.08	−.09
Movies, sports, culture	0.9	0.6		1.0	0.7		−.05	−.08
Visiting, socializing	7.5	7.4		6.9	6.6		−.11	−.13
Exercise, play sports	0.6	1.4		1.1	2.4	**+1**	+.05	−.03
Hobbies	2.1	0.4	**−2**	0.6	0.4		−.06	.00
Telephone, family	7.0	7.0		6.7	7.0		−.06	−.17
TV, videos	9.3	14.7	**+5**	11.9	17.0	**+5**	N/A	N/A
Reading newspapers	2.1	0.7	**−2**	3.0	1.0	**−2**	+.02	+.03
Books, magazines	1.2	1.4		1.0	1.2		−.03	−.02
Radio, records	0.4	0.2		1.0	0.4		.01	.00
PC, Internet	00	1.0		00	1.4		N/A	−.06
Thinking, relax	0.6	1.9	**+1**	0.5	1.9	**+1**	.00	−.03
Total free time	**34.0**	**38.4**	**+4**	**35.7**	**41.8**	**+6**	**+.30**	**+.43**

SOURCE: Robinson and Godbey (1999); Robinson and Martin (2008).
Note: The most notable differences are noted in bold.
a. Changes less than 1.0 hours are not shown to emphasize more significant changes.

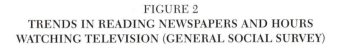

FIGURE 2
TRENDS IN READING NEWSPAPERS AND HOURS
WATCHING TELEVISION (GENERAL SOCIAL SURVEY)

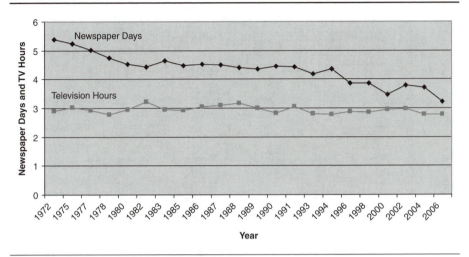

SOURCE: Neustadtl and Robinson (2002).

The dominating impact of TV on free time is further evidenced by recent diary studies in several countries examining the new technologies of the Internet and personal computers. While most Internet usage is at the workplace, U.S. diary studies from 2003 to 2007 show averages of about an hour and a half a week for home use of Internet and computer, which is less than one-tenth of the time devoted to TV. Moreover, evidence from most of these studies indicates little if any displacement of TV by these new technologies (Robinson and deHaan 2004, Kestnbaum et al 2002). Nor do they seem to have affected social life, as indicated by the constancy of GSS social activity questions shown in Figure 3, which is surprising given, for instance, Putnam's (2000) arguments.

What do people do when they're not watching? The data in Table 2b indicate a different pattern of time changes from those indicated in Table 1. Indeed, retrospectively it seems a mistake to think that the decreases in sleep, reading, listening to radio, and visiting in Table 1 would carry over to the current trade-offs in daily activity. In any event, examining in Table 2b the correlations between viewing time and time spent on other activities, one does not find that heavier TV viewers sleep or read less—since both activities had declined among early TV owners, as shown in Table 1. In fact, they spend *more time sleeping and reading newspapers* (ironically, the activities now associated with more TV viewing).

The diary data in Table 2b allow one to examine what daily activities people engage in when they are not watching, possibly indicating what activities people now trade off to watch more TV. Nevertheless, Table 2b, along with Figure 3, displaying data for social activity from the GSS, show that most of these activity

FIGURE 3
TRENDS IN FORMS OF SOCIAL CONTACT (GENERAL SOCIAL SURVEY)

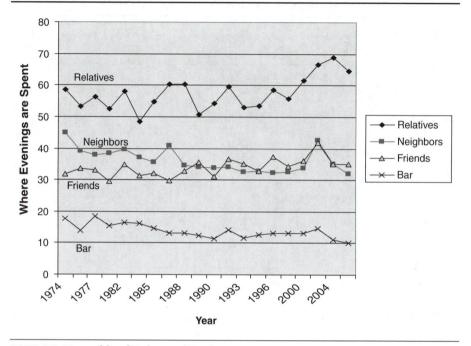

SOURCE: Neustadtl and Robinson (2002).

times have remained rather consistent over the past forty years. Paid work and out-of-home leisure (like visiting, shopping, participating in organizations, and engaging in other out-of-home activities) are mainly associated with less TV viewing time. Although not shown in Table 2, the correlates with TV time are much the same for men and women, although work and (more) sleep and free time are correlated more strongly for men, while child care, shopping, and social activities are correlated more strongly for women.

Perhaps the most telling correlation in Table 2 is the increased correlation of TV with available free time, from .30 in 1965 to .45 in 2005. Along with at-home time and other diary evidence, it suggests that more free time leads to more TV time. These conclusions are reinforced by similar patterns found for longer weekly diary periods (Robinson 1981).

Changes Accompanying These Time Expenditures

The above changes reflect simple units of time and may gloss over the more important nuances accompanying TV's increased domination of time. Thus, recent diary data reveal the phenomenon of "time deepening," mainly in the form of "multitasking," as captured in the "Doing anything else?" follow-up question

(Scheuch 1972). This addition of "secondary activity" in Figure 1 increases TV's share of daily time by more than 30 percent, but this increase in multitasking is evident in other daily activities as well—particularly in housework or child care (as documented in Bianchi, Robinson, and Milkie 2006, 94). While most of this multitasking takes place with other media as well (especially radio), it is intriguing to think that this phenomenon occurred to people as they began to realize that they need not pay strict attention to TV content.

A further important aspect of viewing time is that, particularly as more sets in the home became available and more people live alone, more viewing is *done alone*—producing a more "individualized" experience, akin to that presumably fostered by the arrival of print media centuries earlier. It also means that TV has become less of a social experience, in which others can participate at the same time.

These factors of multitasking or viewing alone raise the question of *attention* to what is on the screen. The nearly universal TV literacy meant that viewers could process content without paying full attention. A number of recent books, as well as the new medical condition of attention deficit disorder (ADD), have raised the question of how much of ADD's origin may be linked to the arrival of TV content that is less demanding of attention.

A similar dysfunction revolves around the problem of *obesity*, not just because TV involves minimal attention but because it reduces bodily activity time as well. While the issue has been of more concern with regard to the lifestyles of children and teenagers, it also applies to the physical fitness of older adults. Newer information technologies may have a similar effect in this regard.

The Social Psychological Impact
and Meaning of TV as an Activity

Finally, there is the question of TV's impact on the overall quality of life (QOL) in society. Studies of the public's satisfaction while engaged in various activities suggest that viewers do not find TV to be a particularly enjoyable activity in the long run. The left-hand column of Table 3 shows that when activities are rated in general, watching TV rates notably below other leisure activities such as active sports, socializing, interacting with children, or book/magazine reading. Moreover, using the more dynamic approach made possible by "beeper studies," in which respondents also report how they were feeling in "real time" during particular activities across the day (and not in general), Kubey and Czikszentmihalyi (1990) also found TV to be not a particularly enjoyable activity—neither challenging nor demanding of concentration, especially as it was viewed for longer and longer periods. Using a separate measure of "time elasticity," Robinson and Godbey (1999) further found that when diary keepers were asked which of their activities they would give up if something more important occurred on the diary day, TV was most often cited, indicating the lesser importance it is accorded in daily life.

However, the right-hand column of Table 3 shows that TV experienced "at the moment" is more highly valued than TV "in general." Some of the diary studies

TABLE 3
ENJOYMENT RATINGS FROM DIARY ACTIVITIES VERSUS IN GENERAL

Activity	1975: In General (Average Enjoyment = 7.0)	1985: In Diary (Average Enjoyment = 6.8)
Sex		9.3
Child care	8.9	6.4
Playing/reading with children		8.7
Play with children	8.6	
Sleep	7.5	8.5
Meals away		8.2
Socialize, visit others		8.2
Socializing, talking	8.0	
Socialize with family		8.0
Work breaks		8.0
Work	8.0	7.0
Meals at home	7.4	7.8
Washing, dressing	7.4	6.5
Hobbies, crafts		7.4
Church, religion	7.3	8.5
Exercise		7.2
Baby care		7.2
Bathing		7.0
Reading	7.0	7.9
Hobbies	6.8	7.5
Cultural events	6.5	8.5
Play sports	6.5	9.2
Help others		6.4
Work commute		6.3
Cooking	6.2	6.6
Dressing		6.1
TV	5.9	7.8
Other housework		5.8
Pay bills, financial etc.		5.2
Home repairs	5.1	5.5
Organizations	5.0	7.2
Yardwork		5.0
Laundry		4.9
Health care, doctor		4.8
Car repair		4.7
Grocery shopping	4.6	5.5
Other shopping	4.3	6.6
Clean house	4.2	4.9

SOURCE: From Robinson and Godbey (1999, appendix O).
NOTE: Scale: 10 (*enjoy a great deal*) to 0 (*dislike a great deal*) (1985 and 1975 national data). Note (1) that all activities except work, child care, and hygiene are rated higher in diary ("at the moment") than in general. However, this may be a partial artifact of the diary data, which include only "doers," whereas the general data include doers as well as nondoers. (2) Diary data is dominated by sex as, by far, the most popular activity. (3) If the ranking is done only for actual activities in both sets, TV rates eighth "in general" and fifth "in the doing." Again, we need to note the different activities and different sample base.

described above indicate that TV does not rate highly in the list of other *general* activities (as shown on the left side of Table 3) and is, in fact, rated lower than work or socializing. Thus, it appears as if respondents are saying, "TV in general is a waste of my time, but the programs I watched tonight were pretty good." More recent confirmation of TV providing rather high enjoyment in the short run of daily life can be found in Kahneman et al. (2004).

In contrast to this short-run enjoyment that makes TV such a popular activity are recent signs that this short-run gain may have more dysfunctional consequences in the long run. In a study spanning thirty-four years of the GSS, with more than forty-five thousand respondents, showing that more frequent participation in most social activities is associated with higher levels of reported happiness, Robinson and Martin (2008) find that more frequent TV viewing is associated with significantly lower reported happiness. If this means that TV provides a refuge for the disaffected and unhappy, that is an important social role. It may also be, of course, that the correlation should be read in the other direction—that is, that TV "causes" unhappiness. Indeed, Kubey and Czikszentmihalyi (1990) find that TV viewing time increased on days when respondents had reported unhappiness but that subsequent time spent with TV did not improve one's morale.

Summary and Conclusion

Periodic national studies of time use indicate that TV has had more impact on daily use of time than other (primarily productive) household technologies and that it continues to consume about half of people's free time in the United States and more than 30 percent in other Western countries. TV has not been greatly displaced by the Internet and other new information technologies. Multinational data indicate that, from the beginning, TV did draw time away from functionally equivalent activities, like movies, radio, and print fiction—and more recently from newspapers. It also appears to have drawn time from social and personal care activities that are harder to argue to be functional equivalents, like sleep, grooming, and household care.

Main gains in viewing time occurred in the United States in the 1970s, apparently related to the arrival of color TV, but with smaller inroads on free time since then. As was true forty years ago, these diary studies show that higher TV time is now correlated with less time at work and in travel and that TV is viewed more by people who are at home and, thus, with more free time. Early activity casualties apparently displaced by TV (like sleep and reading) are now correlated with *more* viewing. Among several possible societal consequences of this greater time spent with TV are increased multitasking, obesity, fragmented lifestyles, and homogenized national culture, with possibly decreased attention spans and lesser appreciation of local culture. Further alleged dysfunctions are persuasively presented in, among others, Postman (1985) and Putnam (2000).

Nonetheless, TV viewing is rated far more positively in "real time" as a daily activity than "in general" or the longer it is viewed, which probably accounts for its predominance in free time. However, such short-term value may translate to long-run dysfunction in terms of longer-term personal happiness.

References

Andrews, F., J. Morgan, and J. Sonquist. 1973. *Multiple classification analysis*. Ann Arbor, MI: Institute for Social Research.

Bianchi S., Robinson J.and Melissa Milkie 2006 *Changing Rhythms of American Family Life* New York: Russell Sage Foundation: Rose Monograph Series.

Bogart, L. 1956. *The age of television: A study of viewing habits and the impact of television on American life*. New York: Unger.

Coffin, T. 1954. Television's impact on society. *American Psychologist* 10:630-41.

Gershuny, Jonathan. 2000. *Changing times: Work and leisure in postindustrial society*. Oxford, UK: Oxford University Press.

Kahneman, D. A. Krueger, D. Schkade, N. Schwartz and A. Stone. 2004. A survey method for characterizing daily experiences. *Science*, December 3, pp. 1176-80.

Kestnbaum, M., J. P. Robinson, A. Neustadtl, and A. S. Alvarez. 2002. IT and social time displacement. *IT and Society* 1 (1): 21-37.

Kubey, Robert, and Mihaly Csikszentmihalyi. 1990. *Television and the quality of life: How viewing shapes everyday experience*. Hillsdale, NJ: Lawrence Erlbaum.

Morgan, J., I. Sirageldin, and N. Baerwaldt. 1965. *Productive Americans*. Ann Arbor, MI: Institute of Social Research.

Neustadtl, A., and J. Robinson. 2002. Social contact differences between Internet users and nunusers in the General Social Survey. *IT and Society* 1 (1): 73-102.

Postman, N. 1985. *Amusing ourselves to death*. New York: Viking.

Putnam, Robert. 2000. *Bowling alone: The collapse and revival of American community*. New York: Simon & Schuster.

Robinson, J. P. 1972. Television's impact on everyday life: Some cross-national evidence. In *Television and social behavior*, vol. 4, ed. E. Rubinstein, G. Comstock, and J. Murray, 410-31. Washington, DC: Government Printing Office.

————. 1981. Television and leisure time: A new scenario. *Journal of Communication* 31:120-30.

Robinson, J., and P. Converse. 1972. Social change as reflected in the use of time. In *The human meaning of social change*, ed. A. Campbell and P. Converse. New York: Russell Sage Foundation.

Robinson, J., and J. deHaan. 2006. Information technology and family time displacement. In *Computers, phones and the Internet*, ed. R. Kraut, M. Brynan, and S. Kiesler, 51-69. Oxford: Oxford University Press.

Robinson, J. P., and G. Godbey. 1999. *Time for life: The surprising ways Americans use their time*. University Park: Pennsylvania State University Press.

Robinson, J., and S. Martin. 2008. What do happy people do? *Social Indicators Research* 89:565-571

Scheuch, E. 1972. The time-budget interview. In *The use of time: Daily activities of urban and suburban populations in twelve countries*, ed. A. Szalai, 69-89. The Hague, the Netherlands: Mouton.

Schramm, W. L., J. Lyle, and E. B. Parker. 1961. *Television in the lives of our children*. Stanford, CA: Stanford University Press.

Szalai, A. 1972. *The use of time: Daily activities of urban and suburban populations in twelve countries*. The Hague, the Netherlands: Mouton.

Vanek, J. 1974 "Time spent in housework" *Scientific American* 11:111-120

Walker, Kathryn. 1969. Housework still takes time. *Journal of Home Economics* 61:621-24.

Weiss, W. 1969. Effects of mass media on communication. In *Handbook of social psychology*, vol. 5, ed. G. Lindzey and E. Aronson, 77-195. Reading, MA: Addison-Wesley.

The Face of Television

By
PAUL FROSH

This article proposes some physiognomic speculations regarding three visual characteristics of television in its pre-digital-broadcasting form: (1) the importance of the head shot as a staple technique for representing the human figure and, hence, the primacy of the human face as a televisual image; (2) the mirrorlike reflective surface of the cathode-ray tube television screen, which makes the viewer's reflected image appear to emanate from the depths of the television set; and (3) the box-like design of television sets that turns them into miniature containers of the pictures they show. It argues that these three characteristics amounted to an integrated communicative structure that made television a key mechanism for the social construction of humanity in the second half of the twentieth century, a mechanism whose future is uncertain in the age of new digital platforms.

Keywords: television; head shot; face; screen; container; humanity; digital platforms

What makes objects expressive are the human expressions projected on to them.
—Béla Balázs, *Theory of the Film*
(1992, 262)

Physiognomy currently enjoys, if that is the appropriate word, a reputation as one of the more dangerously misguided intellectual projects of the modern era (see Weinstein and Stehr 1999). Stripped of its scientific pretensions, however, the idea of physiognomy can usefully convey a concern with the *visible surfaces of things*—and not just people—as expressive of broader social, cultural, and technological

Paul Frosh is a senior lecturer in the Department of Communication and Journalism at the Hebrew University of Jerusalem. He is the author of The Image Factory: Consumer Culture, Photography and the Visual Content Industry *(Berg 2003) and coeditor, with Tamar Liebes, of* Meeting the Enemy in the Living Room: Terrorism and Communication in the Contemporary Era *(Hakibbutz Hameuhad 2006).* Media Witnessing: Testimony in the Age of Mass Communication, *coedited with Amit Pinchevski, was published by Palgrave Macmillan in 2008.*

DOI: 10.1177/0002716209338571

developments. To speak physiognomically of the face of an object is to anthropo-morphize it, certainly; but it is also to claim that the object's physical appearance is a countenance to be read, an expression of the matrix of forces that materially produced it and, moreover, of those that constantly reproduce its identity and meanings *as* a particular kind of object. In the case of an (audio)visual medium such as television, physiognomy has an additional and very obvious resonance: for the object does not simply have surfaces, but one of those surfaces is also a screen—an interface upon which are projected moving pictures and, among them, human faces. To reflect physiognomically upon television, then, is to think about the meanings of television's physical design, the nature of its visual inter-face, and the psychosocial significance of its relentless display of images.

Three rudimentary observations about the face of television guide this article.[1] These concern the importance of the human face as a televisual image, the reflectivity of the television screen, and television's physical appearance as a kind of box. These observations are underpinned by a central assumption: for all the dynamics of change and flux that have characterized the medium since its incep-tion, and despite the fact that historically speaking, "television's identity is a highly unstable affair" (Uricchio 2004), the importance of the human face, screen-reflectivity, and box like design *do* remain meaningfully stable across the era of mass-broadcast television. And a concomitant assumption of this general-ized physiognomy of classic television is that changes in physical design, screen display, and representational practices are altering the face of the medium today. For although one may harbor doubts about the nature and extent of the changes currently affecting television, one thing seems beyond dispute: the physical shape and dimensions of the televisions in our homes have been radically altered, so much so that the traditional TV "set" has all but disappeared.

The Face *on* Television

An advertisement for Philco televisions from 1950 (Figure 1) shows four dif-ferent models.

Among the striking things about this ad is that despite the variety of models, each television displays roughly the same transmission content: a head shot in which one or two human faces look out of the screen toward the viewer. The term *head shot* typically designates a photograph or picture in which the entire head, usually accompanied by the neck and shoulders, appears within the frame, and that focuses on the face of the subject (i.e., an image of the back of someone's head is not a head shot). This face frequently looks directly out of the image at the camera/viewer, but its gaze may also be directed off-center.

Philco was not alone in representing typical television content in this way. Advertisements for Motorola, Admiral, Emerson, General Electric, and other manufacturers from the same period similarly show head shots as the main con-tent of television broadcasts. It may be, of course, that the centrality of the face to ads for televisions is characteristic of a specific time and place (U.S. television

FIGURE 1
PHILCO ADVERTISEMENT, 1950

in the early 1950s) and of a particular conjuncture of marketing strategies, programming practices, representational modes, and audience expectations, all concerned with establishing norms for the newly popular medium (it is also worth noting that the faces depicted are overwhelmingly those of young women, and they are always white).[2] Yet, notwithstanding the particular historical conditions surrounding this emphasis on the face in early advertisements for televisions, I want to suggest that the head shot remains a central, if not dominant, pictorial device of the medium for much of its history, surviving changes in the representational practices and visual technologies deployed in different periods. It endures as a stable way of depicting news anchors and television presenters even today, despite the extension of the televisual repertoire to half- and full-body shots. So, momentarily suspending our suspicion of generalizations about the nature of the medium, what can be made of the importance of the head shot to our encounters with television? What is the significance of the fact that for most viewers in most countries and in most periods, watching television has involved looking at the faces of other people—people they have not usually met in person—and frequently entails being looked at in turn?

Expressive and Deictic Faces

Writing in the 1920s about the cinematic close-up, Hungarian film theorist Béla Balázs made the following observations:

> Now the film has brought us the silent soliloquy, in which a face can speak with the subtlest shades of meaning without appearing unnatural and arousing the distaste of the spectators. . . . The poetic significance of the soliloquy is that it is a manifestation of mental, not physical, loneliness . . . the close up can lift a character out of the heart of the greatest crowd and show how solitary it is in reality and what it feels in this crowded loneliness. (Balázs 1992, 263-64)[3]

Cinematic and televisual images differ in important ways, differences outlined with great clarity by John Ellis (1982) more than twenty years ago, among them the size and position of the image in relation to the viewer: the televisual image is smaller or at best the same size as the viewer, and the image is viewed at roughly head height.[4] Notwithstanding these differences—or rather, because of them—we can consider the televisual head shot as the offspring of Balázs's silently soliloquizing faces. Television's smaller size and head-height viewing position situate its expressive faces *among* those of the audience within an interpersonal (normally domestic) viewing space. This means that while, as in cinema, the expressions on a televised face may indicate a character's feelings within the diegesis of a program, they can also more easily become *expressive of relations with the viewers themselves*.[5] Of course, this quasi-interpersonal expressivity of the head shot truly comes into its own where the televised face looks straight at us out of the screen, a type of shot characteristic of television's direct mode of address (Ellis 1982; Tolson 1996) and rarely found in cinema.[6] The faces of news anchors and presenters, among many others, express *to* us as well as before us— they smile, purse lips, raise eyebrows, pout. One could even claim that the expressivity of televised faces is central to maintaining forms of parasocial interaction with viewers (Horton and Wohl 1956). Hence, in the cinematic close-up, the depicted face is expressive of emotions that can be interpreted by someone watching, but neither the emotions nor their facial signs ostensibly refer to a connection with the viewer: with respect to the face's expressivity, the viewer is a bystander, an onlooker. But the televisual face can not only express referentially (concerning its diegetic context) or emotively (with regard to the character's thoughts or feelings), but also *connatively*: what the head shot "gives off"—in Goffman's sense (1956)—may be directed at those on the other side of the screen.

This connative expressiveness of certain televisual faces—those that address us by looking directly at the camera—also has an important *deictic* function. The eyes of the newsreader looking at the camera designate an exophoric "it" or a "this" to which they refer: neither the camera itself, nor a technician in the news studio, nor the text on a teleprompter that they are reading, but the audience beyond. The audience is not an object of the newsreader's look that is immediately present before his or her eyes but, rather, an absent or virtual object (virtual in the sense of real but intangible) whose existence as the look's ultimate addressee is produced by the look itself within the communicative context of television.[7] Such a deictic gaze is a *learned* and *rehearsed* art of facial control and appearance management that produces an illusion: poor newsreaders can destroy the illusion by failing to hide the movement of their eyes as they scan the teleprompter.

Moreover, this deictic gaze facilitates the transformation of the audience into the viewer: it individuates. Within the context of a head shot—a medium shot to close-up of the head and shoulders—the direct gaze of the newsreader produces a consensual illusion of *proximal deixis*, the notion that that which is being referred to (in this case, looked at) is spatially close to the speaker (Meyrowitz 1986); that it is something the speaker can in fact see. Since the audience is the proximate "that" that is being seen, the deictic gaze positions its addressees as its own inverse: a face *facing* the newsreader, close enough to see him or her at a conversational distance and be "seen" in turn. For the broadcaster, "the audience" is a virtual *generality*, an amorphous collective absence extended spatially in an unbounded beyond outside the studio. But the newscaster's deictic gaze transforms this distant plurality of addressees into the proximate singular viewer, focusing the viewer's attention as both a condition and an effect of being addressed: our eyes "meet" those of the newsreader (it takes sustained effort to look at the screen when a newsreader addresses us without looking at his or her eyes directly), and we are brought "face-to-face" with our distant interlocutor. The deictic gaze issuing from a head shot is therefore a central visual technique to the feeling that Scannell (2000) describes among members of broadcasting's mass audience: that we are addressed as individuals.

Universal Humanity and Emblematic Faces

The expressivity of the televisual face is significant in other respects as well. It exposes individuals, from a very early age, to a larger and more varied physiognomic repertoire of feelings (including extreme emotions), thoughts, and moods than they are likely to come across with any frequency in their everyday personal encounters: anger, ecstasy, humiliation, despair, avarice, fear, hope, love. It helps to train us in the subliminal art of face-reading, and it generalizes this interpretive art by showing expressive faces from distant places and unfamiliar cultures: in effect, television universalizes by presenting these strange faces *as* expressive, as always already *interpretable* by those to whom they are shown. Along with photography, television can be held responsible for constituting and maintaining facial expressivity as part of a universal language of the human, a responsibility with significant political and moral implications. The status of such a putative universal language has, of course, been the subject of much criticism. Especially well known is Barthes's essay "The Great Family of Man" in *Mythologies* (1972), in which he attacks both the universality of the photographic medium and the universality of "man" as myths whose effects are to de-historicize and naturalize the current social order. Against this critique I would argue that the expressive universality of the face, while "mythical," nevertheless socially institutionalizes a space in which each individual's extended and abstract relations of similarity with distant, unfamiliar others become definable under the category of the human. This ideological space of similarity is morally enabling. It may even be that the universalizing expressivity of the photographic and televisual face is a technological and historical precondition of the Levinas-inspired "ethical turn."

This universalization of interpretable facial expressivity—occurring in domestic intimacy and enacted in relation to viewers (and not just as a spectacle played out in front of them)—intersects with another effect of the face on television: the emblematic function of individual faces and their potential aggregation as collectivities. The head shot produces a relationship to depicted social wholes that is physiognomic in nature. One understands the outside world through one's relationship with other (televised) human faces: the human face acts as the interface between viewers and a broader depicted reality. This augments processes already found in photography: entire populations and events of immense scale are encapsulated in encounters with emblematic human faces (Dorothea Lange's "Migrant Mother" photograph standing for all migrant workers, all anxious mothers, all the poor of the Midwest, the Great Depression). This is not to deny or belittle the role of verbal discourse or other visual images. It is to claim that quite often what we see is not the reported event or scene (9/11 was rare in its liveness—most events are reported after they have finished; see Ellis 2006) but, rather, a person telling us what they know and have gone through. And when television presents us with these talking heads, we engage with the head as well as with the talk. When a survivor of the tsunami or of the genocide in Rwanda shares her experiences with viewers via television cameras, her face and its expressions not only speak for the speaker but also may be interpreted as standing for others unseen and for the experience of the events that they faced.

The face's emblematic quality is based on a characteristic that is frequently denigrated: the substitutability of the individual. The face as an emblem seems to come at a price—the face as an index, a singular manifestation of a nameable, unique person: indeed, it can seem but a little way to go from emblem to stereo-type. Furthermore, the endless flow of head shots and faces of which much television consists appears to exacerbate the process of de-individualization: unlike the photograph, which retains the image of the particular face until paper and chemicals fade, televisual faces are *representationally transient*, held before our eyes for a few seconds before being replaced by other images (although the repetition of certain faces—anchors, journalists, and actors—goes against this tide). Yet, this dichotomy between the emblematic and indexical face is by no means inevitable: the substitutability of the emblematic face need not deny the singularity of the face's bearer, but expands its range of significance, creating conditions in which strangers become not only interpretable in their own right but resonant of others who are judged similar because of their participation in a wider reported reality. The emblematic face is therefore both particular *and* general (it shows us "someone-as-anyone," to invert Paddy Scannell's formulation [2000]): it belongs to and speaks for a specific person, and yet, it also speaks for similar others, for social or experiential communities. Taken in conjunction with the face's universalized expressivity, substitutable emblematic faces are a means for television to implicate audiences in forms of extended affiliation and identifi-cation with vast numbers of strangers both as individuals and as collectivities.

Nonreciprocity and Serial Aggregation

The pervasiveness of faces on television normalizes and domesticates a para-doxical communicative structure: nonreciprocal face-to-face communication. Such a communicative structure means that one can be face-to-face with another person and *not* pay him any attention, since the appearance of his face, even when accompanied by direct verbal address, is an indication of his nonpresence at the location of viewing. This relationship seems to bear some affinity with the kinds of nonattentive visual encounters that characterize actual physical proxim-ity and copresence in modern public spaces (especially in cities)—such as Simmel's (1997/1910) analysis of mental life in the metropolis and Goffman's "civil inattention" (1963).[8] Indeed, television appears to introduce such nonatten-tive mechanisms for apprehending unknown others into the home.[9]

Television's domestication of inattentive relations with strangers invites a pow-erful critique: that it is a dire extension, by a major socializing agent (television), of forms of alienation into the private sphere; that it encourages the art of "mis-meeting" (Bauman 1990), which de-ethicalizes others by turning them into mere background figures, and perhaps even establishes inattentive nonintimacy as an appropriate mode of behavior within the home. There is, however, an alternative assessment: that nonreciprocal face-to-face communication pro-motes a desirable cosmopolitanization of the home, allowing the faces of strang-ers to appear in the sphere of intimacy without creating alarm or triggering a defensively hostile response (because these faces can be safely ignored, without offending them in turn).[10] The second, more optimistic judgment sees the multiplicity of ignorable, substitutable, but expressive faces on the television screen as reducing the strangeness of strangers by making them constantly quasi-available, potentially connected to viewers who can choose to engage with them or not. Moreover, even if most individual faces on the television are viewed inattentively,[11] their constant cumulative flickering presence within the home is a novel historical achievement, producing for individuals in their intimate spaces a *serial aggregate* of human similarity and connectedness, an interminably fluctuating and ever-present composite image: the face of humanity itself.

This perpetually changing, aggregate human face participates in and extends television's role as a transcendent *monument*. Monumental structures like churches and government buildings "give a visual and/or auditory focus to the experience of living in a community, allow people to be united in space either vicariously or in actuality, and define here and there . . . by forming a nucleus for social life" (Adams 1992, 126). Television not only conforms to these features, but, according to Adams (1992), it also is consistent with the historical development of monumental forms as they have moved from solidity to ephemerality, sacredness to mundanity, death to life. Whereas traditional architectural monuments attempt to transcend "erosive time" (Berger, quoted in Adams 1992, 127) by using permanent materials that resist decomposition, television achieves transcendence, paradoxically, through perpetual nonpermanence—through the transience and substitutability of its images: "Television—if we mean the flow of images from multiple sources, rather than the individual receivers—does not decompose at all" (Adams 1992, 127). Similarly, the aggregate televisual face is not eroded since it is created by an interminable succession of substitutes. Thanks to the endlessly replenished monumentality of television, the face of humanity never dies.

The Face behind the Screen

When I watch my conventional, seven-year-old cathode-ray tube (CRT) television, I obviously see the colors and forms, figures, and faces of programming content. But I also see something else—especially when the set is turned off: my own reflection and that of the viewing space in which I am located. In fact, it is difficult to remember a time when I did not see my own reflection in the television, and I have occasionally noticed my own children preening before the screen (see figure 2).

There are many tempting possibilities for theorizing this mirrorlike quality of the CRT screen, not least the connection between television and a culture of narcissism, or the deployment of Lacanian models of psychic development (with obligatory references to the ubiquitous "mirror stage"). I will briefly mention only two obvious points, however. The first is that the reflection of the viewer in the television is a virtualization of the viewer's body and physical setting. This is true, of course, of all reflective surfaces and mirrors. Yet, these other reflective surfaces double the space that the viewer already inhabits but do not add to it. The television screen, in contrast, makes the viewer's image a part of a parallel world of

FIGURE 2
REFLECTION IN CRT TELEVISION, 2007

strangers that television creates on the *other* side of the screen, a world that for all its verisimilitude is still very different from the space the viewer physically inhabits. This incorporation of the virtualized viewer into television's universe of strange faces and bodies is most obvious when the lighting in the viewing space and in the program content conspire to make the viewer's reflection overlap with the image on the screen. Even when this does not happen, however, and when my reflection is replaced by the broadcast image, television remains perpetually open to this potential of world-overlap, and not least because I am what appears on the screen when the machine is shut down. The CRT television screen is therefore in a sense never really off: when it shows nothing, what it shows is me.

More than this, it shows me looking back at me. As with one's image in a mirror, one cannot take oneself by surprise: it takes great effort to see oneself without meeting one's own reflected eyes returning one's gaze. To look at my reflection almost always means that my reflection looks back at me as a face that faces it, echoing the structure of the direct deictic gaze to the audience of certain televisual faces described earlier.

How do I look on my television? My image appears to emanate from the dark-ened depths of the set. The screen does not just reflect me; it also presents a mirror image of the three-dimensional space in which I am located. This is important since it constitutes the space *behind* the screen as a world in depth.

The screen appears not only as a surface upon which images are projected but also as the translucent barrier to an anterior space—a space of representation (the illusion of three dimensions) that is mapped onto the physical space of the cathode ray tube. Unlike cinema, then, the space behind the television screen does not appear to be virtual: the screen is not a surface showing only the illusory representation of a three-dimensional world but a looking-glass onto the (inhabitable) inside of the television set itself.

The appearance of a world in depth behind the television screen is, therefore, not simply an effect of the optical illusion of three dimensions that characterizes the pictures shown on television. Instead, the pictorial illusion is made *continuous* with the reflected image of the viewer and his or her setting (walls, sofas, coffee tables), as though both take turns to occupy the same delimited space—a space that is mapped onto the physical depth of the television set. When the television is turned off, and the broadcast image disappears, the space it occupied is filled by the reflection. This gives the inhabitable "inside" of the television, the world in depth on the other side of the glass, a semblance of *permanence*. And this sense of a permanent world-space inside the television intersects powerfully with one of the most obvious aspects of television's physical exterior: its appearance as a kind of container.

Television as a Container

The conventional, predigital television set—whether designed to look like a conventional sideboard in a family room, or as a minimalist square with its own legs, or even as a portable five-inch model from the 1970s—is designed as a *box*: hence the colloquialism "What's on the box tonight?"

Boxes contain things, even if it is only air. What, in representational terms, does the televisual box contain? It contains, first and foremost, space behind the screen, augmenting the sense of permanent depictive depth already aroused by the screen's reflective surface. This space can be understood as a backstage to the images the screen displays, a behind-the-scenes location from which the pictures come, along with the people who appear in them. Television in the 1950s, as Spigel (1992) notes, was often associated with theater; this idea of a backstage space, contained within the box, supplying the screen with its material, further emphasizes its theatrical rather than cinematic antecedents: television as an electronic puppet theater.[12] It is this idea of a backstage location behind the screen whence the pictures come that supplies some of the uncanny effects of television as a separate, horrifying world that is more than merely virtual: the girl trapped inside the television in Spielberg's *Poltergeist* (1982) or Samara's terrifying emergence from the television set in *The Ring* (2002).[13] The horror of these images plays on the uncanny otherness, doubleness, and spatial proximity of the reality that the television set might contain, and that it might therefore unleash: its alternate world is more palpable when confined in a specific physical location.

Moreover, while discourses of connectivity are frequently and rightly empha-sized with regard to television, it is rarely noted that television's box like presence also produces a strong image of self-sufficiency. (Wayne Booth [1982] describes walking around his television to see where its texts were coming from.) In con-trast to cinema, where the apparatus is split between projector and screen, the televisual mechanism appears as a single integrated unit, packed within its shell. Attempts to hide the connectivity of the television through the use of internal antennae and other techniques have contributed to this palpable sense of self-sufficiency. Conjuring up notions of replete isolation even as it was associated with new forms of connectivity, television "was caught in a contradictory move-ment between public and private, and it often became a rhetorical figure for that contradiction" (Spigel 1992, 109)—no less in its physical appearance than in the programs it showed. This material figuration of self-containment within the home acts as a physical correlate to the sense that television *as a whole* is a self-sufficient, self-perpetuating system, replete and impervious to local attempts at resistance (destroying your own television set does not destroy television: it does not prevent the same images being shown on everyone else's set).

The paradox of self-sufficient connectivity has a companion: the paradox of "intimate immensity" (with apologies to Gaston Bachelard [1994]). Television acts as the container of the multiple locales, individuals, homes, and communi-ties that it depicts: the container, in effect, of the multifarious spaces and social relations that make up our sense of the social whole—on an increasingly global scale. Television is a small, self-contained box that nevertheless brings forth mul-titudes. It shares the *multum in parvo* structure of the miniature and so "becomes monumental, transcending any limited context of origin and at the same time neatly containing a universe" (Stewart 1984, 53). As a result, television strangely warps the relationship between macrocosm and microcosm and between interior and exterior.[14] For this container of vast social worlds is itself usually enclosed within the walls of the home. Television provides a framework not only for what Bennet (1995) calls "the exhibitionary complex," putting society on display as a spectacle for its own citizens, but it does so through a form of radical *social min-iaturization*. It shrinks the world, not only through the ideologies and practices of televisual immediacy and connectivity but also by seeming to contain it and magically reproduce it *inside one of its own subunits*: that primary arena of indi-vidual intimacy and strong sociality, the family home.

By appearing to be logically larger than the social whole (how else could tele-vision contain it?), and at the same time being physically present inside it, televi-sion enables simultaneous relations of *transcendence* and *immanence* between the individual and the social totality: transcendent relations through the enhanced connectivity of the individual to the diverse components of the social whole; immanence through the miniaturization of the totality and its ubiquitous embed-ding within the intimate sphere of the individual. The relationship between the physical and representational faces of television is crucial here. The miniature *physical* face of television—its material dimensions as a box that contains society and its multitudes—counterbalances the vastness of the *virtual* aggregates television summons through the unceasing display of expressive and emblematic faces. Thus, television makes the vast, inchoate outside of the social totality seem physically and psychically containable, nesting society as a whole within the homes of its viewers and reducing the scale and threat of its ungraspable immensity. Television is where the teeming masses find their dwelling place.

The Face of the Future

Is this coarsely sketched physiognomy of the face of television in its mass-broadcasting era—based on the primacy of the head shot, the reflectivity of the screen, and the box like design of the television set—likely to be sustained today?

Perhaps one of the greatest impacts upon the head shot concerns the dimensions of the television screen, in particular its "aspect ratio"—the relationship between the width and height of a filmed image. Traditional television has consistently used an aspect ratio of 4:3 adopted from cinema (4 units of width to 3 of height). Known as Academy Standard, after its introduction as the standard format for sound film by the Academy of Motion Picture Arts and Sciences, 4:3 is a convenient and somewhat approximate shorthand for 1.37:1, where 1 expresses the height of the image: in other words, the image is 1.37 times wider than it is tall.[15] While television's adoption of 4:3 made it initially compatible with cinematic film, the development of widescreen cinema (1.85:1 in the United States—Academy Flat)—one of the technical innovations introduced by the film industry to compete with television—meant that the dimensions of the image have also consistently been employed to distinguish between the two media. Technological changes in image display led to the introduction in the 1980s of a new standard aspect ratio of 16:9 (1.78:1)—favored by the large, flat LCD and plasma screens being sold today—a format that takes television firmly in the direction of widescreen cinema.

How might all of this have affected the face on television, and particularly the use of the headshot? While neither 4:3 nor 16:9 exactly suits the orientation of the human face (they are both "landscape" rather than "portrait" formats: unlike the face, they are wider than they are tall), 4:3 encouraged and enabled an intimate focus on the face in close-up, with relatively little attention paid to the background within the same shot—even after the introduction of deep-focus cinematic techniques that allowed both face and background to be kept simultaneously sharp. In contrast, 16:9 necessarily includes more of the background and environmental surroundings of the human face, even in close-up. One of the implications is that the head shot—although by no means entirely eroded—has become less dominant in the televisual repertoire than previously, since it does not fully exploit the more contextual and epic dimensions of the widescreen format. This is perhaps most visible in genres such as television news, where studio sets have been redesigned, screen graphics emphasized, and the presentational techniques of anchors altered in line with the widescreen potentialities of the

16:9 ratio: the use of multiple camera positions within a highly stylized, deep studio space within which anchors and presenters frequently move around (no longer do anchors simply sit behind desks in front of a relatively static background); the use of large screens within the studio space itself, accompanied by full-body shots of the newsreaders and reporters; and the use of on-screen graphics, including multiple windows and textual crawl, to fill the extra width provided by the format. The headshot, it should be repeated, has by no means disappeared, but the change in aspect ratio—among other things—has made it part of a more extensive repertoire of connectivity with the audience in which the conversational and expressive functions of the televised face have been subtly altered.

One interesting example of the shifts involved concerns the deictic function of the newscaster's gaze, one that I have described as traditionally designating the individuated viewer as the anchor's true audience, even though the newsreader cannot see the viewer. An increasingly common practice encouraged by the 16:9 format is to have two or more faces, speaking from *different geographical locations*, placed in their own windows side by side on the screen at the same time and engaging in conversation. This leads to the strange phenomenon of two on-screen faces talking to one another while they both directly look at me, the viewer, rather than at each other. Their faces and gazes designate me as their addressee at the very same time as their conversation excludes me, making me an eavesdropper. By virtue of their facing me, their conversation seems to take place through me (and without me the technological apparatus that makes it possible would not exist), and yet I—its raison d'être—cannot participate in it, am separated from it by a transparent but impermeable barrier. The viewer is simultaneously the interlocutor and spectator of these deictic faces, in a mechanism that makes newly conspicuous the phenomenological complexity, centrality, and uncanny nature of mediation and the reconfiguration of everyday visual and verbal registers that television performs: the paradoxes of the parasocial, dialogue through spectacle, interpersonal interaction made possible by mass dissemination.

We should be wary, of course, about generalizing too greatly from the shift to 16:9 aspect ratio. Not everyone is primarily watching television in widescreen formats, and we should remember that a key characteristic of the transformation in "phenomenal television" (Lotz 2007)—our sense of television's coherence as a particular medium—is that it is now dispersed across a variety of different platforms and screens, including some that are closer to 4:3. Indeed, mobile devices such as cell phones and MP4 players often use screens that are not only smaller but also more face-friendly in their aspect ratio than either 16:9 or 4:3: "portrait" in orientation, like the human face, they are taller than they are wide. If and when a considerable amount of television content is made with these devices in mind, the significance of the head shot is likely to be renewed and reshaped.

In addition, aspect ratio is only one characteristic of screen dimensions that affects the representation of the face on television: screen size is, if anything, even more obvious. The increasing popularity of screens larger than forty inches—coupled with cinematic sound systems, a rhetoric of cinematic viewing, and the high-quality image resolution of high-definition television—means that while watching television still involves encountering the faces of vast numbers of strangers, doing so may more frequently invoke the fetishistic and spectacular pleasures associated with the movie screen rather than deictic physiognomic interfaces with larger worlds beyond. While large screens have yet to erase the practices and experiences associated with the conversational intimacy of news-readers and broadcasters on classic televisions, it surely makes a difference when the face of the talking head addressing us, registered in exquisite detail, has doubled in size. Again, however, large screens are not the whole story. Medium-sized screens are still prevalent, and the viewing of television content on computer screens—especially as the bigger of these are now around twenty-four and twenty-seven inches (i.e., medium-sized televisions)—may ironically perpetuate the screen dimensions of classic television even as computer-based delivery and viewing transform the broadcast mode. Finally, cell phones, MP4s, and other mobile devices showing video and television content reduce the head shot to the size of one's palm. Speculation becomes wilder here, where the relation between viewing and viewed faces is not between conversational or interactional equals but with a countenance one can hold in one's hand. Will this miniaturization of the televised face weaken the sense of affinity and generalized connectivity with aggregated and emblematic strangers, replacing it with a proprietorial fascination with the other as a freakish kind of manipulable toy: the face of Tom Thumb?

Screen reflectivity is another feature that has been altered and is considered a technical advance. Flat LCD or plasma screens do not have the same reflective surface as CRT consoles: my reflection never threatens to overlap or obscure the images they show, nor does it emerge from the depths of a three-dimensional virtual space that is permanently visible on the other side of the screen. There is no serendipitous sense of continuity between the worlds of viewer and viewed, no material correlate to the idea that television is the mirror of society. What we get instead is an opaque and inscrutable void that seems to absorb the surrounding light: television as a black hole.

Finally, these flat, depthless screens are obviously *not* boxes. They do not seem to contain society. Instead, they resemble framed pictures hung on walls or windows that look out onto the world, affinities that appear to embody the duality of spectacle and surveillance more acutely than the box that preceded them. Indeed, it no longer makes very much sense to talk about a "television set" at all—certainly not to a salesperson in an electronics shop. The "set" has disappeared. We speak instead of screens, monitors, or platforms, indications that the self-sufficient design rhetoric of the television box has given way to rhetoric of specific functionality (to screen, to view) and technical interdependence (platform). In contrast to the coherently integrated sociocultural unity between the three faces of traditional television that I have described—broadcast image, screen reflectivity, and physical dimensions—the future face of television becomes dispersed, like the medium itself, in a multitude of emerging contours and possible transformations, all of them, at the present moment, blurred and ill defined.

Notes

1. *Face*, incorporated here into "surface" and "interface," clearly refers to more than the human countenance, a reanimation of its earlier Latin associations with figure and form in general (*faciēs*).

2. A cursory review of U.S. television ads from the 1950s and 1960s seems to show that as the years progressed, more varied images of human figures were employed. Screens were also more frequently left blank (this seems to have characterized much British advertising for televisions from the beginning).

3. See Koch (1987) for an interesting analysis of Balázs's work in relation to Benjamin and Kracauer.

4. Just to reiterate: with the exception of this article's final section, all references to television concern mainstream cathode-ray tube machines associated with the era of mass broadcasting. For an acute discussion of the difficulty of talking about television as more than an aggregate of its programs, see Jacobs (2001). Ellis's views have not gone unchallenged, notably by Brian Winston (1984) and more recently by John Caldwell (1995). However, their disagreements are mainly with Ellis's thesis that viewers glance distractedly rather than gaze attentively at the television screen.

5. This is to accept Ellis's (1982) contention that television, as opposed to cinema, rarely encourages a fetishism of the image.

6. When a face in a film does look directly at the camera, it is usually interpreted as being seen from the point of view of someone present within the depicted scene.

7. This notion of communicative context is meant pragmatically: the basic understanding that television newscasts are intended to communicate with a nonpresent audience rather those physically present before the newsreader is an essential part of the ordinary interpretative practices by which viewers make sense of what they see and hear on television.

8. Getrud Koch (n.d.) has written perceptively on the connection between cinema and the shifts in modern urban public life that foreground the "importance of face-to-face reading as a mutual but silent act."

9. The affinity is limited for two obvious reasons. First, if you are in a public place—a train or a bus—and a stranger looks directly at you for a prolonged period (as many faces do on television), this is a violation of civil inattention and can be interpreted as a potentially hostile act. Moreover, if that person speaks to you, ignoring him or her would violate conversational norms. The lack of copresence between viewer and viewed in the case of television—for all its ideology of immediacy—means that I can ignore or scream abuse at the face of the stranger with not the slightest effect (except perhaps on those watching with me).

10. See Frosh (2006) for a discussion of civil inattention and mismeeting that criticizes Bauman's pessimistic reading of Goffman.

11. Recall Caldwell's witty attack on the thesis that viewers only glance distractedly at the television screen: "Theorists should not jump to theoretical conclusions just because there is an ironing board in the room" (1995, 27).

12. Roald Dahl conveys the impression of television as a habitation for miniature people through the story of Mike Teavee in *Charlie and the Chocolate Factory*. Mike, desperate to be the first boy ever transmitted by television (or "Wonkavision"), finds that he has been drastically shrunk. It is, of course, the only way he can fit into the television set.

13. It is worth noting that the television sets shown in the U.S. version of *The Ring* are cathode-ray tube boxes, despite the fact that the film was made after the advent of flat LCD and plasma screens.

14. For fans of the BBC science fiction series *Dr Who*, I would venture this claim: the *TARDIS* (the Doctor's spaceship/time machine) is a kind of television—larger on the inside than on the outside, carrying us instantaneously across vast swaths of space and time that are experienced as here and now.

15. The reason for its approximate nature is that 4:3 is often quoted as a shorthand for 1.33:1, the aspect ratio used by virtually all films from the beginning of silent cinema until it was altered to 1.37:1 with the introduction of optical sound film around 1930. It is also a common aspect ratio used in photography.

References

Adams, P. 1992. Television as gathering place. *Annals of the Association of American Geographers* 82 (1): 117-35.

Bachelard, G. 1994. *The poetics of space*. Boston: Beacon.

Balázs, B. 1992. From *Theory of the film*. In *Film theory and criticism*, ed. Gerald Mast, Marshall Cohen, and Leo Baudry, 260-67. Oxford, UK: Oxford University Press.

Barthes, R. 1972. *Mythologies*. London: Jonathan Cape.

Bauman, Z. 1990. Effacing the face: On the social management of moral proximity. *Theory, Culture and Society* 7: 5-38.

Bennet, T. 1995. *The birth of the museum*. London: Routledge.

Booth, W. 1982. The company we keep: Self-making in imaginative art, old and new. *Daedalus* 111 (4): 33-59.

Caldwell, J. 1995. *Televisuality: Style, crisis and authority in American television*. New Brunswick, NJ: Rutgers University Press.

Ellis, J. 1982. *Visible fictions*. London: Routledge.

———. 2006. Witnesses or bystanders: What models are appropriate in understanding the media act of witnessing? Paper presented at the ICA Conference, Dresden, Germany, May.

Frosh, P. 2006. Telling presences: Witnessing, mass media, and the imagined lives of strangers. *Critical Studies in Media Communication* 23 (4): 265-84.

Goffman, E. 1956. *The presentation of self in everyday life*. New York: Doubleday.

———. 1963. *Behavior in public places: Notes on the social organization of gatherings*. New York: Free Press.

Horton, D., and R. Wohl. 1956. Mass communication and para-social interaction: Observations on intimacy at a distance. *Psychiatry* 19: 215-29.

Jacobs, J. 2001. Issues of judgement and value in television studies. *International Journal of Cultural Studies* 4 (4): 427-47.

Koch, G. 1987. Béla Balázs: The physiognomy of things. *New German Critique* 40: 167-77.

———. n.d. Facing modernity: Facial expression and new reading. Manuscript.

Lotz, A. 2007. *The television will be revolutionized*. New York: New York University Press.

Meyrowitz, J. 1986. Television and interpersonal behaviour: Codes of perception and response. In *Intermedia: Interpersonal communication in a media world*, 3rd ed., ed. G. Gumpert and R. Cathcart, 253-72. Oxford, UK: Oxford University Press.

Scannell, P. 2000. For-anyone-as-someone structures. *Media, Culture and Society* 22 (1): 5-24.

Simmel, G. 1997. The metropolis and mental life. In *Simmel on Culture: Selected Writings*, ed. D. Frisby and M. Featherstone, 174-76. London: Sage. Originally published in 1910.

Spigel, L. 1992. *Make room for TV: Television and the family ideal in postwar America*. Chicago: University of Chicago Press.

Stewart, S. 1984. *On longing: Narratives of the miniature, the gigantic, the souvenir, the collection*. Baltimore: Johns Hopkins University Press.

Tolson, A. 1996. *Mediations: Text and discourse in media studies*. London: Arnold.

Uricchio, W. 2004. Television's next generation: Technology/interface culture/flow. In *Television after TV: Essays on a medium in transition*, ed. L. Spigel and J. Olsson, 163-82. Durham, NC: Duke University Press.

Weinstein, J., and N. Stehr. 1999. The power of knowledge: Race science, race policy, and the Holocaust. *Social Epistemology* 13 (1): 3-35.

Winston, B. 1984. Television at a glance. *Quarterly Review of Film Studies* 9 (3): 256-61.

The self-presentation of ordinary people on TV took some time to develop. An early game show from British ITV demonstrates the many pitfalls encountered in developing even the most basic of self-presentational codes. So the presentation of sincerely felt emotions did not develop as a style until the late 1980s with the changes in daytime talk and the growth of reality TV. The cult of sincerity, however, has had profound cultural effects, reaching into the political sphere.

The Performance on Television of Sincerely Felt Emotion

By
JOHN ELLIS

Keywords: television; sincerity; politics; self-presentation; game show; reality TV

Television has brought a new visibility and hence prominence to many aspects of human life. It has shown us the inside of other people's homes and the surface of the moon, modes of consumption that are almost within our grasp, and the desperate poverty of many of our fellow humans. It has shown us the world from space and, in so doing, has helped to bring about a perception that we share a planet with finite resources (Poole 2008). Above all, though, television has given visibility and prominence to the emotional. TV has enabled us to take a close look at people who previously were distant or invisible: we have a close-up view of the faces of our politicians and an inside view of the private lives of celebrities. We see our fellow citizens as they experience stress in documentaries or talk about stress on daytime TV. Duncan, in Shakespeare's *Macbeth*, may claim

John Ellis is a professor of media arts at Royal Holloway University of London. He is the author of TV FAQ *(I. B. Tauris 2007),* Seeing Things *(I. B. Tauris 2000), and* Visible Fictions *(Routledge & Kegan Paul 1982). Between 1982 and 1999, he ran Large Door Productions, making documentaries for British TV. He was elected vice-chair of PACT (the film and TV producers' trade association) and is now chair of the British Universities Film and Video Council. He is associated with several research projects aimed at making historical TV available for study.*

DOI: 10.1177/0002716209339267

that "there is no art to find the mind's construction in the face" (act 1, scene 4: 11-12), but television allows us to presume that we can. We scan these faces for signs of emotions, seeking above all an assurance that whatever emotion we find is sincerely felt.

Yet, at the same time, the emotions that we find are performed. They are disclosed to us by more or less conventional indicators, by the expressions and gestures known as "body language," a language that can be involuntary just as much as consciously performed. Someone who is "wooden" in front of the camera can be achingly sincere in what he or she has to say but nevertheless nervous about having to say it. What we as viewers tend to see is the nervousness rather than the sincerity, and this serves to undermine the value of what is being said. Groups encountering or "using" the media nowadays take this into account when choosing their spokespeople; public figures are routinely trained to produce the appearance of sincerity in those who are likely to be interviewed in the course of their work.[1]

Performance, sincerity, and emotions go together. Public concern focuses on the possibility of performance of emotions insincerely held (the "crocodile tears" of public figures); but the other side of the coin, that of sincere emotions inadequately performed, is perhaps the more common problem. It lies at the core of the criticisms that many have made of Kate and Gerry McCann, the Scottish couple whose daughter Madeleine was abducted from a Portuguese resort in April 2007. Kate McCann has repeatedly been criticized for not crying in the initial days after the abduction, for "her flat sadness, or the very occasional glimpse of a wounded narcissism that flecks her public appearances" (Enright 2007, 44). Gerry McCann is criticized because "the sad fact is that this man cannot speak properly about what is happening to himself and his wife, and about what he wants. The language he uses is more appropriate to a corporate executive than to a desperate father" (Enright 2007, 44). These reactions are to the visibility of the couple's emotions, as displayed on television in press conferences and statements to the media. The McCanns deliberately made use of television to spread the message about their child's abduction (which remains an unsolved mystery). But many commentators deemed their television performances to be inadequately sincere. As a result, speculation has wreathed around them, encouraged by elements in the Portuguese police, that they were somehow responsible for their daughter's disappearance and that they might even have murdered her. Clearly, then, the correct performance of sincere emotion is a problem for our age.

This problem is a relatively recent development, the product of television's sixty-year history. The new medium required new styles of performance right from the outset, but the need for that performance to communicate sincerity came later. In the initial phase of television, performance styles had to be developed, especially for nonprofessionals. In a second phase, the expression of emotions became more elaborated and confident, especially as TV fictions became more complex. Only then could the centrality of sincerely felt emotion begin to emerge, and at the same time the medium freed itself from the expectation that it should provide explanatory meta-discourses. Audiences were left to judge for themselves the degree of sincerity in the emotions displayed before them in factual material. The definitive emergence of emotionality as the key means of under-standing people and events appears toward the end of the period of scarcity of television (Ellis 2000), at the moment when regulatory expectations were reduced in the 1980s. Thus, the development of the performance of sincerely felt emotions has three stages. To demonstrate the first, the emergence and naturalization of a televisual performance style, I use an example from the early days of television that shows vividly the problems in securing a new performance style appropri-ate to the new medium. I then look in more general terms at the development of emotional complexity in television. Finally, I examine the implications of the apparent paradox of the performance of emotional sincerity on TV.

Early TV and the Negotiation of Performance Styles

At 8 p.m. on Monday, September 26, 1955, the new British commercial televi-sion channel, ITV (which had opened two days previously), showed the first episode of *Double Your Money*. This game show, hosted by Hughie Green, became a mainstay of ITV's schedule until 1968. Green was already an estab-lished broadcaster who had hosted the precursor of *Double Your Money* since 1952 on Radio Luxembourg's popular station directed toward the United Kingdom. He became one of the most familiar TV show hosts in Britain and maintained that status for thirty years. This first TV edition of *Double Your Money* takes considerable pains to explain the format, and when the show gets going, Hughie Green is clearly anxious to secure a properly televisual perfor-mance from his guests.

This being Britain, even the question "What is you name?" is a minefield. The first contestant replies, "Mr. Harding." Green responds by repeating what the contestant has just said, but this time as a question: "Mr. Harding?" "Alan Harding" is the sheepish response. "May I call you Alan?" "You may." This exchange, remarkable now (television has since put us all on first-name terms with each other) but mundane in its time, establishes Harding's place in the social geography and the limits he wants to put on the intimacy of the exchange being initiated. Green now has to maneuver Harding into the correct stance for interac-tion before an audience. "I want you to turn around so you can see all our nice friends in the audience and our nice friends at home," he says as he puts an arm around Harding's shoulder and a hand on his chest to guide him to face three-quarters forward rather than face-to-face with Green. This is the only point in the show where Green verbalizes the need for contestants to behave in a particular way. Elsewhere, his interaction is highly tactile. He has his arm around the shoul-der of male contestants and the waist of the females. Only with a newlywed couple does he hold back with his arms clasped behind his back (the husband imitates this stance), but he gently puts his reassuring arm around the wife's waist when the husband is having difficulty with a question.

Green converses with the contestants before the formal contest questions begin, but he follows no conversational logic. He asks a series of questions, repeats the answer, and then makes a trademark bad joke. One exchange goes badly wrong when he prompts Alan Harding to say that he is a clerk at the Arsenal football club. Green seems unaware of Arsenal's enduring reputation as the club everyone loves to hate, so he asks, "Any Arsenal supporters here tonight?" to which the studio audience replies with some polite applause and plenty of boos. Harding ruefully flaps his hands, acknowledging that he knows his club's unpopularity but trying to move things on. Green's emollient "Well some of them are for you anyway aren't they?" bridges to a question about the club's prospects, ending with a characteristic Green gag ("Well I'm available and I'm only twenty-five") accompanied by some outrageous mugging. Later, when he finds that contestant Polly Matthews ("Mrs. or Miss?") is a physiotherapist, he jokes, "That's interesting . . . we had one at home but we got rid of it [light laugh from audience] . . . yeah, the wheels dropped off." He has his arm round her waist, but she still manages to pull away from him at this point, clearly nonplussed. Green's populist recovery tactic is to appeal for audience applause for the great work done in hospitals by Matthews and people like her.

Such is Green's formula, and it places him at the center of attention. This first edition of *Double Your Money* shows the many levels of adjustment needed in Britain to produce a distinctively televisual form of performance. Green's ideal is demotic, superficially intimate, and dominated by a high level of inconsequential or phatic exchange. However, he encounters problems on many levels with achieving this kind of performance. He has problems with his studio audience (the anti-Arsenal boos) as well as with his contestants. His contestants need guidance on how to stand on stage, how to handle the double address to audience and interlocutor. Contestants do not know what style of exchange to engage in, whether it is a conversation despite the audience or a performance for an audience. They therefore are unsure about how to adjust the normal forms of social intercourse to this new format, beginning with the basic problem of naming in a class-aware society. There is also a delicate and unverbalized negotiation about physical intimacy: Green's tactile style goes well beyond what was accepted in everyday life and is also more marked than that of contemporary British game show hosts like Michael Miles. Finally, there is the inheritance of existing public performance styles, some of which fit uneasily into the new performative regime that Green is trying to usher into being. It is, however, not a straightforward task. The evolution of performance appropriate to television can be observed across the early years of the medium.

Sincerity was not the central aim of television performance at that time, however; rather, it was initially concerned with the management of how to be oneself in public. If anything, the eruption of sincerity was disconcerting, upsetting the process of developing a repertoire of performance styles within the new medium. A clear example can be found in the BBC's *Face to Face* series, each episode of which was devoted to a single interview with a distinguished personality held in close shot as he or she answered delicately probing questions from John Freeman, a former Labour politician who was later the British ambassador in Washington. In 1960 Freeman interviewed Gilbert Harding, a well-known television personality of the early years of TV in Britain, famous for his no-nonsense approach in the BBC's popular panel game *What's My Line?* Harding was an irascible, portly, middle-aged figure, once called "the rudest man in Britain." In Freeman's interview, however, he became demonstrably nervous, and in response to the question, "Have you ever been in the presence of a dead person?" he answered with a choking "yes" and began to cry. Freeman did not push the questioning to make Harding reveal himself further. If he had, Harding would have confessed that he was referring to his mother, who had died a few weeks earlier. Instead, Freeman moves quickly to another subject. Even so, the program was extensively criticized for being grossly intrusive (Medhurst 1991). In the revelatory close-up format of *Face to Face*, sincerity was seen as an undesired element, something that disrupted the performance of self rather than confirmed its presence.

Emotionality was, at that time, still a difficult issue for television; many years passed before it emerged as one of the key desired characteristics of factual TV. The process was a slow one and took place both in factual programming and, perhaps surprisingly, in fiction as well. In Britain, the lexicon of performance styles was extended a little later by series like *Man Alive* in the 1960s, which specialized in the frank and moving interview on personal issues (Ellis 2000, 51). The series editor, Desmond Wilcox, encouraged his directors to probe further than any documentary had gone before, to ask ordinary people questions along the lines of "How does it *feel* to be . . ."; the group put a premium on footage in which the interviewee began to cry. Tears were the sign of the depth of feeling being put on display. But this emotionality stayed carefully within certain bounds. *Man Alive* programs were organized around themes (adoption, pedophilia, homosexuality, terminal illness, etc.), and the plight of the characters was tied to a particular issue. The focus of the program is the issue to which it is devoted, and the interviewee's tears attest to the importance of that issue and not, in the first place, to the sincerity of the interviewee.

Industrial Fiction

The second stage of the development of the performance of sincerely felt emotions took place in fictional television as much as it did in factual television. Developments in television fiction made a crucial contribution to the evolution of the televisual performance of sincerely felt emotions. Television has developed an industrial series-based form of fiction that produces many episodes of the same format featuring the same core characters. Initially, these characters showed no development from episode to episode for series at a time. But as TV fiction developed, it began to explore the implications of following characters through different incidents and stories. Increasingly, industrially-produced series fiction began to show characters who develop emotionally, weaving in "character development" to the onward rush of events.

More things happen to regular TV characters than happen to their viewers. TV series storytelling provides its viewers with frequent resolution of narrative incidents rather than the definitive closure of a narrative with all the loose ends tied up and the characters dispatched to death or a serene future. It is "off they go back to all their other worries" rather than "they all live happily ever after." The threat of the sequel hangs uneasily over all their futures. The types of incidents that are contained and resolved within the larger narrative include the resolution of a police investigation or a law case, the reconciliation of arguing neighbors, or the agreement of reluctant parents to a marriage. They provide a sense of narrative closure. The enduring characters in the series may well have learned from them and been changed by them. And they offer the seeds of further narrative incidents: a fresh row between neighbors or the subsequent divorce of the happy couple. It seems that these incidents are enough to satisfy the demand for satisfactory stories and that definitive endings are not essential.

With television, the delay of narrative closure means that characters can learn from their mistakes. What television seems to offer through this process is a modern and secular form of salvation. Characters in TV series are saved in this world and not the next, and they see their rewards in this world. Those who redeem themselves are saved by learning through experience and understanding their experience. Learning, and with it salvation, take the form of the transformation of character. Bad-tempered antisocial characters begin to show signs of consideration and generosity. Aggressive characters rein in their tempers, often with visible effort. Backsliding and major relapses occur as with any reformed sinner, but the characters will be treated as reformed increasingly as the series evolves. This transformation through socialization is a major theme of factual programming and reality TV as much as it is of series fiction.

From the audience point of view, we see all too clearly the imperfections of characters. We know them for their faults as well as their strengths. As TV has evolved, the heroes of yesterday have given way to more vulnerable or damaged people as central characters: the decisive Dr. Kildare gave way to the prevaricating and overprincipled Dr. Green or the weird and edgy Dr. House, the wholesome Saint to NYPD Blue's unsavory Andy Sipowitz. For viewers, the imperfections of the characters are the source of the continuing drama. When this is the case, viewers also learn not to rush to judgment on characters. They may not be what they first appear; they are certainly likely to change and mature as Sipowitz did. TV characters are there for the long term (if not for life), buffeted by the weekly supply of incident, and it is by no means clear how they will end up.

The industrial form of TV series production provides for this double level of narrative. The successful series will be planned meticulously in its individual incidents, so that each episode will work efficiently toward the closure of those particular incidents. But the longer story arcs of the series and of the characters are worked out as the series develops. In the team writing that is necessary for long-running series on the American model, scriptwriters base their work on the "bible": a defining document that describes the characters and their "backstory" (their life before the series began) and a mine of potential revelations as the series evolves. The nature of each character will often be defined in terms of oppositions. But their eventual finishing point, their closure, will be left open to be defined as the series develops. It will not be determined by the progress of the story itself so much as by the popularity of the character and of the series, by the success or otherwise of the performer's contract renewal negotiations. These industrial factors are external to the fictional world itself, but they frame the potential for storytelling.

Within this industrial form of storytelling, the most intimate and everyday is the soap opera. Soap operas are overwhelmingly domestic in setting and put relationships and emotions at their heart. They provide regular, even daily, episodes involving familiar characters in a serial form, with plotlines carried on from episode to episode. Soap opera characters regularly face new crises and are changed by them. They remember their pasts and, in a few cases, manage to learn from them. Jostein Gripsrud has pointed out that soap characters inhabit a kind of parallel world (Gripsrud 1995). They live their lives at the same pace as those of their viewers, so that the daily or weekly visit to their world shows that the program has moved on by the same period of time. Soap opera characters live in our time, growing old with their viewers. But soap opera characters live a different kind of life, and as all soaps are not identical, the character of those lives differs remarkably between cultures and even within one national broadcasting system. In soap operas, events take place that are frequently beyond the scope of most people's lives. They are often exaggerations of real-life dilemmas, but the characters explore each other's emotions around them in exhaustive detail. The ordinary soap character will go through more traumas in a few years than most people could suffer in a whole lifetime. Soaps dramatize: they are fiction. Soaps exaggerate because they are melodrama, using clearly defined emotions to explore complex moral issues. But soaps are also mundane, involving familiar characters, comprehensible reactions, and an everyday time scale. Soaps have the rhythm of everyday life but the narrative range of fiction.

Long-series fiction and soap operas have developed, slowly over time, a more sophisticated and universally recognizable lexicon of emotions and their expression. They have explored, time and again, the issues of sincerity and duplicity, of emotional honesty and deceit. After a quarter of a century, the lexicon of TV performance styles had likewise developed and settled down. The habits became recognizable, and TV performance had become the source of humor. *Not the Nine O'Clock News* (1979-1983) based many of its sketches on TV formats, from news to youth programming. Spike Milligan's wayward occasional *Q* series (1969-1989) was based on frustrating the conventions of TV performance, from looking down the camera to revealing the backstage to even failing to complete sketches. TV performance, which emerged so haltingly in early shows like *Double Your Money*, had become a recognizable repertoire of ways of being in public. At the same time, the pervasive presence of these televisual fictions has enabled the development of a general cultural knowledge of the performance of emotions. This is now beginning to produce a generalized cultural ability to perform emotions "adequately."

Nowadays, the emotions of ordinary people are explored everywhere in television. In the past two decades, new opportunities have been offered to examine those emotions and particularly to apply the forensic skills (Ellis 2007) of looking below the immediately apparent (behind the mask) at the emotional displays of real individuals. Factual television has been overhauled by the emergence of "reality TV," which provides an arena for the examination of the emotions. Reality TV effectively fuses the forms of game show with those of documentary. From the game show, the genre takes the emphasis on explicit rules and the kind of inconsequential exchanges that Hughie Green was trying to develop in the first edition of *Double Your Money*. From documentary, reality TV takes the require-ment for the explicit expression of sincerely felt emotions. They are recombined to create the performance of sincerely felt emotions.

Reality TV and the Issue of Sincerity

Reality TV thrives on speculation and participation. It has reinvented partici-patory television and the television event. By combining elements from the game show (the controlled challenge) and documentary (fascination with real people), it has discovered a fresh way of linking TV into the present moment of its viewers. It creates shows that excite an immediate common interest. Participants become known by their first names, as in "Did you see what Craig did last night?" Reality TV allows unfettered opportunities for gossip and speculation by all the means that are now available in blogs and message boards, radio phone-ins, newspapers and magazines, as well as everyday face-to-face conversation. A successful reality show will have substantial daily coverage in popular newspapers and will receive distanced attention from the broadsheets as well. Its official Web site will keep viewers informed of the latest events and may even charge for access to streamed live footage. In this sense, reality TV is the reality of TV: pervasively present in everyday life.

Reality TV shows encourage speculation about sincerity and the limits of per-missible behavior. These are two aspects of contemporary life that TV has been instrumental in bringing to the fore. Sincerity is a constant issue with reality TV participants; with it comes the issue of trust: do we trust that these people are sincere, and would we trust them? Since they have volunteered to take part in the reality TV game, they are to a significant degree performing a version of themselves, or even trying to get away with a constructed persona. In game-based formats, the participants may have a substantial prize to win; in challenge-based formats, they are being offered a solution to problems in their lives. In either case, it is left to viewers to judge how much they are hiding of themselves behind their performance of what they would like us to think they are. Reality TV is based on a paradox. Its situations are unreal or artificial, yet reality is what we seek from them: the reality of the individuals involved. Viewers are keenly engaged in the process of decoding the "real" people, of judging the sincerity of what they are putting on display. They are required to perform "naturally," to give the kind of performance of self for a viewership that was created in the early years of TV. But it has to be a performance of sincerity itself since it will be judged harshly if it seems to be evasive, duplicitous, or scheming. Reality TV depends on putting the reality of ordinary people into defined artificial situations and letting viewers discover and condone the sincere and trustworthy. Research has reported that frequent conversations about reality TV events relate directly to this issue: is it a performance, or are they being sincere (Hill 2004)?

The second set of speculations around reality TV relate to the limits of acceptable behavior. Reality TV formats tend to place participants in stressful situations, and their response to stress can often trigger behavior that many viewers find objectionable. As Annette Hill (2004, 133) points out, "Ethics are at the heart of reality programming. Rights to privacy, rights to fair treatment, good and bad moral conduct, and taste and decency are just some of the ethical issues that arise." The programs themselves simply display behavior: they have no theme or issue. Anyone who seeks moral guidance from what happens within them is, exactly, taking them out of context. Documentary formats can provide explicit or implicit moral evaluation, but reality TV shows do not. Instead, reality shows provide raw material for comments and discussions that take place around them; these discussions are where moral and ethical questions are worked through. They are worked through in the "public" media, in celebrity magazines like *Heat* or *Closer*, in newspaper coverage, on radio shows. They equally generate comments on message boards and blogs (sometimes attached to the program, sometimes attached to public media), where people speculate freely about the possible motives of participants and what led them to behave in a particular way. They roundly condemn particular behaviors and then have to justify their views. Similar exchanges take place in everyday conversations and are reflected in the comments of radio presenters, columnists, and other media-based commentators. These reactions feed into the commentary programs that surround the most prominent shows (e.g., *Big Brother's Little Brother*, *Big Brother's Big Mouth*, etc.). The reality show may be at the core of this process, but its social importance lies in the activities it produces rather than in the series itself. As TV events rather than as TV programs, reality TV enables public, informal discussions about the motives behind particular behaviors and the limits of acceptable behavior.

Reality TV is part of a general social trend toward the blurring of leisure and information. It looks like entertainment; it is treated like entertainment. But it gives rise to conversations that, while still compelling and enjoyable, have wide implications. Reality TV enables social talk about moral values and about how to understand human behavior. Reality TV conversations are different from sport conversations or most other conversations around event TV. Reality TV provides neutral common ground for talking about issues of trust and the credibility of our fellow humans. Conversations about reality TV are gossip that will not get back to the subjects of that gossip and are an opportunity for finding out what colleagues and acquaintances think about interpersonal issues without the need to confront problems together. Issues of trust and sincerity come to the fore and then impact on other areas where these are important issues, not least the realm of politics and how politicians are regarded.

A new emotional complexity has been brought to everyday and public life. TV has blurred the boundaries between the domestic and the public spheres, between leisure and information, and between the emotional and rational in public life. By bringing politicians visibly close to their citizenry, it has given those citizens a new intimacy with their rulers. We now understand their actions by reference to emotional criteria as well as policies, judge them by their sincerity, and even refer to them by their given names as if we knew them.

Politics and Emotional Sincerity

TV has given a new visibility to politicians, bringing them into the everyday world of people on TV, so their every expression and mood can be closely scrutinized (Turnock 2006). Few have ever met a president or prime minister, but everyone knows their voice and style of speech, their hairstyle, their grins and frowns, their particular gestures and involuntary body language. Most people will claim to be able to gauge their sincerity from these indicators, just as they do about people who appear in documentaries or reality shows. Some refer to prominent politicians by their first names only, as though they were actually acquainted, so close is the seeming link to these individuals through television.

The democratic political process has found it hard to adapt to this new visibility brought by TV. Radio broadcasting had proved to be a useful tool for traditional politics. In the 1930s, American radio began to provide its political leaders with a new platform, which they adapted to provide "fireside chats" with the electorate, addressing citizens as individuals rather than as a mass in a public meeting. This was simply a new means of achieving an age-old need of those in power: to communicate their decisions to those they govern and to secure consent for those decisions. Broadcasting allowed rulers to speak directly to the ruled. However, TV has brought a new personalization of politics, reducing the traditional distance of national politicians from their people. All people now know what their rulers look and sound like. Impressionists have provided instantly recognizable lampoons of British prime ministers since Willie Rushton's Harold Macmillan on *That Was the Week That Was* in 1962. Yet, just twenty years before that moment, it was possible to keep hidden from the American people that President Franklin Delano Roosevelt was effectively confined to a wheelchair. Cinema newsreels and radio did not provide the same visibility as TV does.

TV gives us politicians in close-up. By appearing on TV, in broadcasts under their own control or on news or discussion programs, politicians submit themselves to the same regime of understanding as any other TV performer. Their sincerity can be judged just like that of any other documentary or reality show participant. This has thrown the emphasis of the political process onto the question of trust. Now that average citizens can see politicians daily and come to think they know them well, it is natural that they place more emphasis on a politician's personal characteristics rather than the policies that they claim to represent. We ask not what policies they stand for so much as whether we can trust them to do the best for us. Politicians have responded in kind, proposing themselves as sincere and trustworthy when seeking election and invoking the bond of trust that they believe they have created. Television enabled British citizens to see Prime Minister Tony Blair furrowing his brow and presenting his decision to join the U.S. invasion of Iraq in 2003 as a struggle with his conscience. He explicitly appealed to the overwhelmingly skeptical British public to trust him. Many citizens (the majority according to opinion polls) responded with the slogan "Not in my name." This ruthlessly highlighted the inherent problem of representative democracy that has been intensified by the development of TV. Blair was appealing to the trust he thought he had won from the electorate. A majority responded that he did not represent their views on this important issue. It was an issue that no political program or set of policies could have foreseen.

Television has exposed a problem at the heart of the process of democratic representation. Two principles of representation are involved: the idea of an individual whom you trust and the idea of an individual who represents a set of ideas and values that you share. The process of democratic voting is one of picking an individual to represent one's views and desires at governmental level. According to political theory, these individuals are elected as representatives of political programs rather than as individuals. They represent a set of explicit aims (e.g., the Greens) or a general tendency (e.g., New Labour). Under some democratic systems, citizens vote for lists of candidates rather than for an individual. Nonetheless, each list has its stars (who feature at the top of the list and are likely to be elected) and its known individual leaders. In other systems, like the United Kingdom and the United States, voting is for a particular individual as representative of a particular program or party.

The double system of representation (trusted person versus explicit program) exists in an uneasy balance. Television has tipped this balance decisively toward the personal, by creating the feeling of a direct connection with individual politicians, usually the party leader. Voting for a party program has given way to voting for the appeal of a party's leader. Those leaders will propose a particular approach to politics rather than a concrete program. They express themselves across their policy pronouncements and through them. Their programs, such as they are, are more a vehicle for demonstrating their trustworthiness than a firm commitment to a particular course of action. Any politician putting forward a policy with less than total conviction is liable to be found out by the forensic viewing of voters, so those policies still matter. Nevertheless, a shift has taken place in how the democratic process works; democracies are still coming to terms with it. Democracy is beginning to work on the basis of a personal contract of trust between leaders and their citizens, but the system scarcely works well.

Modern politicians mobilize the idea of trust as the bedrock of their relationship with citizens. They will base their appeal on offering themselves as a trustworthy person, a person "like you" or "who you can do business with." They appeal for the trust of the electorate on the basis of a show of sincerity, which viewers may judge according to many other such appeals across TV. Politicians are then forced to present themselves as blameless in matters of personal morality to justify the trust of the electorate. In the prevailing morality of TV, trust requires that a person be open and sincere: to be caught being two-faced, duplicitous, or hypocritical is one of the worst sins of reality TV. However, politics is a process in which it is unwise to reveal everything that you hope for or intend to do, and this creates problems for many candidates. The area of personal morality is a further problem, as candidates usually want to present themselves as morally blameless rather than risk alienating part of the electorate. This provokes the inevitable investigations into their past or present acts of a dubious or unacceptable moral nature and to the spectacle of attack commercials in the United States at election time. It is a rare politician who declares his or her past mistakes and uses this honesty as the basis of an appeal for trust. Rather, as with Bill Clinton and many others, the problems of personal morality quickly become issues of trustworthiness, not so much because of what they did or did not do but because they lied to cover up.

The politics of seeming sincerity and trust involves a considerable amount of image management. Leaders are taught how to speak sincerely. This was famously the case with Margaret Thatcher, tapes of whose elocution lessons were widely circulated while she was prime minister, precisely to demonstrate that she lacked real sincerity. All senior politicians calculate when, where, and how they should appear and employ teams of advisers whose role is to ensure that some aspects of how they conduct their business remain hidden from their citizens. These image managers, or spin doctors, ensure that their charges continue to give an impression of sincerity and trustworthiness.

Sincerity is a performance for many politicians, not least because they are called upon to make many different kinds of pronouncements in different situations. In negotiations, sincerity is of little use, whereas other characteristics are: stubbornness, the ability to compromise, and the ability to imply something without actually saying it. Public political discourse still remains relatively formal in order to provide a flexible way of communicating on several levels at once, often by implication. Despite their seeming sincerity, politicians still use formal forms of speech most of the time. They frame their pronouncements carefully, even if they spice them increasingly with down-to-earth demotic phrases. Nevertheless, it is still a shock to hear how politicians speak to each other when they think the microphones are switched off. George W. Bush and Tony Blair made the mistake of thinking they were off-mike at a G8 conference in Russia in July 2006. The conversation recorded was also widely broadcast to reveal the distance between their performance as public figures and how they speak in private. Bush's greeting, "Yo Blair," Blair's reference to "this trade thingy," and Bush's proposed solution to war in Lebanon ("what they need to do is to get Syria, to get Hezbollah to stop doing this shit and it's over") all revealed a discourse somewhat less elevated than the average daytime talk show, let alone a TV current affairs program. It equally showed the hesitant and deferential attitude of Blair to Bush, both through his speech and his body language, standing while Bush sits munching a sandwich.[2]

Such glimpses of the actual interaction of politicians reveal how little we really know them. Our politicians are visible to us, but they still largely control the terms of that visibility; they determine when and how they are seen. TV may have enabled a visibility and brought a new relationship of familiarity with politicians, but this relationship can still be controlled and manipulated. It also carries with it a danger of disillusion with the political process itself, especially if attempts to manipulate the relationship begin to go wrong. TV has introduced an "up close and personal" approach to politicians that has intensified the representational contract by enabling citizens to make a judgment about the sincerity of politicians and whether they are "sympathetic." In this new political landscape, disappointment and disillusion with a once-trusted politician is a common experience. It can contribute to a disillusion with the whole process of politics and the negotiation of collective endeavor. The show of sincerity and the appeal for trust are easily abused. The resultant disillusion can be felt more keenly as a personal betrayal than, for example, the attempts by politicians in the past to abandon or revise a central plank of policy. Disillusion with politics, in other words, may not be the result of an increasing distance from those in power at all. It seems more to be the result of the feelings of closeness to politicians that TV has brought about and the subsequent disappointment when that personal relationship is betrayed.

The pervasive nature of television has enabled such a development. It would be wrong, however, to argue that politics has in some way been degraded by this process or that one form of inadequate democratic process has been replaced by another. The process has been far from simple, as it has involved the development of a lexicon of performance styles fitted to the new audiovisual media, along with a greater awareness of emotional expression and a greater cultural confidence in our ability to assess the sincerity of the feelings being bodied forth in particular, and by now familiar, regimes of public performance made universally visible by television.

Notes

1. The contrast between successive British prime ministers demonstrates this. Tony Blair appeared "sincere" in front of the cameras; Gordon Brown "dour" and "uncomfortable". However journalists report that in personal interactions, Brown's sincerity of belief was striking compared to Blair's hesitations and searches for the right things to say.

2. This is a British reaction to the exchange. American reaction tended to concentrate on the president's use of the word *shit*.

References

Ellis, J. 2000. *Seeing things: Television in the age of uncertainty*. London: I. B. Tauris.

———. 2007. *TV FAQ: Uncommon answers to common questions about TV*. London: I. B. Tauris.

Enright, A. 2007. Diary. *London Review of Books*, October 4.

Gripsrud, J. 1995. *The Dynasty years: Hollywood television and critical media studies*. London: Routledge.

Hill, A. 2004. *Reality TV*. London: Routledge.

Medhurst, A. 1991. Every wart and pustule: Gilbert Harding and television stardom. In *Popular television in Britain*, ed. J. Corner. London: BFI.

Poole, R. 2008. *Earthrise—How man first saw the earth*. New Haven, CT: Yale University Press.

Turnock, R. 2006. *Television and consumer culture: Britain and the transformation of modernity*. London: I. B. Tauris.

Cultural and Moral Authority: The Presumption of Television

By
DAVID E. MORRISON

This article shows how British television has lost cultural authority due to social shifts in British society whereby no single moral voice can expect to find an audience. The author argues that there is no longer a moral language by which to address moral issues nor any common agreement about the rightful constitution of the cultural and moral universe. The central point is that technological development leading to increase in television channel proliferation did not fragment the audience, as is often assumed, but that it was the fragmentation of the audience that allowed the uptake of the varied and various channels.

Keywords: culture; secularization; Lord Reith; law reform; Sir Hugh Greene; audience; moral authority

Acentral theme that emerged from our study, *Media and Values: Intimate Transgressions in a Changing Moral Landscape* (Morrison et al. 2007) was the absence in Britain today of a moral language with which people could engage with cultural issues. Based on interviews with twenty-seven senior media personnel, regulators, and members of media interest groups, plus twenty-two general population focus groups and three nationally representative surveys, the study is by far the largest and most detailed empirical examination of the media's cultural performance as viewed by the public and media personnel. The report's key finding, however, of the absence of a moral language by which to evaluate media performance must be

David E. Morrison is a professor of communications research at the University of Leeds in the United Kingdom. He has written about the history of communications research and the institutionalization of knowledge, journalists and war reporting, moral protest movements, audience response to social issues, and methodological developments. His most recent coauthored book, Media and Values: Intimate Transgressions in a Changing Moral Landscape *(Intellect 2007), examines moral coherence in the contemporary world as revealed in empirical research into individual attitudes, opinions, tastes, and judgments.*

DOI: 10.1177/0002716209338351

seen as part of a wider historical story of the secularization of culture. The aim of this article is to examine British television's response to social change and its cultural outcomes from a moral perspective.

The Secularization of Culture

In the spring of 1964, John Reith, the first director general of the BBC, wrote in his retirement to Arthur Fforde, chairman of the BBC, bitterly attacking what he saw as the BBC's desertion of its cultural duty by the broadening of its audience appeal: "The BBC has lost dignity and repute; in the upper reaches of intellectual and ethical and social leadership it has abdicated its responsibility and its privilege. Its influence is disruptive and subversive; it is no longer on the Lord's side" (Stuart 1975, 143). Reith unknowingly put his finger on fault lines of stress appearing within broadcasting in the 1960s, when it lost its claim to speak for an identifiable set of values drawn from cultural assumptions about Britain as a Christian nation.

The impact of secularization on cultural production has not simply meant the disappearance of religious symbols from art, literature, and theater, nor a pervasive cultural content that has little or nothing to do with the "salvation of the soul" (Lowenthal 1961, xviii). It has collapsed the possibility of a central moral authority capable of providing any overarching cultural meaning acceptable to society as a whole. Indeed, the twin processes of industrialization and urbanization, which led to secularization, have made it impossible to speak of an audience as a whole and impossible to identify any moral voice capable of gaining general acceptance. Industrialization and urbanization not only destroyed the features of the old order to which religion gave symbolic expression, and within which a religious view of the world made sense, but in doing so also fragmented experience and created groups, classes, and cultures that stood in opposition to each other. The changed structure of modern society, as Alasdair MacIntyre has pointed out, "made it only too obvious to all parties that the alleged authoritative norms of the whole community to which appeal is made are, in fact, man-made, and that they are not the norms of the whole community to which in their own way men of every rank are equally subject" (MacIntyre 1967, 12, 14).

What MacIntyre (1967) captures in his discussion of the secularization process is the increasing fragmentation of the social world that denied religion an authoritative moral voice. What is important in terms of broadcasting, however, is that in the absence of such possibility of appeal, broadcasting had nowhere to turn other than to the popular by way of judging performance. While Reith castigated the BBC for attempting to extend its appeal at the expense of its "ethical and social leadership," the reality of the situation was that it could do no other; it no longer had a moral compass by which to steer a course of instruction.

Each culture must be examined separately for the meaning that religion holds for it and for the meanings of institutional attachment, a point Bryan Wilson (1966, 114, 115) makes in discussing the marked difference in church affiliation between the United States and England. In England, it is true that for the Irish immigrant, Catholicism provided a point of Irish identity in a manner suggested by Wilson in relation to the social function of religion in America. However, the description of the Church of England as the "Tory party at prayer," while overly simple, nevertheless captures a process of religious and sociopolitical fusion and, by extension, the process by which religious influence permeated general associations in a manner not possible through its own direct appeal. This religious capture of culture through such sociopolitical fusion meant the permeation of Christianity into general culture so that even classes and groups that were formally removed from clerical Christianity could not escape its imposition. Indeed, as David Martin (1969) points out, the English urban working class was never especially churched, but the Church of England as the established Church, and closely interlocked with the establishment, had permission to address audiences, most notably in the nation's schools, where it would not otherwise have been invited.

Loss of Moral Authority

Tom Burns, writing on the early days of the BBC under the management of Reith, likened it to a "kind of internal diplomatic service, representing the British–best of British to the British." BBC culture, like that of standard English vocabulary and pronunciation, was, according to Burns, "not peculiar to itself, but an intellectual audience composed of the values, standards and beliefs of the professional middle classes" (Burns 1964, 20; see also Burns 1977). While the British upper and middle classes may not have shared the Presbyterian fervor of Reith, Christianity had a common enough drawing-room presence among such groups to provide a sense of a refracted common culture. In effect, as Burns notes, this sectional elite culture operated as official culture. The point to stress, however, is that this official culture was infused with a moral language and purpose drawn from Christian sentiment, which provided broadcasting with moral purpose.

The application of moral purpose to broadcasting was made all the more possible by the absence of any alternative channels to the BBC to carry other voices. By the late 1950s, one begins to see the fading of the Anglican Church as an authoritative source of public pronouncements about the way to live. A whole raft of government legislation governing "moral performance"—the Obscene Publication Act of 1959, the Murder [Abolition of the Death Penalty] Act of 1965, the Abortion Act of 1967, the Sexual Offences Act of 1967, the Theatres Act of 1968 (abolishing stage censorship), and the Divorce Act of 1969—separately and together offer evidence of a loosening of moral certainty, a loss of confidence in the right of the State to rule on how individuals shall live and, in the case of the abolition of the death penalty, how they shall die.

This movement in moral legislation away from Christian-informed precepts to a secular regard for pragmatic practice is reflected in movements within broadcasting that denote a shift in the intellectual location of senior policy makers away from a distinctly Christian-informed rule to one of "moral pluralism." For example, if one compares statements of principle by past directors general of the BBC—for example, Reith (in Stuart 1975), Haley (1948), Greene (1965), and Curran (1971)—there is a distinct shift from Reith's and Haley's commitment to solid Christian principles to Greene's support for what he described as "basic moral values" (that is, non-Christian) and Curran's acceptance that, in a post-Christian era, the responsibility of broadcasting was to give full voice to all the various ideas current within society. Curran's position (in Stuart 1975) is reflected in the thinking of the Independent Television Authority (ITA) in its submission to the Longford Committee on pornography in 1970. As the regulator for the whole of the commercial sector of television, the ITA acknowledged the difficulty of providing production directives in the form of codes of practice to the companies under its direction. It submitted,

> One of the main difficulties underlying [the codes of practice] has come as a result of the philosophical shifts over the last few years. The black and white value system accepted in the 50's emerged into the grey area of the 60's and led to the rejection of absolute standards in the thinking of many in today's society. (Longford 1972, 247)

The ITA was not alone in voicing such difficulties. A little later the Church of England Broadcasting Commission (1973), reflecting on the moral context in which decisions about program content were made, remarked that

> it would be useless for the broadcasting authorities to seek for such principles from the practice of modern society. The trouble is that the present pluralist society not only lacks any universally, or even generally, accepted moral norms, but instead simultaneously pursues the widest variety of independent aims.

In short, like the ITA, but from a theological perspective, the commission saw the "problem" with broadcasting as trapped within the prevailing orthodoxy of the so-called new morality, which, it went on to say, was often sheer social expediency: "Its ethics are situational and its ultimate goals seldom bear any relationship to Christian hope."

There is a clear recognition from the Church and broadcasting authorities, and as evidenced by legislation, that by the 1960s there was no longer an available common moral language by which to judge cultural performance. In this context, a vigorous protest at declining moral values in broadcasting made itself heard through the Clean Up TV campaign launched by Mary Whitehouse, a retired schoolteacher. The campaign was consolidated into the National Viewers and Listeners Association (NVALA), which functioned as a moral watchdog, ready to protest about indecency, obscenity, and bad language in television output.

Moral Protest and Language

As a social movement organized around television, NVALA was a unique phenomenon on the British political landscape. Its paid-up membership consisted of no more than around twenty thousand people, but its demand for a curb on swearing, violence, and explicit sex struck a chord of support among large numbers of the population and made Mary Whitehouse a household name and potent lobbying force. Demographically the movement was a microcosm of the Church of England, to which most members belonged. It was middle-class, middle-aged to elderly, and predominantly female in its composition (Tracey and Morrison 1979). Fervently Christian and Anglican, NVALA was driven by the desire to save television from Hugh Greene's "basic moral values" and restore John Reith's principles of Christian leadership (Whitehouse 1967). As far as Whitehouse was concerned, television had not just lost its way; it had taken society with it. As she said in an interview, "If you ask me to name one man who more than anybody else has been responsible for the collapse of this country I would name Greene" (Tracey 1983, 231).

NVALA protests, campaigning, and political lobbying, although an irritant to broadcasters and annoyance to the liberal establishment, were tracts against the times. However, in terms of understanding the trajectory of British television, its existence and activities assist in defining a moment in history and also a sociological truth. The BBC had been forced to take note of its audience, increasingly so after the advent of commercially funded television in 1956. As it gradually did so, it retreated from its role of moral and cultural leadership. The forces that produced NVALA are the very forces that pronounced, or delivered, the end of television in Britain as a force of moral and cultural endeavor. The idea of moral and cultural service becomes transformed to that of organizational striving, unencumbered by principles, for the immediate satisfaction of audience tastes. The fate of NVALA was to recognize the necessity to reassert the assumed core values of a shared universe of Christian meaning that had informed British culture, while failing to understand what the broadcasters and even the established church so readily understood: that the long process of cultural fragmentation dissolved any framework of discourse within which moral questions applicable to the whole of society could be articulated.

Without a shared moral language, it is difficult to proclaim a moral order or indeed a cultural order. Instead, moral appeal is replaced by appeals to taste, individual preferences of consumption. Yet, what was certainly understood by NVALA, in both its attack on the established Church for what was seen as its lack of moral leadership and on the BBC as the broadcasting establishment for pandering to popular sentiments, was that the appeal to individual taste was a sign of lost moral purpose in the first instance and of lost cultural purpose in the second. As worrying as such developments may have been to Whitehouse and her followers, the sociological fact in reference to NVALA, as Roy Wallis pointed out, was that the fragmentation of beliefs in contemporary society were such that "no man can expect his norms and values to hold exclusive sway" (Wallis 1976, 279-280).

It is the mark of the moral entrepreneur to dissolve the differing features of the social landscape into a leavened moral plain of possible achievements. Judgments of performance are not to be modified by any recognition of the social circumstances within which they occur. This was precisely what occurred in both legislation and in broadcasting during the sixties: recognition of how lives were in fact lived, rather than how they ought to be lived. The Divorce Reform Act of 1969, to take one example, viewed marriage as a legal contract, not a binding, lifelong sacramental union. At the same time, the BBC's path-breaking realist *Wednesday Play* series, which ran from 1964 to 1970, held no message of common appeal to Christian instruction either, or even Christian hope, but revealed a mundane world of ordinary people and ordinary lives, often lived on the margin of social inclusion. The plays informed some parts of the population about how others lived—those who were not accustomed to public attention other than, often as not, as a social problem in need of control.

The Sixties: A Cultural Watershed

It is here, at the juncture between ideas, culture, and social structure, that matters become complex, marking the sixties as a watershed in the history of television in Britain. If public service broadcasting is taken to involve some idea of culture in the sense of meanings drawn from, or relating to, collectively shared understandings, then it begins to unravel as a normative ideal in the face of empirical facts, namely, that there is no common culture to which appeal can be made. Television in the sixties demonstrated this to itself by highlighting differences in living, something that grew apace in the decades following with the development of lifestyle and reality television. It was the weekly *Wednesday Play* broadcast during Greene's reign at the BBC that broke the rules of play concerning the manner in which television talked to its public and talked about sections of the public. *Cathy Come Home* (November 1966), the most famous and controversial of the plays, dealt with the effects of homelessness on a young white, working-class family. It was a damning indictment of the fate of the poor and had a huge and immediate impact on public opinion.

Cultural struggle is political. A new generation of reforming Labour Members of Parliament (see Pym 1974) returned to power in 1966 and continued to push forward legislation related to cultural expression and social conduct, especially in relation to sexual behavior—which may be viewed as evidence of the reworking of authority that television also exhibits. Yet, if the general ethos of reform relating to cultural expression and personal conduct favored the exploration by television of ways of life existing at the margins of the respectable, the inclusion of such groups and behaviors as legitimate foci for discussion and portrayal assisted the promotion of tolerance to varieties of lives and, in some cases, even sympathetic concern. The launch in 1966 of Shelter, a leading charity for the homeless, benefited enormously from the national debate that followed the showing of *Cathy Come Home* just prior to its founding. Indeed, to an unusual degree, this period sees a fit between political sentiment and public broadcasting.

At the level of culture as symbolic representation of the world, the period following the ending of the Second World War saw the unshackling of the ethic of performance underpinned by notions of Christian stewardship to be replaced by thoroughly secular expression. This transformation, however, given witness by the legislative changes governing ways of living, as well as in broadcasting content, is reflective of the recognition of structural and cultural change. That is, the fracturing of traditional associations that had given rise to sets of fairly readily defined cultural expressions was replaced by a range of associations, and hence range of cultural expressions, that came to be identified through, or associated with, consumption. The austerity of the immediate postwar years and into the fifties begins, certainly by the 1960s, to give way to a more affluent consumer culture and a diversity of expression and display focused around objects of consumption. Although not to be accounted for by consumption itself, the period sees a move to enjoyment and away from the kind of hardship that had previously provided solidarity to working-class experience and sharpness to its politics (Abercrombie, Keat, and Whiteley 1994; Micheletti, Follestal, and Stolle 2004).

Although class remained, as ever, a strong predictor of life chances, class as a rhetorical organizing category of experience began to lose its purchase in the sixties. The period, although not devoid of issue politics, saw a shift from collective consciousness, be that informed by religion or class, to a particularization of experience informed by consumption. Freed from general organizing principles of experience in the manner of collective properties, the movement was toward seeing everything as the individual expression of personal preference. Culture lost its value associations and became a question of taste. As such, culture became the subject and object of measurement. Indeed, taste became open to measurement in the way that culture as a value was not. This movement had far-reaching consequences for the moral performance of television and the values of public service broadcasting.

Audience Measurement

Hardly anything captures the change in the moral logic of television from the 1950s to the present better than the rise of audience research, a central feature of which was the realization that television could no longer reference the audience as if it were a unified and uniform whole. Neither could it exercise moral authority without exposing itself to charges of representing only a particular elite stratum of society. Put simply, broadcasting had lost the right of cultural imposition on its audiences and was increasingly obliged to investigate and understand them. The provision of culture was to be pursued by the pursuit of the audience, and the pursuit of the audience was to be pursued by knowledge of its tastes, and those tastes were to be discovered through audience research.

Yet, the desire to know the audience through research, prompted by the realization of its plurality and the impossibility of a single moral voice, is only part of a larger story that sees the replacement of moral language with the language of technical reason. The effect of this has been to turn questions of culture into behavioral questions amenable to measurement. Thus, harm, although it has become a central plank in the debate over symbolic representations of the world, is not construed in a manner that suggests the transgression of values but as the transmission of behavior that if acted upon would be socially disruptive. Even consideration of material that gives offense is not conceived of as offense to values but in terms of upset to the sensibilities of people. This is technical reasoning, and not moral judgment. As such, taste, or cultural preference, becomes a research question: the scientific exploration of social arrangements. It does not presuppose standards drawn from an ordered moral position.

While this transformation of the moral into the technical fits with the general rise of research as a way of managing performance in the face of a fragmented audience, the problem emerges in terms of intellectually understanding social processes when instrumental rationality becomes amplified in the face of technology itself. Stripped of moral content through the absence of moral language, people are seen to stand in relationship to the world in operational terms. That is, they are seen as decision makers responding to opportunities to maximize satisfactions. Indeed, the preeminence of economic rational choice theory in policy making on broadcasting and other public service matters today (health, for instance) rests on more than its explanatory power and exemplifies a particular social-scientific view of the individual. The evaluation of the individual is based on the decision made—a kind of technical competence—rather than on the moral base of the decision making. Lost to sight, in other words, is the human aspect of performance.

This frame of thinking defines the current regulation of British television by the Office of Communication (OFCOM), the national regulatory authority. A particular view of the ecology of the audience has emerged, namely, a fracturing of the audience. From an econometric viewpoint, this has been an almost individualization of the audience—brought about by technological development that saw the entry, first by cable, then satellite, and then digital compression, of hundreds of television channels. However, while this creation of a multichannel viewing environment has undoubtedly split the profits of television companies as they struggled to hold market share, it cannot be argued that the technologies of channel proliferation split the television audience. The fragmentation of the audience came as a result of social change that was already taking place and that heightened social differentiation. Multichannel cable and satellite television provide new commercial opportunities to cater to an already diversified and culturally fragmented society. They are not the cause of social and cultural fragmentation.

In the official discourse of OFCOM, which privileges the "citizen-consumer," we see a view of the audience as an appendage of technical achievement and not a living expression of social experience. The triumph of this technical framework of instrumental reasoning, as it applies to the audience, is a far cry from the reasoning that surrounded the initial public discussion in the 1970s of the expansion of TV channels and the social purposes of the proposed new television services. In the deliberations of the Annan Committee's report on the future of broadcasting (Annan 1977), and in the launch of Channel Four (1982), which resulted from the deliberations of Annan, there was a clear recognition of the pluralistic makeup of the national audience that was not addressed by the existing three national TV channels. Channel Four was expressly set up to cater to minority tastes and interests largely unacknowledged and ignored in existing mainstream television provision.

The Acknowledgment of Pluralism: Annan and Channel Four

The collapse of a shared social and moral order acknowledged in the submissions of the Independent Television Commission to the Longford Committee in 1970, and the Church of England Broadcasting Commission of 1973, was in reality the coming into view of the cultural diversity of British society. The recognition of this new reality—and of the loss of moral authority by the old elites—was central to the workings of the Annan Committee on the Future of Broadcasting. Reporting in 1977, it accepted that any judgment on the future organization and performance of broadcasting had to take into account the changed and changing nature of the composition of British society. Britain, the report declared,

> is now a multi-racial and pluralist society: that is to say, people adhere to different views of the nature and purpose of life and expect their own views to be expressed in some form or other. The structure of broadcasting must reflect this variety. (Annan 1977, 30, quoted in Freedman 2001, 203)

What Annan illustrates is not simply recognition of the increasingly diverse character of the British population but the need to recognize this diversity in broadcast output. The fragmentation of British society precedes the fragmentation of the British audience for television. What we see in Annan is not just recognition of the plural nature of the television audience but a moral prescript to open up the airwaves to a plurality of voices. It is a demand for the democratization of culture and a recognition that the traditional cultural elites could no longer expect their values to hold sway. The committee's proposal to establish an Open Broadcasting Authority that would act as a publisher was designed to "allow for the transmission of opinion not normally sanctioned by other channels" and was at the heart of its stated aim to open up broadcasting (Freedman 2001, 206).

This opening up had to wait until the introduction of Channel Four, which began transmission in 1982 with Jeremy Isaacs as its first executive director. Isaacs's position on the function and purpose of a fourth channel had already been laid out in a talk given at the Edinburgh Television Festival (1979) in which he argued that the proposed new channel had to cater to substantial minorities neglected by other parts of the television industry (Docherty, Morrison, and Tracey 1988, 5). Isaacs was quite clear about the nature of Channel Four and the more general nature and purpose of broadcasting: "My view of what a liberal society is about [is that] you tolerate people's activities as long as they don't harm you." He referred to political support that "understands the need for a tolerant society, to have broadcasting that allows all sorts of opinions and attitudes" (Docherty, Morrison, and Tracey 1988, 19).

Isaacs's position offers a view of broadcasting as more than a mere reflection of cultural change but, rather, as forming an active part in change itself. The whole drift in postwar British society was one of the loosening of control over how individuals should conduct their private lives and a recognition and acceptance of difference. Television was no passive witness to this. It assisted in forcing the pace of change through bringing into the public domain much that had previously remained hidden, and this was taken further in the 1980s by Channel Four. Indeed, especially in the realm of sexuality, Channel Four offered legitimacy to behaviors and groups that had hitherto been withheld visibility and respect. The opening up of the airways proposed by Annan saw the inclusion of hitherto marginalized social groups who now claimed a right to representation not simply as worthy subjects for dramatic attention, but as citizens. Their inclusion in routine television output marked a move toward the cultural democratization and away from the cultural control of broadcasting.

If Channel Four developed out of the recognition by the late 1970s of the cultural diversity of British society, it nevertheless ran ahead of public opinion in its liberal-minded sexual politics. In the case of the representation of homosexuality, the channel very much went against the grain of public tolerance of sexual difference, as shown by the fact that five years after it went on air, only 3 percent of the population accepted that homosexuals should have regular programs, with the majority, 61 percent, totally opposed to any such programs (Docherty, Morrison, and Tracey 1988, 126). The opening of the airways to same-sex relationships by Channel Four represented an imposition of liberal ideology and not the reflection of popular sentiment. It may be seen as an attempt to give recognition and acceptance to what had been legalized by the Sexual Offences Act of 1967—to give it a kind of cultural second reading. It certainly shows television as an active reformer in the effort for the acceptance of difference while acting as an early indicator of the pluralization of audiences ahead of the multichannel environment begun in the 1990s. Channel Four might have catered to homosexual interests and tastes; it certainly did not create them.

How far exposure to difference makes for acceptance of difference is an open empirical question, but it is reasonable to assume that the familiar is easier to accommodate than the unfamiliar. In that sense, television can claim in the period under examination to have been a liberalizing force, but that liberalization was bought at a cost: the collective expression of culture as a shared set of values. Indeed, the loosening of moral authority that allowed entry to a range of alternative values, norms, and ways of living proved a mixed blessing. Once cultural expression fails to be guided by a central agreement on what constitutes the moral order, there is no end to the demands for cultural representation. And indeed, each particular demand for cultural inclusion is as valid as any other, and all that holds back the satisfaction of the demands is the physical impossibility of granting reward to every request. Without a substantive moral order, everything is reduced to technical expediency. Nothing stands in the way of satisfying a multitude of demands beyond the technological capacity to cater to them. Channel Four in the 1980s was only one station on the way to the multichannel world of cable and satellite delivery systems of the 1990s. Technology did not fragment the audience; rather, a culturally plural population with diverse tastes already existed, which new delivery systems were able and willing to meet.

The End of Television

The upshot of these social changes and the cultural realignments that accompanied them is not the end of television in any apocalyptic sense but, rather, the eclipse of that sense of moral purpose that was crucial to the original concept of public service broadcasting. The increasing difficulty of invoking the moral precepts of the British political, cultural, and religious establishment increasingly eroded the meaningful possibility of a genuinely national culture. Over a thirty-year period, from the 1960s to the 1990s, watching television became less and less a public act in the sense of accessing a nationally common offering—except in rare instances of collective celebration and mourning—and more and more a private act of consumption reflecting individual preferences without intruding on those of others. If today viewers each go their own way without hindrance or acknowledgment and if viewing is an individual and no longer a public matter, it becomes impossible to invoke the notion of a common culture or a shared way of life. What is is, and requires no more justification than that it is accepted.

References

Abercrombie, Nicholas, Russell Keat, and Nigel Whiteley. 1994. *The authority of the consumer*. New York: Routledge.

Annan, Lord. 1977. Report of the Committee on the Future of Broadcasting, Cmnd 6753. London: Her Majesty's Stationery Office.

Burns, Tom. 1964. *Cultural bureaucracy: A study of occupational milieux in the BBC*. Edinburgh, UK: University of Edinburgh, Department of Sociology.

———. 1977. *The BBC: Public institution and private world*. London: Macmillan.

Church of England Broadcasting Commission. 1973. *Broadcasting, society and the church: Report of the Broadcasting Commission of the General Synod of the Church of England*. London: Church Information Office.

Curran, Charles J., Sir. 1971. Broadcasting and society: A speech given [at the] Edinburgh Broadcasting Conference, 23 March 1971. London: British Broadcasting Corporation.

Docherty, David, David E. Morrison, and Michael Tracey. 1988. *Keeping Faith? Channel Four and its audience*. London: John Libbey.

Freedman, D. 2001. What use is a public enquiry? Labour and the 1977 Annan Committee on the Future of Broadcasting. *Media, Culture & Society* 23:195-211.

Greene, Hugh, Sir. 1965. Conscience of a programme director. In Sir Hugh Greene, *The third floor front: A view of broadcasting in the sixties*. London: Bodley Head Ltd.

Haley, W. 1948. Moral values in broadcasting. Address to the British Council of Churches, London.

Longford, Lord. 1972. *Pornography: The Longford report*. London: Coronet.

Lowenthal, Leo. 1961. *Literature, popular culture and society*. Palo Alto, CA: Pacific Books.

MacIntyre, Alasdair. 1967. *Secularization and moral change*. The Riddell Memorial Lectures. London: Oxford University Press.

Martin, David. 1969. *The religious and the secular: Studies in secularization*. London: Routledge & Kegan Paul.

Micheletti, M., A. Follestal, and D. Stolle. 2004. *Politics, products and markets: Exploring political consumerism past and present*. New Brunswick, NJ: Transaction Publishers.

Morrison, David E., Matthew Keiran, Michael Svennevig, and Sarah Ventress. 2007. *Media and values: Intimate transgressions in a changing moral landscape*. Bristol, UK: Intellect.

Pym, Bridget. 1974. *Pressure groups and the permissive society*. Newton Abbot, UK: David and Charles.

Stuart, Charles, ed. 1975. *The Reith diaries*. London: Collins.

Tracey, Michael. 1983. *A variety of lives: A biography of Sir Hugh Greene*. London: Bodley Head.

Tracey, Michael, and David Morrison. 1979. *Whitehouse*. London: Macmillan.

Wallis, R. 1976. Moral indignation and the media: Analysis of the NVALA. *Sociology* 10 (2): 271-95.

Whitehouse, Mary. 1967. *Cleaning-up T.V.: From protest to participation*. London: Blandford.

Wilson, Bryan R. 1966. *Religion in secular society: A sociological comment*. London: Watts.

Television, Public Participation, and Public Service: From Value Consensus to the Politics of Identity

By
PETER LUNT

The proliferation of popular television genres in which the public are key participants (talk shows, reality TV, and makeover and lifestyle television) on the surface may seem less to do with engagement and more to do with entertainment and voyeurism. However, this article explores an alternative to the idea that popular television based on personal experience is a marker of the end of television in general and the weakening of the public service tradition in particular. Two programs, *Oprah!* and *Little Angels*, are shown to address the agendas of reflexive modernity and governmentality and potentially to contribute to a normative social order based on the project of the self. The fact that both traditional public service providers and commercial channels are engaging with these social issues suggests that new ways of legitimizing television in the public interest are emerging, with implications for the character of public service television.

Keywords: public service broadcasting; popular television; public participation

Television is alive and well as part of the convergent global mix of communications. The proliferation of channels, the growing global communications market, and innovations in technological modes of delivery such as WebTV continue to transform television. In contrast to the first age of television in the two decades following the Second World War, however, television now is less and less the main source—the trusted provider of information with the potential to bring nations together and reflect on the key social and political issues of

Peter Lunt is a professor of media and communications at Brunel University in London. His research interests include the social psychology of the media and consumption, focusing on issues of public understanding and participation. He is the author of Mass Consumption and Personal Identity *(with Sonia Livingstone, Open University 1992) and* Talk on Television *(with Sonia Livingstone, Routledge 1994). He recently completed a book on Stanley Milgram and is researching public understanding of the regulation of financial services and the media in the United Kingdom in collaboration with Sonia Livingstone (Palgrave 2009).*

DOI: 10.1177/0002716209338457

the day. In particular, the role of television as a public service provider is under threat as the social, market, and technological contours of the mediascape change. One sign of the changing nature of television appears every day on our screens in the proliferation of participatory TV genres such as talk shows, reality TV, and lifestyle TV. These programs have not replaced traditional, valued genres of factual broadcasting such as news and documentary, but they do appear to dilute the quality and alter the meaning of the public information project of broadcasting.

The age of television coincided with a particular moment in the liberal democratic politics of Western societies in which the imperative of postwar reconstruction, the developing conflict of the cold war, and the emergence of consumer society combined. These conditions of social change, new opportunity, increasing threat from abroad, and dispersal and fragmentation at home created the context in which television was both constitutive of individualism and consumerism and also offering the potential for social cohesion by connecting people together through a shared, mediated culture and the provision of public information. The postwar social democratic liberal democracies in the United States and Europe had a number of shared features:

> They were liberal in the sense that they had constitutions which protected citizens' basic rights and freedoms. They were democratic, since people could vote for political parties to represent them in the legislative institutions of the state. They were more specifically *social democratic*, since they engaged in a degree of income distribution, welfare provision and economic planning. Finally, such societies were based on the assumption that nations and states should coincide, so that each nation should be governed by a single, unified political authority. (Thompson 2006, 1)

In this social and political context, traditional public service broadcasting (PSB) embodied values of social cohesion and the provision of public knowledge through high-quality factual broadcasting typified by news and documentary (Blumler 1991).

In contrast to these serious intentions of traditional genres of factual broadcasting, a number of genres of popular television such as talk shows, reality TV, and lifestyle television have emerged in recent years in which members of the public are the protagonists and participants. Such programs are hybrid forms of "infotainment" combining information and entertainment reflected in program content that covers a variety of lifestyle issues such as healthy living or fashion and a range of social, psychological, and political issues that are discussed, debated, or reacted to by members of the public (Andrejevic 2004; Bondebjerg 2002; Hill 2005; Livingstone and Lunt 1994; Lunt 2008; Ouellette and Hay 2008). These genres of popular television are aimed at individuals rather than collectivities and address questions of personal development and entertainment rather than questions of cohesion through the enhancement of shared values, public engagement, and the provision of public knowledge.

It is possible, perhaps tempting, to interpret talk shows, reality TV, and makeover, and lifestyle television as examples of the way that contemporary television has lost its public purpose and instead appeals to voyeurism, narcissism, populism, and the fetishism of identity (Brunsdon 2003). It might have once been possible to think of television and the public interest in the same breath, to hope that television might play a central role in the democratic process by providing a cultural forum that could both reach all of the public and connect them in a coherent way resulting in an informed public and sovereign opinion, but no longer. Such optimism seems incredible today as PSB gives way to the development of commercial media systems with global reach, and more complex technology driven by the market and oriented toward the individual consumer viewer. Popular television programs that focus on the personal issues faced by individuals seem an unpromising arena for public service, apparently doing nothing for democratization, the formation of social collectivities, and the citizen viewer. Instead, these programs seem to typify the new age of television focused on the consumer and entertainment rather than the citizen and public value.

In this article, I argue the contrary: that in important respects, new genres of factual broadcasting provide examples of a form of television in the public service oriented to public education and social order. I explore examples from genres of talk shows and lifestyle programming to develop this case, but first I outline briefly the key features of traditional conceptions of public service television to provide a comparison against which to develop an account of changes in the way that television serves the public interest.

Blumler (1991) outlines the common features of the public service legacy in Europe. First, PSB offers a comprehensive range of programming in recognition of the levy of a license fee on all listeners and viewers. Traditional PSB has a comprehensive remit addressing the diversity of public tastes and interests and articulated in a mandate to inform, educate, and entertain. The second principle is the independence of PSB from government and commercial interest. In addition, the PSB tradition also asserts independence from populism, working in the public interest rather than being guided by popular demand.

Blumler (1991) links the legitimation of traditional PSB to the potential of television and radio in liberal social-democratic states. He draws on Katz's (1985) suggestion that PSB offered "the opportunity of shared experience . . . contributing to authenticity by connecting the society to its cultural center and acquainting the segments of society with each other" (Katz 1985, in Blumler 1991, p. 11). In other words, traditional PSB seeks legitimation through the provision of public information while also constituting an institutional cultural sphere aimed at enhancing social coherence in a complex, fragmented society (Bohman 2000).

Indeed, independent PSB, funded by license, demands a range of conditions of legitimation. The public must feel that their voices and interests are reflected in program choice and content. The industry must agree that the market is not distorted by the activities of the public service broadcaster to the determinant of consumer interests. Politicians must feel that independence from political influence is matched by widespread public access and ideological neutrality in program content. The legitimacy of the arrangements for maintaining a public service broadcaster with the scope and remit of a body like the BBC comes into question if any of these conditions are not met.

Each of these issues has been raised against the PSB tradition in recent years (Blumler 1991). The traditional PSB was the result of a particular political settlement reflecting a debate from the 1940s and 1950s between advocates of elite democracy and those favoring pluralism—a debate that is arguably no longer the central issue in the relation between media, culture, and society (Held 2006). Nevertheless, the architecture of PSB reflects a compromise between these two accounts of the facticity of liberal democracy articulated in a normative discourse of public interest. Pluralism is reflected in the principles of diversity of content and balance in factual broadcasting in which diverse views, opinions, and ways of life compete for representation. However, a self-regulating elite decides upon the presentation and production of content, with the public limited to expressing their tastes and preferences through their choice of programs and, in the political sphere, through the potential increase in their understanding and appreciation of their social and political world. Both sides of this settlement have subsequently come under attack as outdated versions of elite democracy. The prerogative and desirability of elites to manage media content and representation and the notion of citizenship as consisting of making choices from among those presented have both been criticized.

New Genres of Popular TV and Public Service

Set against these arguments about the nature of PSB, the rise in new genres of popular TV such as talk shows, reality TV, and lifestyle TV appear as evidence of the triumph of popular taste over the traditional model of public service. Such programs, at face value, seem alien to public service because they do not conform to the traditional model of PSB. Infotainment challenges the traditional public service settlement that aligned informative and pedagogic aims with factual broadcasting and separated the product from entertainment. In addition, talk shows, reality TV, and lifestyle programming are all cheap, daytime TV and therefore do not meet the "quality" threshold for programming that delivers public service. Questions also surround the knowledge claims of programs in which the authority of traditional genres such as news and documentary is replaced by a new form of expertise grounded in practical advice and aimed at the problems of everyday life. The programs aim to help people to improve their lives rather than raising them to the higher plane of knowledge, experience, and consciousness that was the purpose of the public knowledge project of traditional PSB (Corner 1991).

I argue that such programs combine practical purpose with normative aims that potentially empower viewers, by encouraging them to take charge of their lives and attain a degree of autonomy and self-determination, while simultaneously constituting social order through the self-regulation of individuals (Lunt and Lewis 2008). These two principles, of emancipation and social order, are important dimensions of talk shows and reality TV, although they are achieved in the absence of the articulation of shared values and rather through the practical accomplishment of everyday life.

Let me begin with what is new in the increased visibility of the public on television. Talk shows, reality TV, and lifestyle television change the mode of address from the mass or the nation to the individual and involve shifts in the nature of expertise, topic, and purposes when compared to news and documentary. Equally important, the audience is no longer configured as the recipients, the end point of communication, but as participants who have migrated from the home to the studio and form part of the process of production as well as reception. The content of such programs is constructed from participants' ideas, actions, and reactions. Participatory program formats take this basic stuff of human existence and social interaction and mold it into narratives of self-improvement, reflections on the human condition, and social interaction between participants. The focus on self and identity echoes the way that individuals engage in the social world as reflexive subjects who pursue the project of the self (Giddens 1991). In such programs, "public service" takes on a new meaning that makes sense against the background of neoliberalism or late modernity.

Diversity and Change in Public Service Broadcasting

To some degree, PSB has already changed in practice to include greater diversity and new forms of public participation. In the United Kingdom, for example, one response to the criticism that public service had not represented the diversity of identities and experiences of British citizens was the establishment of Channel 4 in 1982 with a different public service remit to the BBC. Instead of comprehensive scope, the idea was to target previously underrepresented groups and innovations in program style and content (Born 2003). In addition, the development of the BBC Web site moved away from a traditional mass communication model to offer a range of interactive services and connections to broader online content as a context for TV programs. A new channel, Radio 5Live, combines news and sports coverage with radio phone-in. A more recent innovation is the availability of content on demand through BBC iPlayer (see www.BBC.co.uk). In addition, the BBC developed a range of program content innovations including twenty-four-hour rolling news and, significantly for this article, a variety of talk shows and reality TV programs.

In other words, PSB has changed, and the change is in the direction of more popular, niche, interactive delivery and diversity of audience participation and engagement. These changes do not sit comfortably with the ideals of social purpose: dissemination of knowledge to a mass audience through quality programming with the purpose of social cohesion, which is the cornerstone of the traditional public service model. In the case of talk shows, reality TV, and lifestyle TV, the populist nature of the programs and the potential vulnerability of participants adds to concerns about their place in PSB. If this is public service, what model of public service does it exemplify? Whatever value participants and audiences might gain from such programs (see Hill 2005), it is open to debate whether they are part of the public knowledge project or a means of enhancing social cohesion. Can programs contribute to public service if they neither engage the public in discussion and debate that might lead to consensus nor disseminate expertise and knowledge? More problems arise from questions about quality of production, the knowledge claims of program content, and the seriousness of purpose that supposedly characterizes PSB: how can popular television claim to reflect the public interest in the face of such questions? In what follows, I consider how the concept of public service would be changed if we included such programs, which are not easily covered by the rationale for traditional PSB.

The Social Value of Popular, Participatory TV as Mediated Civil Society

To explore the potential public service values in participatory programs, I discuss two programs: *Oprah!*, a hybrid of talk show and lifestyle program linked to the Web site Oprah.com (Lunt and Lewis 2008), and *Little Angels*, a BBC lifestyle program in which a clinical psychologist gives advice to parents with troublesome toddlers (Lunt 2008). These two examples are taken from a traditional public service provider in the United Kingdom (the BBC) and a commercial producer in the United States. This is important because the question of overlap between commercial and public service broadcasters raises two questions: should public service broadcasters continue to provide comprehensive program content including participatory programs, and to what extent can commercial broadcasters produce programs with public service content? The answers to these questions depend on what counts as public service.

Oprah! *and Oprah.com*

The *Oprah!* program, originally a therapeutic talk show, now fuses talk show and reality TV and is part of the extended cultural presence of the Oprah brand (Arvidsson 2006). In addition to the television program, the Oprah empire includes a Web site (Oprah.com), a magazine (*O, The Oprah Magazine*), a highly influential book club, and a variety of charitable and civil society activities in the United States and abroad (Illouz 2003; Lunt and Lewis 2008). The talk show *Oprah!* has been transformed through its integration with these other platforms. While intimate, therapeutic discussions between Oprah and her guests remain a central feature, the role of experts on the show has been developed. For example, British celebrities Trinny and Susannah, who have their own show, *What Not to Wear*, in the United Kingdom, appear on the *Oprah!* show to dispense advice on clothing to members of the studio audience. In addition to their appearances on the show, Trinny and Susannah appear on the Web site (Oprah.com), where they provide more generic advice on dressing accompanied by an interactive online survey, which asks questions about body size and shape and then dispenses "personalized" advice in the form of rules of clothing style choice.

   The example of Trinny and Susannah on Oprah.com illustrates the changing nature of expertise on lifestyle programs and contrasts with the authority and knowledge claims of traditional public service programs (Hartley 2008). A variety of lifestyle experts appear on Oprah's program, and their ideas are documented on the Oprah.com Web site, which constitutes an archive of advice in the form of guidance, suggestions, tips, and rules of thumb on a range of issues such as personal finance, relationships, fashion, style, fitness, health, and interior decorating (Lunt and Lewis 2008). This archive does not contain abstract, authoritative knowledge disseminated to a mass audience but rather mediated practical knowledge, which is both performed in the programs and presented as rules of thumb that constitute an ethic of personal growth and development. This form of expertise constructs a relationship between the lay participants, the host of the show, and the experts, organized around the rhetoric of personal growth and transformation (Lunt and Lewis 2008).

   There have always been "advice" programs on radio and television, such as the U.S. radio program *Car Talk*, in which reviews and advice on all matters related to car ownership, purchase, and maintenance are offered. Also, advice has often been included in entertainment genres; for example, soap operas have often been used as a vehicle for public information on health, crime, and other subjects (Livingstone 1998). However, I would argue that two things have happened to the nature of advice with the advent of lifestyle and makeover programming (Lunt and Lewis 2008; Taylor 2002). First, the development of lifestyle television involving programs oriented toward the development and enhancement of the self has proliferated in recent years through the development of talk shows, reality TV, and lifestyle TV. Second, the nature of expertise has changed from the provision of knowledge in the form of useful information to a format in which expertise and the adoption of advice is performed in programs and backed up by the accumulation of a repository of advice. The role of the expert has shifted from the authoritative provider of public information to that of therapist or coach offering advice to participants in the practical accomplishment of the transformation of the self.

Little Angels

   Little Angels is a lifestyle program in which parents who are experiencing difficulties with their toddlers call on the advice of a clinical psychologist. The family home is equipped with cameras and microphones to record the "naturalistic" behavior of parents and children over a period of weeks. When the psychologist arrives for her initial discussion with the parents, she brings clips of the live shot material recorded by the cameras in the family home. She then talks the parents through examples of their interaction with their children, offering an analysis of the problems of communication, parenting strategy, and emotional expression and suggesting alternative ways of handing such situations. Although there is an implicit reference to a variety of psychological concepts during this analysis and advice phase of the program, it is very much in the background. The focus is on identifying problems experienced by the parents, followed by the psychologist's guidance on how to, for example, manage temper tantrums, bring order to mealtimes, and get children to go quietly to bed.

The next part of the program consists of attempts by the parents to implement specific "positive parenting practices" that emerged from their discussion with the clinical psychologist. The psychologist then returns to the family home to give more concrete advice on parenting technique. In this phase of the program, one of the parents and the psychologist are fitted out with a microphone and earpiece to communicate while the psychologist watches the interaction between parent and child on a TV monitor in another room or just out of sight of the parent and child. An activity, previously identified as problematic in the discussion of live shot material, is chosen, such as putting the child to bed, going on a shopping trip or to the park, engaging in mealtime, or washing the car. The parent and child perform the activity with the psychologist watching on the monitor and offering a stream of instructions and advice to the parent over the earpiece. Expertise is represented in action oriented to the practical accomplishment of parenting in the setting of the home and judged by the effects on the parent-child relationship and ultimately the behavior of the children. Needless to say, remarkable transformations are achieved in making children happier, less aggressive, and able to go to bed on time and eat their meals in a civilized fashion.

Analysis and Conclusions

Popular, participatory programs may not conform to traditional criteria of public service by forming the basis for consensus and enhancing social cohesion, but they might provide a different kind of public service that reduces neither to populism nor to the tastes of the elite. The programs *Oprah!* and *Little Angels* illustrate that popular television genres such as talk shows, reality TV, and lifestyle television reflect a normative social order oriented to self-regulation and development in which expertise is constituted as an aid to everyday living. If we are to think of these programs as serving the public, they do so as part of processes of self-actualization and/or social control through the internalization of norms of conduct. Two social theories provide ways of thinking through these possibilities: reflexive modernity theory, which provides an account of the way that social institutions are oriented to individuals, providing support for the project of the self (Giddens 1991), and governmentality theory (Dean 1999), which provides a way of thinking through relations of power/knowledge whereby social order results from an ethic of self-control dispersed through social institutions that instigate training and surveillance in the ethics of self-control.

Governmentality theory treats TV as an agent of the state addressing audiences in a normative discourse, which enrolls them as self-governing subjects. This view of governance suggests that power is dispersed beyond the state through culture, in this case popular culture (Oullette and Hay 2008). Lunt and Lewis (2008) summarize as follows:

Central to governmentality theory is a reconceptualisation of power in modernity from a sovereign to a discursive mode, a shift that for many exemplifies the modus operandus of the neoliberal state with its concern to devolve questions of social and political responsibility to the level of the individual consumer-citizen. A pivotal characteristic of discursive power is that it operates productively and that a key site of its operation is subjectivity; the minds, bodies and conduct of subjects. (P. 17)

On this reading, popular culture has become a site of social control, mobilizing individuals in processes of rationalization (the adoption of psychological discourse), self-surveillance, and confession (Andrejevic 2004). This account supports an interpretation of popular television as an institution of civil society focused on the training of normative political subjects rather than as a medium that educates, informs, and engages people in discussions of issues of public interest aimed at the acceptance of social values. In contrast, reflexive modernity theory offers an interpretation of such programming as providing resources for individuals to develop and realize their identities, to develop "pure" social relationships oriented toward equality and mutual satisfaction (even between parents and children) as part of a perpetual reflexive project of the self (Giddens 1991).

It is significant that these programs are open to interpretation as both examples of governmentality and reflexive modernity. In this, they play out a key dilemma of contemporary society and social theory. Do the increasing individualization and reflexivity of contemporary life and the way that social institutions target individuals rather than collectives signify a new environment of risk and opportunity for individuals supported by reflexive social institutions? Alternatively, does the increasing focus on the interiority of the individual, on his or her potential for self-reflection and change, constitute a new, subtle form of social control in which the individual takes on the task of governing the self?

In both *Oprah!* and *Little Angels*, there is a strong focus on embodiment and performance as individuals discuss, enact, and transform their bodies, their dress, and their conduct. The critical issues of whether this constitutes normative or counter-normative reflection on bodies and performance notwithstanding, the programs offer a mode of engagement, reflection, and experimental material transformation of the self. Value is given to personal problems that reflect social issues.

We have come full circle. Programs that appeared as the epitome of the breakdown of public service television now appear as part of social relations of control, reflection, and self-realization. Just as traditional PSB reflects the welfare consensus of liberal democracy, so popular participatory television reflects the centrality of the individual to power and order in contemporary society. Television is no longer the main source, but it still reflects the social contours of its time, although serving the public has shifted from establishing common values and unifying social groups to supporting a normative ethic of the self.

These arguments link to broader debates about the role of institutions in democratic societies. The arguments for traditional public service are problematic in relation to social complexity, pluralism, and the need for an institutional basis for participation in contemporary society (Bohman 2000). Recently, social theorists have moved away from the monolithic architecture of the public sphere while seeking to retain the focus on openness and democracy (Dean 1999). Habermas's (1996) original formulation of the public sphere focused on value consensus, a noninstitutional context, and the differentiation of the public sphere from both the life world and the institutions of the state and commerce. In contrast, the concept of "civil society" retains the focus on democracy and openness in a society that takes the form of a "network of institutions, movements, associations, and discourses" (Dean 1996, 220). Habermas himself, in *Between Facts and Norms*, rethinks the public sphere as dependent on civil society as a distillation and expression of diversity and social difference acknowledging the importance of social institutions in civil society.

The complexity and pluralism of contemporary society suggests that issues of identity rather than problems of communication and consensus are of central concern. Rather than establishing the conditions for mutual understanding as a basis for reaching agreement, civil society is seen as the site where mutual recognition of diverse identities can take place (Honneth 1995; Dean 1999). Civil society, constituted as "mutually interlocking and overlapping networks and associations of deliberation, contestation and argumentation" (Benhabib 1996, 74), is a context in which engagement and mutual recognition (respect) can emerge.

Something intriguing is happening in relation to the blurring of the boundaries between factual broadcasting and entertainment, the shifting nature of expertise, and the proliferation of the representation of everyday life problems (Bondebjerg 2002). A different conception of public service television is emerging that combines elements of surveillance with self-help resources as part of the mediation of civil society. The question remains whether the best interpretation of such programs is that they provide a way in which participants and audiences internalize a normative psychological vocabulary under conditions of surveillance leading to docile subjects or whether the programs represent an institutionalization of civil society that pragmatically facilitates self-help and furthers the potential for a politics of recognition.

In terms of debates about the future of PSB, the proliferation of new genres of factual broadcasting complicates matters in two directions. First, public service broadcasters have already adapted to new modes of programming in the public interest that reflect the shift to individualization, the project of the self, and the changing nature of expertise, as we have seen in the case of the BBC's *Little Angels*. Whether such programming should be considered PSB is open to debate; some would like to see public service concentrate on traditional genres of factual broadcasting such as news, current affairs, and documentary. Second, television in the public interest is dispersed beyond the boundaries of traditional public service broadcasters since programs such as *Oprah!* are produced by commercial broadcasters. It will be interesting to see whether and how public service broadcasters can continue to innovate in the arena of popular broadcasting while retaining a distinction between programming in the public interest and PSB.

References

Andrejevic, M. 2004. *Reality TV: The work of being watched*. Oxford, UK: Rowman & Littlefield.

Arvidsson, A. 2006. *Brands: Meaning and value in media culture*. London: Routledge.

Benhabib, S. 1996. Toward a deliberative model of democratic legitimacy. In *Democracy and difference: Contesting the boundaries of the political*, ed. S. Benhabib, 67-94. Princeton, NJ: Princeton University Press.

Blumler, J. G. 1991. *Television and the public interest: Vulnerable values in Western European broadcasting*. London: Sage.

Bohman, J. 2000. *Public deliberation: Pluralism, complexity, and democracy*. Cambridge, MA: MIT Press.

Bondebjerg, I. 2002. The mediation of everydaylife: Genre, discourse and spectacle in reality TV. In *Realism and "reality" in film and media*, ed. A. Jerslev, 159-92. Copenhagen, Denmark: Museum Tusculanum Press.

Born, G. 2003. Strategy, positioning and projection in digital television: Channel Four and the commercialization of public service broadcasting in the UK. *Media, Culture & Society* 25: 774-99.

Brunsdon, C. 2003. Lifestyling Britain: The 8–9 slot on British television. *International Journal of Cultural Studies* 6 (1): 5-23.

Corner, J. 1991. Meaning, genre and context: The problematics of "public knowledge" in the new audience studies. In *Mass media and society*, ed. J. Curran and M. Gurevitch, 267–84. London: Edward Arnold.

Dean, M. 1999. *Governmentality: Power and rule in modern society*. Thousand Oaks, CA: Sage.

Giddens, A. 1991. *Modernity and self identity*. Cambridge, UK: Polity.

Habermas, J. 1996. *Between facts and norms*. Cambridge, UK: Polity.

Hartley, J. 2008. *Television truths*. Malden, MA: Blackwell.

Held, D. 2006. *Models of democracy*. Cambridge, UK: Polity.

Hill, A. 2005. *Reality TV: Audiences and popular factual television*. London: Routledge.

Honneth, A. 1995. *The struggle for recognition: The moral grammar of social conflicts*. Cambridge, MA: MIT Press.

Illouz, E. 2003. *Oprah Winfrey and the glamour of misery: An essay on popular culture*. New York: Columbia University Press.

Livingstone, S. 1998. *Making sense of television: The psychology of audience interpretation*. London: Routledge.

Livingstone, S., and P. Lunt. 1994. *Talk on television: Audience participation and public debate*. London: Routledge.

Lunt, P. 2008. *Little Angels:* The mediation of parenting. *Continuum* 22 (4): 537-46.

Lunt, P., and T. Lewis. 2008. OPRAH.com: Lifestyle expertise and the politics of recognition. *Women and Performance: A Journal of Feminist Theory* 18 (1): 9-24.

Ouellette, L., and J. Hay. 2008. *Better living through reality TV: Television and post-welfare citizenship*. Malden, MA: Blackwell.

Taylor, L. 2002. From ways of life to lifestyle: The "ordinari-ization" of British gardening lifestyle television. *European Journal of Communication* 17 (4): 479-93.

Thompson, S. 2006. *The political theory of recognition: A critical introduction*. Cambridge, UK: Polity.

Gender and Family in Television's Golden Age and Beyond

By
ANDREA PRESS

Images of women, work, and family on television have changed enormously since the heyday of the network era. Early television confined women to the home and family setting. The increase in working women in the 1960s and 1970s was reflected in television's images of women working and living nontraditional family lives. These images gave way, in the postnetwork era, to a form of postfeminist television in the 1990s when television undercut the ideals of liberal feminism with a series of ambiguous images challenging its gains. Women's roles in the workplace, increasingly shown, were undercut by a sense of nostalgic yearning for the love and family life that they were seen to have displaced. Current television presents a third-wave-influenced feminism that picks up where postfeminism left off, introducing important representations more varied in race, sexuality, and the choices women are seen to make between work and family.

Keywords: gender; family; feminism; women; sex; lesbian

Any discussion of the end of the network must address the importance of television's imaging of women and domestic life. An extensive literature (Spigel 1992; Spigel and Mann 1992; Haralovich 1989; Taylor 1989; Press 1991; Brown 1994; Lipsitz 1992; Lotz 2006; Oren 2003) has examined the development of images of women and the family on television, particularly during television's "golden age" from the 1950s to the 1970s. The consensus is that television's depiction of gender and of the family has been influential in American culture

Andrea Press is a professor of sociology and chair of the Media Studies Department at the University of Virginia, where she is also executive director of the Virginia Film Festival. She is the author of Women Watching Television: Gender, Class and Generation in the American Television Experience *(University of Pennsylvania Press 1991). Her new projects concern media culture among fundamentalist political activists in the United States, the use of new media in American political culture, and the new versions of feminism common in popular culture and popular consciousness.*

DOI: 10.1177/0002716209337886

(Coontz 1992). Television's early family images, in particular, have become cultural icons that feature extensively in scholarship on the importance of early television in American life (Haralovich 1989; Lipsitz 1992; Spigel 1992, 2001). As Oren (2003, 78) notes, the white suburban sitcom genre of the late 1950s and early 1960s has "had a curious afterlife. These visions of domestic bliss continue to fascinate." This article explores television's imaging of women and the family, by discussing their iconic cultural and scholarly importance, and argues that current representations of family and gender on television in the new postnetwork era continue to be culturally significant, though not in the iconic fashion of television's golden age.

Scholars have noted that in its golden era, television worked to create a "unifying address with which to capture an American majority" and created "an immediate 'mainstream' through which notions of proper behavior and a desirable lifestyle were represented" (Oren 2003, 89). These attempts, and this effect, have now given way to a more fragmented mode of address that explicitly questions television's former assumption of an important, mainstream majority and recognizes the importance of various racial, sexual, and ethnic minorities. In its new role, television in part reflects our increasing cultural recognition of the true diversity of gender roles and family forms that constitute our culture.

Early television's representations of gender and the family presumed a unified American majority identity, an identity many scholars have attempted to specify, if only to criticize. Yet, it is interesting to note that it took almost a decade of programming for this convention to emerge. The earliest television representations of the family included images of ethnic and socioeconomic difference that dropped out of later representations (Lipsitz 1992). Family shows in the early 1950s—*I Remember Mama* (1949-1957), based on an immigrant Swedish family; *The Goldbergs* (1949-1956), based on a Jewish family; and most popularly *The Honeymooners* (on and off from 1952-1967), a cornerstone of classic television history based on an avowedly working-class family—were more diverse than the white middle-class pattern of a few years later. Due explicitly to sponsor influence (Barnouw 1990), this white, middle-class model came to be identified—against much of the sociological evidence—with the majority collective American identity in the 1950s. Some assert that the 1950s white middle-class television family has "come to stand in as an icon for the 1950s decade in total" (Oren 2003, 78).[1]

Alongside its portrayals of ethnic diversity, very early television had occasionally depicted single working women, such as the schoolteacher in *Our Miss Brooks* (1952-1956), the cruise director in *My Little Margie* (1952-1955), or the secretary in *Private Secretary* (1953-1957). However, the independence of these women was tempered by their representations as seeking marriage and/or their continued connection to their families of origin. The spirited heroine of *I Love Lucy* (1951-1957) was wife to Ricky and later mother to little Ricky, yet she never gave up her repeated attempts to escape the confines of her domestic situation to enter show business, start a business, get a job, or generally to play a role in the extradomestic sphere.[2]

Many have noted the themes of women's rebellion present in these early sit-coms (Press and Strathman 1993; Oren 2003; Mellencamp 1986). Quite explic-itly, in the plotlines women's domestic roles were often parodied and noted as boring or confining, particularly in the successful and still-popular *I Love Lucy* (1951-1957). Mellencamp (1986) and Oren (2003) note that these early television sitcoms reflect the rise of the strong woman comedienne in the personae of Gracie Allen (*The George Burns and Gracie Allen Show*, 1950-1958), Joan Davis (*I Married Joan*, 1952-1955), in addition to Lucille Ball. These shows ironically featured strong and memorable women actresses playing housewives who did not work outside the home, although their roles featured elements of rebellion toward the domestic sphere.

The ethnic and diverse representations of women early in television's history were replaced by a plethora of white, middle-class families showcasing very simple problems—the happy people with happy problems, as the saying goes (Taylor 1989; Coontz 1992), which constituted television's "golden era" (Spigel 1995). The commercial nature of television dictated that it feature a middle-class ambiance, in association with the nature of the products that formed its com-mercial basis. Therefore, a proliferation of middle-class family images character-ized most situation comedy programming of American television's prime-time from the mid-1950s through the late 1960s, television's "signature" years in many respects, at least where family television is concerned (Lotz 2006; Lichter, Lichter, and Rothman 1986).

Television families of the period tend to be white, middle-class, intact, and suburban, all appearing in much higher percentages than they did in actuality. Women in these families overwhelmingly do not work outside the home and are shown primarily in the activities associated with their roles as wives and mothers, which are shown to be the center of their lives and identities. By the early 1960s, the earlier vestiges of independence and strength had disappeared almost entirely. Family values—presented in a straightforward way, without irony—came to predominate in the television sitcom, tempering even the image of fathers as breadwinners and certainly taming the earlier independence of televi-sion's domestic women. Oren (2003) notes how widely the phenomenon of the family-oriented dad was noted in reviews and commentaries of the time.[3]

The Donna Reed Show was one of the most popular of the golden era televi-sion situation comedies, running from 1958 to 1966 in a prominent prime-time evening slot. The show starred former film actress Donna Reed, playing a whole-some wife and mother, Donna Stone, married to a physician, with two children. The show revolved around mostly rather mundane family issues and dramas, scrapes the children would get into, problems Donna's friends might have, friends whom she made through her women's club associations and her card play-ing, all set in a large white home in an unnamed American suburb.

Viewer reaction to the iconic nature of programs of this era can be observed in online comments, for example, the following observation on watching *The Donna Reed Show*:

> I remember watching this show sometimes when it was on Nick at Nite back in the '80s. I was a kid at the time and I remember Donna Stone just being so nice. She always solved any problem in such a sweet, wholesome and sensible manner. Sure it's another example of that "perfect picturesque fifties family lifestyle" but it's part of television heritage. Just like those messages embedded in the show telling you to have good manners, drink more milk and marry a doctor. Still, the theme song brings back memories that are warm and endearing. Donna Reed will always be there to give us our milk and cookies. (Internet Movie Database)

In interviews with women and girls, I have encountered nostalgic references to television families of the classic period that indicated that viewers read these shows as reflective "of an earlier period of American culture in which families often stayed together rather than divorced, in contrast to the present" (Press 1991). While Coontz (1992), Oren (2003), and Spigel (1992) address the fact that the reality of American family life was very different from television's golden representations, given that more and more women were entering the workforce during the 1950s—ironically in part to achieve the dream life of a suburban, single-family-home lifestyle—they also describe in great detail the mythic power of these oft-repeated images. How, if at all, we must consider, has the decline of network television affected such mythic power of television in our culture? Has there been a fundamental shift in television's cultural function?[4]

The particular representation of the relationship among women, work, and family characteristic of early 1960s television families begins to change on prime-time television in the late 1960s as alternative images of women in the workplace as well as in the family slowly begin to proliferate. For example, the television situation comedy *That Girl* (1966-1971), starring Marlo Thomas, is the first show of the new period to feature a young, unmarried girl living on her own. Ann Marie wants to become an actress and leaves her family's home in Brewster, New York, to occupy her own apartment in Manhattan while she searches for fame and fortune in the entertainment business. Daddy and boyfriend Donald are both prominently featured, so we hardly see Ann as unprotected; yet, she does live on her own to seek a career, a clear departure for a young girl in the world of television situation comedy prior to this show.

The Mary Tyler Moore Show (1970–1977) was the next major departure from the early images. In this path-breaking show, we are introduced to what is perhaps television's first true "career woman." Mary leaves a broken engagement to "make it on her own," as the theme song tells us, presumably because a woman "on her own," without husband or family, is so unusual as to be worthy of note on the prime-time television of the 1970s. The show revolves around what becomes her workplace "family" once she finds a job as a television producer and her apartment neighbors Rhoda and Phyllis, both of whom are strong characters, although each contrasts with Mary's nontraditional image (Rhoda is looking actively to get married; Phyllis is married with children and speaks humorously of her family).

In the wake of *The Mary Tyler Moore Show*, television family shows began to exhibit a marked differentiation from the old pattern. While some single-parent families always appeared on television prior to this period, all of them—in direct contradiction to the reality of single-parent households—were male-headed households. *My Three Sons*, for example, with its long run from 1960 to 1972, was one of the most successful and popular shows of early television, yet for most of its run, it had no regular female characters at all; neither did *The Courtship of Eddie's Father* from 1969 to 1972 or the earlier *Bachelor Father* from 1957 to 1962.

In a new turn toward relevance, television of the 1970s and 1980s began to feature the single mother, or ensemble mothers, or combined families. *The Brady Bunch* (1969-1974) had focused on a combined remarried family (with a nonworking mother *and* a full-time housekeeper). *Kate and Allie* (1984-1989) featured two single-mother friends sharing a household, and *Who's the Boss?* (1984-1992) focused on a single mother and her household helper. Images of gender, and family, and women's roles in society really began to shift with the establishment of the women's network Lifetime in 1984 (Byars and Meehan 1994), and later with the rise of postfeminist television in the 1990s (Lotz 2006). These key events followed the breakdown of the network era in the late 1970s and the concomitant changes in the structure and organization of television programming.

Byars and Meehan (1994) argue that television "discovered" the female prime-time market in the 1970s, as evidenced by a spate of what they call "hybrid" prime-time shows, which combine melodramatic elements with traditionally male genres like the cop show or the action show. Beginning with the female cop show *Cagney and Lacey* (1982-1988), television witnessed a spate of the hybrid genre, evidenced in shows such as *Spenser for Hire* (1985-1988), *China Beach* (1988-1991), and *L.A. Law* (1986-1994), which combined action, adventure, detectives, and workplace with melodramatic elements. Byars and Meehan discuss how the image of women populating prime time, in particular their relationship to work and sexuality, shifted as well, toward a more "feminist" image that was less passive, more powerful, and more independent—though still heterosexual and romantic—than earlier television women.

While Byars and Meehan (1994) discuss primarily the Lifetime network, which arose in the 1980s and was marketed as "television for women," their observations apply as well to other images on network television. Beginning in the 1970s, television's norms of representing women overall began to shift. While previously most women on prime-time television were positioned squarely within the nuclear family as homemakers and mothers, thereafter images of working women became first acceptable, with *That Girl* and *The Mary Tyler Moore Show*, then common, and finally unremarkable.

With the breakdown of network television—as cable television claimed a larger share of the airways—came a decidedly postfeminist proliferation of women's television images. Postfeminism, as Lotz (2006) and others argue, is characterized by a clear and constant undercutting of the ideals and visions of liberal feminism (Dicker and Piepmeier 2003; Heywood and Drake 1997), which stressed the need for women to achieve equality with men in the workplace, the home, and the bedroom. Postfeminist television opened up a new set of possibilities for the representations of women, work, and family. Television's representations of women throughout the 1980s and 1990s focused on women making "choices," usually between work and family. While some shows (*L.A. Law* [1986-1994], *Thirty-Something* [1987-1991]) make the case that fulfilling both roles is impossible, others (*The Cosby Show* [1984-1992], *Family Ties* [1982-1989]) portray the easy fulfillment of both as a given (Heide 1995; Press and Strathman 1993).

In an analysis of the popular television show *The West Wing* (1999-2006), Lotz (2006) points out how strong female.characters exist alongside references to a pair of female underpants being found in a diplomat's suite and the search for a boyfriend. Lotz comments that "I use these examples from *The West Wing* to indicate how a series that professes liberal politics and offers female characters narrative space still undercuts and minimizes their professionalism. These devices only can be identified by examining the stories told by the series; the characters' status as single women in career roles provides no suggestion of the ambivalent nature of their narrative construction" (p. 162). Thus, does Lotz illustrate the postfeminist quality of postnetwork shows in which feminist themes about women's professional status are systematically ignored and undercut in favor of a focus on the details of women's romantic personal lives, in narratives that could just as easily have been featured in a Rock Hudson–Doris Day comedy of the 1950s.

Lotz (2006) finds that the "choice" theme is also limited to women who actually have such choices to make—mostly upper-middle-class, educated, white, and attractive women: "Employment in a professional career remains a crucial component of female representations that critics consider progressive" (p. 146). Although feminist second-wave ideals are critiqued, the postfeminist critique does not extend to the more sophisticated critique of third-wave feminism, which spotlights the white, middle-class, heterosexual biases of the second-wave feminist movement and the stories it spawned.

These themes are evident in popular shows of this era, such as *Ally McBeal* (1997-2002) and *Sex and the City* (1998-2004). While *Ally McBeal* features a single, successful attorney shown largely in her workplace, her preoccupation is with marriage, with dating relationships and the search for a partner. *Sex and the City* focused primarily on the personal (and sexual) lives of four women in New York City. While all have successful careers, the show combines an acknowledgement of the importance of women's independence with a very traditionalist focus on "the search for Mr. Right." This emphasis is so strong that it undercuts the way the women's careers might be seen to underscore their (and the show's) support for second-wave feminist values.

One episode of *Ally McBeal* featured Ally defending a woman in court who was suing a company for allowing more time off and flexible hours to women with children than women without. Ally's main defense of her criticism of these policies was that "women now have the 'choice' to have children, and when they do, they should be forced to bear the consequences for this," an argument that has been amply invalidated by current feminist scholarship (Douglas and Michaels

2004). This narrative ignores what has been perhaps the most prominent thrust of the women's movement in the United States, that is, the push to allow family benefits for both women and men (Douglas and Michaels 2004).

On another topic in the same vein, an episode of *Sex and the City* involved an abortion decision made by Miranda, one of the show's main characters. A surprise pregnancy makes Miranda consider having an abortion, causing her friend Carrie to reflect with extreme sadness and regret on her own abortion when she was younger. We see Carrie unwilling to admit to her current boyfriend that she had the abortion, changing the details so that she seemed to be younger at the time (and thus perhaps less responsible), and narrating the incident with a regretful voice.

This episode epitomizes postfeminism, as the choice feminist abortion activists have made possible for these characters is simply assumed and then undermined by the show's multiple critical perspectives toward the act. In the end, Miranda changes her initial decision to abort into a decision to have her baby and become a single mother, and is toasted and supported by all the women. Can the prime-time audience—even the audience for a paid subscription service like HBO—not be trusted to sympathize with a character who obtains an abortion without regret, or even without much second-guessing? Despite this backtracking from one of the most hard-won goals of second-wave feminism—women's reproductive freedom—this is one of the shows that has been most heralded as an icon of the era of feminist television. While its portrayal of women and their sexuality has certainly been progressive in many respects, the postfeminist qualities of *Sex and the City* (and its overall adherence to traditional values of glamour and consumerism) tend to mitigate the radical impact the show can have on its eager and committed female audience (Arthurs 2003; Akass and McCabe 2004).

In what has come to be called "third-wave" feminism, an attempt has been made to retain a feminist "essence" while redressing some of the deficiencies of second-wave feminism such as a lack of ethnic, racial, and sexual diversity in the movement and a sexual Puritanism that many found alarming. Gill (2003) argues that a third wave or "new era" of feminism in which women wear T-shirts proclaiming sexually explicit slogans—in the guise of asserting women's right to sexual freedom—has not really proved to be a feminist advance for women. Television shows like *Sex and the City* or *Ally McBeal* invoke a third-wave feminist perspective in the explicit "sexiness" of their lead characters but, at the same time, feature the upper-middle-class, professional, educated, white, glamorous women so widely criticized in third-wave literature as precluding any real diversity in televisual portrayals.[5]

While issues like women's relationship to work, family, and romance, or women's reproductive rights were not always (if ever) presented in a feminist manner, television of the 1990s did come to reflect the feminist victories of the preceding decades in the form of many new and innovative images. *Ellen* (1994-1998) featured the first overt lesbian "outing" on prime time; *Murphy Brown* (1988-1998) starred a hard-driving career women who chose to become a single mother; *Roseanne* (1988-1997) centered on a working-class family whose female head did not fit the bill of the typical slim, white, and glamorous television woman; and *Buffy the Vampire Slayer* (1997-2003) featured an extremely powerful, feminist, and capable young woman heroine. All of these shows were popular successes, and all helped pave the way to the increasingly innovative television images of the new millennium.

A New Critical Rhetoric: But Not for Women?

Current television reveals a different comment on postfeminism and third-wave feminism in comparison with the 1990s. For example, the recent HBO show *The Wire* (2002-2007) offers a new level of diversity in its representations. It is a police show that introduces depth in its portrayal of the criminals and members of the "underclass." For example, one narrative line follows an African American drug-dealing dynasty in some depth, including many of the members of the drug dealers' families, children who are recruited by the business, informants, and the wealthy kingpins.

The female characters featured on *The Wire* provide the kind of diversity that Lotz and others failed to find in the past decades of network television. Particularly noteworthy are the characters of Brianna Barksdale, sister of one of the drug dynasty kingpins (Avon Barksdale) and mother of D'Angelo Barksdale, a character who finds himself facing a twenty-year jail sentence. In one subplot, Brianna's son is offered a deal that could shorten his sentence significantly if he offers information on the drug-dealing. We see the mother visiting her son and urging him *not* to testify, because it will help her and her family, even as he faces possible death as a result. It is certainly an unconventional portrayal of motherhood—and one totally new to prime time. Another unconventional mother is De'Londa Brice, mother of Namond, a fourteen-year-old whom she urges to skip school and join the family drug business.

Detective Shakima "Kima" Greggs, an African American lesbian cop (played by Sonja Sohn), with a live-in lesbian lover (Cheryl), is yet another significant and unconventional character in *The Wire*. Kima is an extremely tough cop. She is also a glamorous woman who often goes undercover to ferret out information about the drug dealers the cops are following throughout the show. In one episode, she gets shot, and we are shown how difficult this is for her girlfriend, particularly when she recovers and insists on going back to police work rather than accepting the desk job she is offered. What has changed here? Social class, sexuality, and race are more diversified in these portrayals than in the vast majority of the shows portraying women on television throughout the preceding decades.

The *L-Word*, a new Showtime show about the lives of lesbians, displays young lesbian women as though they were heterosexual glamour girls. While at one level, it is transgressive to portray a group of lesbians openly at all on television; at another level, it should be noted that every woman featured in the show could be considered glamorous—thin and beautiful in conventional terms. Although not all the women in this show are white, they all have the kind of beauty that belongs to the social class that possesses enough time and money to acquire glamorous clothing, to maintain the perfect body shape, and to correct obvious facial flaws by cosmetic means. The new Showtime show *Weeds*, about open drug-dealing and drug use among middle-class white America, features a single mother, played by Mary Louise Parker, who supports her white, middle-class family with drug-dealing. Certainly *Weeds* breaks new ground in its social mores and perspective through its matter-of-fact portrayal of drug use and drug-dealing among white middle-class Americans, but at the same time, it retains the norm of focusing on thin, conventionally beautiful women.[6]

These shows illustrate the "narrow-casting" that has become a feature of television in the postnetwork age, playing to audience groups who find open lesbian lifestyles or drug use acceptable but in large part clinging to visual portrayals of women that remain conventional and straightjacketed, impervious to decades of feminist critique. Yet, this array of new images on prime time opens up possibilities for diversity in images of women, work, and family never hinted at during television's golden era. The impact of these images is strengthened by the general mode of address established in television's golden age. Walters (2001) argues that television has played a key role in the struggle for gay and lesbian rights in the United States. The presence of the *L-Word* on prime-time cable television provides an updated illustration of her argument. As social minority struggles for women's, gay, lesbian, and minority rights continue, prime-time television will continue to play an important role in establishing for the public what can be acceptable in modern American life. Both an African American and a woman ran in the 2008 presidential primary, so it is hard to deny that social consciousness about the rights of gender and minority groups has changed fundamentally in the United States. And an examination of changing images on current television indicates that the ever-popular medium has potentially played a considerable and important role in these changes.

Television has even taken a step toward a more honest portrayal of women's choice issues, as seen in the prime-time hit *Desperate Housewives*. A key breakthrough image on this show is on-again, off-again working mother Lynette, who left a successful advertising career to become full-time stay-at-home mother. Yet, the portrayal of her role contrasts markedly with families of television's golden era. Unlike the television of an earlier era, motherhood in this instance is not idealized, as Lynette is shown having many regrets about her choice, and then trying to go back to her career and realizing the difficulties involved in this choice as well. In this instance, women's need to choose among motherhood, work, and their combination are fairly and critically portrayed, although it should be noted that like the golden age of family television, the show has a white, middle-class bias and errs on the side of portraying conventionally beautiful actresses. Nevertheless, in some respects, with *Desperate Housewives*, we travel beyond postfeminist television to family television written with a more overt consciousness of the real social and political issues women now face, in the family, in relationships, and in the workplace.

Conclusion

Images of women, work, and family on television have changed enormously since the heyday of the network era. Early television offered a rather restricted set of images, confining women to the home and family setting. The increase in working women in the 1960s and 1970s precipitated a concomitant rise in later television images of working women, and in women living nontraditional family lives, as this increasing market of working women was not lost on the television industry. As well, an increased number of television women in action genres marked television of the later golden period. These images gave way, in the post-network era, to a form of postfeminist television in the 1990s, in which television undercut the ideals of liberal feminism with a series of ambiguous images challenging its gains. Women's roles in the workplace, increasingly shown, were undercut by a sense of nostalgic yearning for the love and family life that they were seen to have displaced.

Current television presents a third-wave-influenced feminism that takes up where postfeminism left off. The recent popularity of *Sex and the City* perhaps best illustrates this paradox. As Tukachinsky (2008) notes, *Sex and the City* is read by young college women today as both a paean to traditional romantic feminine values and a diatribe against them. Precisely this ambiguity is the key to its enormous success, both with viewers of different ages, and in the feminist critical television literature.[7] With a culture that remains decidedly ambivalent about feminism for women, the most successful cultural products will reflect this ambivalence, which can be read as the celebration of diversity that characterizes what has come to be known as third-wave feminism. Yet, on prime time, diversity remains limited for women, as thin, young, and conventionally beautiful images predominate even as portrayals become sexually and racially diversified. Even newer shows illustrate some of these marked though limited gains. Perhaps we have moved beyond a simplistic nostalgia for 1950s' life, so shaped by television family images of the period, to a new sophistication in our ability to consider the choices women continue to make between the roles that family, work, and career will play in their lives. If so, television may be playing a progressive role in facilitating this change of mood.

Does postnetwork television still reflect consensus values in our culture? If maintaining a multitude of positions—all portrayed as equally valid—is the key to relevance in a hybrid culture, television can be said to remain on our cutting edge. And given the lack of actual cultural consensus previously masked by the television medium, television's multiplicity may be playing an increasingly progressive role for women and minority groups in our culture. While television may never again provide the iconic symbols of the golden era, it nevertheless will continue to play a central cultural role in the United States. At least for now, it continues to maintain its status as the most used medium,[8] even as we experience the vast technological changes and the proliferation of new media that characterize life in the new millennium.

Notes

1. See Coontz (1992, 1997) and Spigel (1992) for detailed discussion of differences between, as Coontz notes, "the way we really were" in the families of 1950s America.

2. Consider the following episode titles: "The Girls Want to Go to the Nightclub," "The Audition," "Lucy Writes a Play," "Job Switching," "Lucy Becomes a Sculptress," "The Girls Go into Business," "Equal Rights," "The Million Dollar Idea," "Lucy Writes a Novel," "Lucy Gets into Pictures," "Lucy's Italian Movies," and so on.

3. Oren (2003) cites a slew of current reviews and commentaries that take note of this apparent "weakening" of the strong masculine aspect of fathers, which now became tempered with domesticity, in such publications as *Time* magazine, *Cosmopolitan*, the *Saturday Review*, and *American Mercury*.

4. One plotline of *The Donna Reed Show* indicates that even in the white, middle-class, nonethnic family of early 1960s television, the theme of women's rebellion remains. Donna and her friend Midge get the idea of starting their own business after a card game in which their husbands repeatedly belittle and dismiss women's financial acumen. They visit a bank for a loan but again are belittled by the bank manager, who states he is often inclined to lock up the vault when women come to request loans. Very condescendingly, he explains how difficult it is for women to make money in business, and he tries his best to discourage them. The episode ends with Donna and Alex talking in their (separate) beds, with Alex protesting that he does not think Donna will fail in business, but his resistance comes from his desire to keep her efforts all to himself and his family. Hearing this, Donna protests that she could not imagine any other role seriously for herself aside from wife and mother, and the episode is resolved on a happy, contented note for all involved. Thus is the "mother-milk-cookies" heritage expressed and reproduced in this as in so many episodes of early television situation comedies.

5. In fact, *Ally McBeal*'s star Calista Flockhart was the widely publicized victim of a life-threatening eating disorder that kept her dangerously thin almost throughout the production of the show. Her adherence to an excessively thin body ideal flew in the face of one of the main cultural critiques of second-wave feminism (Orbach 1978), and this in pursuit of a third-wave defined sexiness.

6. I am indebted to Amanda Stuckey for pointing out these facets of the show *Weeds*.

7. The evidence that viewers respond to the ambiguity about feminism in *Sex and the City* is not unlike the evidence that audiences of *All in the Family*, the controversial 1970s (1971-1979) hit show about a bigot, was read favorably by conservative audiences who liked bigoted lead character Archie Bunker and liberal or radical viewers who read the show as a criticism of Archie's beliefs (Vidmar and Rokeach 1974).

8. See del and ins. http://www.podcastingnews.com/2008/12/26/internet-overtakes-newspapers-as-news-source-in-2008/ for recent figures supporting this point.

References

Akass, Kim, and Janet McCabe, ed. 2004. *Reading Sex and the City*. London: I. B. Tauris.

Barnouw, Erik. 1990. *Tube of plenty*. New York: Oxford University Press.

Brown, Mary Ellen. 1994. *Soap opera and women's lives*. Thousand Oaks, CA: Sage.

Byars, Jackie, and Eileen R. Meehan. 1994. Once in a lifetime: Constructing the working woman through cable narrowcasting. *Camera Obscura* 33-34:12-41.

Coontz, Stephanie. 1992. *The way we never were: American families and the nostalgia trap*. New York: Basic Books.

————. 1997. *The way we really are: Coming to terms with America's changing families*. New York: Basic Books.

Dicker, Rory, and Alison Piepmeier, eds. 2003. *Catching a wave: Reclaiming feminism for the 21st century*. Boston: Northeastern University Press.

Douglas, Susan, and Meredith Michaels. 2004. *The mommy myth*. New York: Free Press.

Gill, Ros. 2003. From sexual objectification to sexual subjectification: The resexualization of women's bodies in the media. *Feminist Media Studies* 3 (1): 100-105.

Haralovich, Mary Beth. 1989. Sitcoms and suburbs: Positioning the 1950's homemaker. *Quarterly Review of Film and Video* 2:90-91.

Heide, Margaret. 1995. *Television culture and women's lives: Thirtysomething and the contradictions of gender*. Philadelphia: University of Pennsylvania Press.

Heywood, Leslie, and Jennifer Drake, eds. 1997. *Third wave agenda: Being feminist, doing feminism*. Minneapolis: University of Minnesota Press.

Internet Movie Database. The Donna Reed Show: User Comments. http://www.imdb.com/title/tt0051267/

Lichter, Robert, Linda Lichter, and Stanley Rothman. 1986. The politics of the American dream—From Lucy to Lacey: TV's dream girls. *Public Opinion* 9 (3): 16-19.

———. 1992. The meaning of memory: Family, class and ethnicity in early network television. In *Private screenings*, ed. Lynn Spigel and Denise Mann, 71-92. Minneapolis: University of Minnesota Press.

Lotz, Amanda. 2006. *Redesigning women: Television after the network era*. Urbana: University of Illinois Press.

Mellencamp, Patricia. 1986. Situation comedy, feminism, and Freud: Discourses of Gracie and Lucy. In *Studies in entertainment,* ed. Tania Modleski, 80-98. Bloomington: Indiana University Press.

Orbach, Susie. 1978. *Fat is a Feminist Issue*. New York: Berkeley.

Oren, Tasha. 2003. Domesticated dads and double-shift moms: Real life and ideal life in 1950's domestic comedy. *Cercles* 8:78-90.

Press, Andrea L. 1991. *Women watching television: Gender, class and generation in the American television experience*. Philadelphia: University of Pennsylvania Press.

Press, Andrea L., and Terry Strathman. 1993. Work, family and social class in television images of women: Prime-time television and the construction of postfeminism. *Women and Language* 16 (2): 7-15.

Sex and the City. Episode no. 59., first air broadcast, 5 August 2001 by HBO. Directed by David Frankel and written by Jenny Bicks.

Spigel, Lynn. 1992. *Make room for TV*. Chicago: University of Chicago Press.

———. 1995. From the dark ages to the golden age: Women's memories and television reruns. *Screen* 36 (1): 16-33

———. 2001. *Welcome to the dreamhouse*. Durham, NC: Duke University Press.

Spigel, Lynn, and Denise Mann, eds. 1992. *Private screenings*. Minneapolis: University of Minnesota Press.

Taylor, Ella. 1989. *Prime-time families*. Berkeley: University of California Press.

Tukachinsky, Riva H. 2008. Feminist and postfeminist readings of romantic narratives: Heterosexual romantic experiences versus *Sex and the City*. *Feminist Media Studies* 8 (2): 181-96.

Vidmar, Neil, and Milton Rokeach. 1974. Archie Bunker's bigotry: A study in selective perception and exposure. *Journal of Communication* 24:36-47.

Walters, Susannah. 2001. *All the rage: The story of gay visibility in America*. Chicago: University of Chicago Press.

Half a Century of Television in the Lives of Our Children

By
SONIA LIVINGSTONE

The quintessential image of the television audience is of the family viewing at home—sitting together comfortably in front of the lively set. Accompanying this happy image is its negative—a child viewing alone while real life goes on elsewhere. This article reviews evidence over five decades regarding the changing place of television in children's lives. It argues that, notwithstanding postwar trends that have significantly changed adolescence, the family home, and wider consumer society, there was time for the 1950s *family* experiment to spawn the 1960s and 1970s *family television* experiment, thereby shaping normative expectations—academic, policy, and popular—regarding television audiences for years to come. At the turn of the twenty-first century, we must recognize that it was the underlying long-term trend of individualization, and its associated trends of consumerism, globalization, and democratization, that, historically and now, more profoundly frame the place of television in the family.

Keywords: children; television; family; audience; historical change; individualization; parental mediation

Television and the Family: What Do We Want to Know?

The quintessential image of the television audience is of the family viewing at home—children and parents sitting together comfortably in front of the lively set. Accompanying this happy image is its negative—a child viewing alone, square-eyed and trancelike, while real

Sonia Livingstone is a professor in the Department of Media and Communications at the London School of Economics and Political Science. She is author or editor of eleven books and more than one hundred academic articles and chapters on media audiences, children and the Internet, domestic contexts of media use, and media literacy. Recent books include Audiences and Publics *(Intellect 2005),* The Handbook of New Media *(edited with Leah Lievrouw; Sage 2006), and* The International Handbook of Children, Media and Culture *(edited with Kirsten Drotner; Sage 2008).*

DOI: 10.1177/0002716209338572

life goes on elsewhere. The former image was quickly popularized by broadcasting industries in many Western countries after the Second World War. It represents the hope of shared pleasure that motivated the public to purchase and install this new technology as quickly as they could afford to do so (Butsch 2000; Spigel 1992). The latter image, reproduced by newspapers, parenting magazines, and public policy pronouncements, represents the fear that motivated funding for empirical research by social science designed to investigate television's potentially harmful effects (Rowland 1983; Wartella and Reeves 1985). So who was right? Can we, after half a century or so of television in our homes and, furthermore, half a century or so of research, identify what difference television made to the family?

The moral panics associated with the arrival of each new medium, which demand that research address the same questions over and again—about the displacement of reading, exercise, and conversation; about social isolation and addiction; about violent and consumerist content (Barker and Petley 2001)—have a long history. Bettelheim (1999) traces them back via Goethe's *The Sorrows of Young Werther*, blamed for a wave of suicides in eighteenth-century Germany, to Plato's ideal state that banned imaginative literature for corrupting the young. But what this makes plain is that society's perennial anxieties about children, childhood, and the family are catalyzed by "the new," the popular hope being that by fixing the technology, society can fix the problems of childhood. However, a critical rejection of both moral panics and technological determinism does not permit us to conclude that television played no role in the unfolding history of the family in the twentieth century. Indeed, I am partly provoked to write this article by the notable absence of answers to the "so what?" question from the many scholars who, over the decades, have zealously charted the facts and figures on the prominence of television within the family.[1] Surely television must have made some difference. Equally surely, family life would have been different without television or had television been itself different.

To avert the charge of technological determinism hovering in the minds of this volume's readers (MacKenzie and Wajcman 1999), I stress that the starting point must be the recognition that television, both the domestic set and its broadcast forms and contents, was developed, designed, financed, regulated, and marketed by the very society that then worried about the consequences. Crucially, society has itself undergone profound changes over the past half century, so that television is just one of many factors that have influenced family life in the second half of the twentieth century. These changes include the urbanization and education of the population, the growing emancipation of women, the growth of affluent individualism and the rise of consumer society together with an increasingly dispossessed poor, the gradual inclusion of the diversity of the population in terms of ethnicity and sexuality, the decline in public participation and political commitment, and, specifically relevant here, the posttraditional family and research on adolescence. Together, these factors have refashioned the family during the twentieth century in the direction of individualization and democratization, ever further away from the Victorian family (Beck and

Beck-Gernsheim 2002; Coontz 1997; Gadlin 1978); they have therefore also shaped the context within which television was appropriated, acquiring a meaningful place within the family.[2]

Parallel changes in media and in childhood must be considered in tandem if we are to avoid either technological or cultural determinism. However, this short article can only sketch the outline of an analysis of television's place in the lives of parents and children, and in so doing, it must rely on an even sketchier account of the major societal shifts during the past half century to contextualize the arrival of television. Specifically, I argue, first, that the coincidence of mass television in the 1950s and what Stephanie Coontz (1997) has called "the 1950s family experiment" meant that for a time the arrival of television signaled a temporary but culturally significant grouping of the family around the living room set (and the nation around the prime-time terrestrial schedules). However, historical evidence reveals that this only briefly bucks the longer-term trend toward the multiplication and diversification of media that has facilitated what Patrice Flichy (2002) calls "living together separately" or, more abstractly, the processes of individualization, consumerism, and globalization that characterize Western societies in late modernity.

"Family Television": An Accident of History

Research conducted from the 1950s on, when television reached the mass market in many Western countries, showed a collective coming together of the family around the set, with domestic living space rearranged to create the family room (i.e., television room; Spigel 1992) and the domestic timetable adjusted to fit the television schedules (Scannell 1988).[3] Compared with those without television, Hilde Himmelweit and her colleagues found in 1955 to 1956 that children in television households were slightly more likely to stay indoors and to share both time and interests with their parents. Television rapidly became children's main leisure activity, to some extent displacing reading and "doing nothing" and providing functionally equivalent leisure with little detrimental effect on schoolwork. Viewing figures quickly reached just under two hours per day (the greatest amount of time spent on any leisure activity; Himmelweit, Oppenheim, and Vince 1958).[4] From the early years of television, viewers spent less time alone and more time indoors with the family (though not necessarily talking to each other!), with television tending to displace going to the cinema and socializing with others (Andreasen 1994; Katz and Gurevitch 1976; Robinson and Godbey 1997).

Although in the 1950s family life and gender roles became unusually predictable and settled, this was, as historical trends in social statistics show, "a very short interlude that people mistakenly identify as 'traditional'" (Coontz 1997, 54). I suggest that a similar misconception, occasioning a similar nostalgia, has become associated with "the 1950s family experiment," namely that of "family television". For several decades, television has been seen as—and for many people has been—what the family watched together, after father came home from work and when mother had finished tidying the house for the day. Television represented a key means by which father, by choosing to watch "his" programs, asserted his economic power; while mother, who regulated the children's viewing while father was at work, showed her moral proficiency in managing her family. Yet, as Morley's (1986) account of family television illustrated, fundamental tensions between genders and generations were often exacerbated rather than alleviated by these normative expectations regarding the family.

In short, family television was more a popular ideal than an actuality. Himmelweit, Oppenheim, and Vince (1958) showed that even in the 1950s, children stayed up late watching television, watching "inappropriate" programs and conflicting with their parents. Oswell (2002) adds that though television was promoted as a joint activity for parents and children (consider the title of the popular British preschool program *Watch with Mother*), it was widely understood as providing a babysitter that allowed mother to do something else. In short, the signs of individualization as the dominant trend were already present. Interestingly, notwithstanding the decades of research on whether the television was or was not beneficial for the family, it was apparent from the outset that physical colocation does not guarantee emotional cohesiveness. In a statement that one could still write today, Himmelweit, Oppenheim, and Vince wrote,

> Television does keep members of the family at home more. But it is doubtful whether it binds the family together more than in this physical sense, except while the children are young. As they grow older, their viewing becomes more silent and personal. Also, as children grow into adolescence, the increased time spent with the family may set up strains, since it runs counter to their need to make contacts outside. (P. 25)

Compared with radio, which took children for granted within the family audience, its mode of address asserting a unifying voice to bring the family together around the hearth, television arrived when the trend toward individualization was well under way (Oswell 2002). Family members were dispersing around the home, developing diverse lifestyle tastes and identities, partly because of the coincidental arrival of central heating (though few public discourses attack central heating for breaking up the family!). Faced with the task of addressing an already heterogeneous audience, television drew more on the techniques of market research to distinguish the child audience from the adult audience than it attempted to draw the generations together. Thus, television has progressively distinguished kid, teen, and, later, toddler and tween market segments through programming form, content, and style (Kenway and Bullen 2008), addressing each as distinctive from each other and from adults, encouraging certain activities, interests, and even subversive joys (Seiter 1993), while associating peer culture and youthful identity with the messages of marketing, merchandising, and distinction (Kline 1993).[5]

Locating Television in the Longer History of Individualization

Individualization[6] refers to a social change with a much longer history than the half century addressed here: as early as the end of the seventeenth century, one could identify "the privatization of families from each other, and the individual-ization of members within families" (Luke 1989, 39). But for young people, the change has been more recent, for the notion of "teenager" emerged only in the 1950s (Abrams 1959; France 2007), this in turn resulting from the conjunction of several key changes—from children having a productive role in the economy to that of children as consumers (Cunningham 1995), the extension of formal edu-cation from mid- to late teens and a commensurate rise in the average age of leaving home (France 2007), and the advent of consumer culture that created youth culture to fill the new space between childhood and adulthood (Osgerby 1998).[7] The consequence is not simply the replacement of the traditional norms and values by which parents socialized their children (Gadlin 1978) in favor of the peer group but, rather, the emergence of the new responsibility, namely, "the reflexive project of the self which consists in the sustaining of coherent, yet con-tinuously revised, biographical narratives" (Giddens 1991, 5). Here, the media play a key role, providing the resources for identity construction and display and the occasions for negotiating and defining aspects of one's identity against the expressions of others.

Comparing the 1950s with the 1980s, Ziehe (1994, 2) argues that the new consumer opportunities of postwar Western societies were framed in terms of ambivalent desires for ever higher domestic and personal living standards, result-ing in "an increasing orientation towards questions of life style" that in turn became crystallized in the parallel discourses surrounding youth, thereby encod-ing cultural change in terms of generational conflict. Ziehe stresses the impor-tance of music here, but for Osgerby (1998), television was also crucial as it addresses young people as distinctive in identity, lifestyle, and attitudes, encour-aging their construction of a leisure career that, being itself subject to pervasive market forces and peer pressures, is perceived by parents as making them "grow up faster and earlier" (while postponing adult responsibilities longer). As Coontz (1997, 13) puts it, "In some ways, childhood has actually been prolonged, if it is measured by dependence on parents and segregation from adult activities"; this dependence is in a state of tension with young people's growing autonomy in the realms of leisure, consumption, appearance, and identity. It is this tension, surely, that is expressed in the conflicts of adolescence that are, in turn, so often expressed as conflicts over the use of media at home.

Not only children and teenagers but also the family and television have changed, coevolving (Andreasen 1994) through the postwar decades. For many, family life in the 1950s was undoubtedly cohesive and stable, with sufficient afflu-ence to fuel the consumer boom to which both the birth of youth culture (Osgerby 1998) and the golden age of television (Spigel 1992) were linked. While television diffused rapidly, rising in the United States from 9 percent of house-holds in 1950 to 87 percent by 1960, the significant change over the next thirty years was not so much the saturation of the market, though this occurred (with 98 percent of households having television by 1990), but rather the growth of multiset households. Along with the linked technologies (satellite and cable chan-nels, videocassette recorders, electronic games, etc.), this transformed the home into a multimedia environment capable of supporting not only a shared interest in the nightly news, the national soap opera, or the Saturday film but also the diverse and niche interests of each individual separately.

In this manner, television followed the trend established for electronic media throughout the past century: the gramophone from the start of the twentieth century, the telephone from the 1920s, radio from the 1930s, television from the 1950s, the VCR from the 1970s, the computer from the 1980s, and now the Internet. Each has begun its career in the main collective family space of the living room, but as prices fall and multiplication and mobility of goods become feasible, each has moved into more individualized, personalized, and, for children, unsupervised, spaces, particularly the bedroom but also the study, playroom, and kitchen, thereby spreading both spatially and temporally—from defined and prioritized spaces and times to casual use throughout the home and throughout the day (Flichy 2002; Livingstone 2002).

Ratings show that television as a shared experience is in steady decline, for children and adults, with the increasing diversity of channels resulting in greater fragmentation of the audience and ever less adherence to a scheduled timetable of viewing. Today, few programs attain mass audiences on the scale of, say, U.K. soaps twenty years ago (with 15 to 20 million viewers in a nation of some 60 million). Even mass audiences may not share their experiences: in the late 1980s, I observed a family of six, all fans of the Australian soap opera *Neighbours*, who watched on different sets or at different times—a dispersed mass audience, eschewing colocation in the family room (Livingstone 1992).[8]

In 1955, watching alone was relatively rare: 24 percent of ten- and eleven-year-olds watched children's programs alone, as did 23 percent of thirteen- and fourteen-year-olds; for evening programs, the proportions were 11 percent (ten- and eleven-year-olds) and 9 percent (thirteen- and fourteen-year-olds). Viewing with parents, on the other hand, was very common, particularly for evening programs: 81 percent (ten- and eleven-year-olds) and 88 percent (thirteen- and fourteen-year-olds); though even at that time, children's programs were more often shared with siblings than parents (Himmelweit, Oppenheim, and Vince 1958). Four decades later, watching alone had not risen among ten- and eleven-year-olds, but for thirteen- and fourteen-year-olds, viewing alone rose sharply to 32 percent. Meanwhile, viewing with parents fell, both for the ten- and eleven-year-olds and, more strikingly, for the thirteen- and fourteen-year-olds (33 percent with father, 40 percent with mother) (Livingstone, Bovill, and Gaskell 1999).[9] A longitudinal study conducted in Iceland found that the percentage of ten- to fifteen-year-olds who usually watched television alone rose from 2 percent in 1968 to 40 percent in 2003, while the proportion who watched with their parents fell commensurately (Broddason 2006).

There has been, in short, a discernible shift away from shared toward privatized viewing over the past four decades, and, arguably because adolescents began to be labeled "teenagers" from the 1950s onwards, this shift is more evident for thirteen- and fourteen-year-olds than for ten- and eleven-year-olds.[10] Although multiple sets and competing program preferences facilitate this trend (having television in one's bedroom adds half an hour to daily U.K. viewing time and one and a half hours in the United States; see Livingstone 2002; Roberts, Foehr, and Rideout 2005), the primary driver is children themselves—the Young People, New Media project found children wish to watch alone even more they actually do.[11]

Looking Ahead: The Changing Public Agenda

I had first thought to argue that, for its first twenty years or so, television brought the family together but then, from the 1970s onward, it began to pull them apart. But a better account is one that recognizes the signs of individualization from the very early years of television (and before)—in strategies of audience segmentation, in a history of multiplication and personalization of domestic media, in youthful desires to escape the parental gaze, and so on. Before these signs gathered strength, which took some decades, being dependent on longer-term trends regarding adolescence, the family, and consumer society, there was time for the 1950s *family* experiment to spawn the 1960s and 1970s *family television* experiment. This moment in time, it seems, shaped normative expectations—academic, policy, and popular—regarding television audiences for years to come. But at the turn of the twenty-first century, we must recognize that it was the underlying long-term trend of individualization, and its associated trends of consumerism, globalization, and the democratization of the family, that more strongly shaped and was itself facilitated by television. Two consequences of individualization are worth signaling by way of conclusion. These concern parental mediation and media literacy, concepts that are central to today's research and policy agendas, yet they barely figured fifty years ago. Parental mediation, I suggest, gains a new importance in what Giddens (1993, 184-85) calls "the democratization of the private sphere," while media literacy arises in the context of the individualization of risk (Beck [1986]2005)—in this case, risk of media harm.

The social trends of the twentieth century combined to transform the Victorian family, a model of domestic life that prioritized a culture of stability, hard work, security, duty, and respect, into the democratic family that prizes role flexibility, gender and generational equality, and a culture of self-fulfillment and individual rights. As Giddens (1991, 7) put it, in the democratized private sphere, children have gained the right to "determine and regulate the conditions of their association" within the family, while parents have gained the duty to protect them from coercion, ensure their involvement in key decisions, be accountable to them and others, and respect and expect respect. For young people, this resulted in part from the economic and legal hiatus that opened up in the past fifty years between dependent child and independent adult, resulting in tensions between the discourse of needs and that of individual rights. The new child-centered model of the family offers some resolution insofar as it advocates that parents should provide for their children economically for an extended period while simultaneously recognizing their independence in terms of sociality and culture, for now "the

goal of individual self-realisation overshadows community solidarity and stability"
(Gadlin 1978, 236). However, this creates new difficulties in balancing the
requirements of parents and children, difficulties to be resolved through negotiation rather than, as before, strict discipline, and that are often expressed
through conflicts over space (the front door, the bedroom door), time (what to
do, and watch, when), and media (personal vs. shared media, content preferences, etc.; see Andreasen 1994; Livingstone 2002).[12]

Given this context, it is intriguing to note that Himmelweit, Oppenheim, and
Vince (1958) asked few questions about parental mediation or regulation of television, observing simply that one in five do control (ban, restrict, encourage) their
child's viewing and concluding that "control, then, is rare, and where it exists, it
is aimed at preventing the child from watching horror or frightening pro-
grammes" (pp. 378-79). Possibly, Himmelweit, Oppenheim, and Vince said little
about parental mediation in the 1950s because its importance was obvious rather
than because its role was then unanticipated. In early American research, the
importance of parental mediation received a little more consideration, especially
as a problem among supposedly negligent working-class families, who tended to
treat television as the electronic babysitter, permitting their children access to
content appropriate only for adults (Butsch 2000; Klapper 1960).

Today, parental mediation is conceptualized as combining three distinct strategies of restriction (on time, length, or content of viewing), evaluation (guiding
children on quality, interpretation, criticism), and co-use (discussion while viewing, sharing the viewing experience). But in the work of Himmelweit, Oppenheim,
and Vince (1958), Klapper (1960), and Schramm, Lyle, and Parker (1961), parenting was understood in terms of the Victorian model, with only restrictive mediation being considered. For example, Schramm, Lyle, and Parker discuss parental
authority by noting that "late bedtimes tend to occur in homes where parental
control is lax," and they stress the parental duty "to shield a child from undue
fright resulting from television" (p. 148). But they say nothing that conceives of
parents as equals who may share (or conflict over) the entertainment of viewing
or as supporters who help their children get ahead or keep up in education or
consumption. By contrast, in today's democratic family model, the latter strategies are instead emphasized (Valkenburg et al. 1999). Nathanson (2004) asks
parents to discuss screen violence with their children, for example, rather than
banning their viewing. States seek to roll back national regimes of broadcasting
regulation; public policy is again determined that parents should bear the primary responsibility for managing and controlling their children's media exposure,
even though this demands a restrictive approach that problematically casts parents back into precisely the gatekeeper and rule-enforcer role they have escaped
from, albeit ambivalently, in recent decades (Livingstone and Bober 2006).[13]

Notwithstanding these shifts, children's escape from authoritarian parents has
been curtailed, especially by comparison with the comparative freedoms of fifty
years ago, though for different reasons. Childhood and youth have, over the
period we are concerned with here, become key sites for the anxieties of the risk
society—a term by which Beck ([1986]2005) points to the reflexive recognition
of postwar recent society that it faces vast yet uncertain and unmanageable risks

of its own making.[14] Not only are parents responsible for protecting their children from such risks, including the risk of media-related harms (Millwood Hargrave and Livingstone 2009), but children, too, in a context of the individualization of risk, are responsible. In the media and communication landscape, these risks are signaled by digital convergence. As the EC's information society and media commissioner, Viviane Reding, said in December 2007,

> In a digital era, media literacy is crucial for achieving full and active citizenship. . . . The ability to read and write—or traditional literacy—is no longer sufficient in this day and age. . . . Everyone (old and young) needs to get to grips with the new digital world in which we live. For this, continuous information and education is more important than regulation. (Europa 2007)

Media literacy was not, it seems, a term in Himmelweit's vocabulary, though she was very interested in differential levels of intelligence as a mediator of television's influence (Himmelweit, Oppenheim, and Vince 1958). As Luke (1990, 282) observes, the prevailing behaviorist tradition meant that "the possibility that viewers bring anything other than demographic variables to the screen was conceptually excluded." But following the cognitive reframing not only of psychology but also, therefore, of the psychology of the viewer, media literacy, we saw both a new focus on critical literacy as empowerment (Pecora 2007) but also, more critically, that "the discourse cleared a space for institutionalized practices of intervention"—notably, media education, parental mediation, and devolved content regulation (Luke 1990, 282). Today, media literacy continues to grow in importance on both academic and policy agendas, given current efforts to devolve media risks to an empowered and media-savvy public (Livingstone 2008). The family's role in mediating the television (and also an array of other media, including the Internet) is, therefore, increasingly an educational one, an informal extension of the formal requirements for children's learning, protection, and participation. But television's role in mediating the family means that the children are somewhere else, evading parental guidance, and, precisely, doing their own thing even when at home.

Notes

1. I will not, here, review research on television's effects on individual attitudes and behaviors, except to note the growing body of findings that, broadly, support the conclusion that television has cultivated certain assumptions, beliefs, and mores in the population as a whole, reinforcing a normative status quo of consumerism and do-it-yourself lifestyle identity, along with a mainstreaming of public opinion and a fear of crime, strangers, and the unfamiliar (Millwood Hargrave and Livingstone 2009).

2. As Hill and Tisdall (1997, 66) observe, "The idea of family is to some degree a fluid one, with a mix of concepts at its core—direct biological relatedness, parental caring role, long-term cohabitation, permanent belonging." Indeed, given limitations of space, I will not here stress the complex, multidimensional, and historically contingent nature of family, childhood, youth, and television—but I hope the reader will not take this to mean that I intend them in any simple fashion.

3. Indeed, the marketing and design of television still seeks to shape family space and time to its expectations—unusually for media both before and since. The home computer notoriously does not fit well into the home, print media never sought to, and the radio quickly adjusted to fit people's schedules rather than the other way around.

4. This figure has risen today to nearly two and a half hours in the United Kingdom (Livingstone 2002) and to three hours per day in the United States (Roberts, Foehr, and Rideout 2005). I thank Friedrich Krotz for drawing to my attention a German project published by Gerhard Maletke (1959) as *Fernsehen im Leben der Jugend* (Hamburg, Germany: Hand-Bredow Institut). As in the United Kingdom and the United States (Schramm, Lyle, and Parker 1961), this showed that family viewing quickly reached fifteen to twenty hours per week, a level from which subsequent research in Western countries shows little increase (see also Broddason 2006; Johnsson-Smaragdi 1992).

5. Ironically, throughout the dominance of mass communication, popular fears regarding "kids' culture" stressed the homogenizing effect of commercialization; today, the more commercially effective strategy capitalizes upon the process of individualization, providing—and profiting from—fast-changing niche markets and diversified taste cultures. Yet, television's power has its limits: children and, especially, teenagers remain a notoriously hard market for either advertisers or broadcasters to reach; children still generally prefer to play with friends or ride their bikes than watch television (Livingstone 2002), and when they do watch, they reinterpret the meanings offered to them in ways that fit their own perceptions, such reinterpretation being sufficiently creative for the media industry itself to hire so-called cool hunters and incorporate the inventions of youth culture in developing its own innovations (Jenkins 2003).

6. *Individualization* refers to the thesis that traditional social distinctions (particularly social class) are declining in importance as determinants of people's (especially young people's) life course, resulting in a fragmentation of (or perhaps liberation from) traditional norms and values (Beck and Beck-Gernsheim, 2002).

7. It is noteworthy that, although Himmelweit, Oppenheim, and Vince (1958) did not find television to have any impact on children's aggression, they did find that those with television became more ambitious and middle class in their aspirations and values, and girls also became more conformist in their desire to adopt feminine roles.

8. This is not to say that television is no longer important in the family but, rather, to reveal the diverse and sometimes counternormative ways in which it is embedded in the dispersed family, providing a common or private leisure activity, symbolic resources for family conversation and negotiation, and an occasion for the socialization of children regarding the wider world (Goodman 1983). For many families, family time is also media time, especially television time, and television may be positioned as scapegoat, boundary marker, escape, time manager, stress reducer, bartering agent, babysitter, companion, and more.

9. Himmelweit asked in 1955, "With whom do you most often view?" (see Himmelweit, Oppenheim, and Vince 1958). The Young People, New Media project asked almost the same question in the United Kingdom in 1997 ("With whom do you watch television for more than half the time?") but did not distinguish children's from evening programs.

10. Note that today, research extends the age range of "children and young people" up to eighteen, while Himmelweit researched only those from ten to fourteen years old—after all, in mid-1950s Britain, pupils left school at fourteen or fifteen and entered the adult world, as apprentices if not as fully independent (see Himmelweit, Oppenheim, and Vince 1958).

11. This is not to classify young people as social isolates: note the discussion above of the changing nature of childhood. Nor should we overstate the case: most six- to seventeen-year-olds, including older teens, said they eat a main meal (75 percent) and watch television (68 percent) with their parents on most days of the week, and most talk to them about something that matters at least once or twice a week (70 percent). For parents, television viewing remains the activity they most commonly share with their children (Livingstone 2002).

12. Much of this privatized use of media is focused on the bedroom, once a rather chilly and uncomfortable, sometimes forbidden, place in which to escape the demands of family life but now positively valued for opportunities for socializing and identity work, saturated with media images, sounds, technological artifacts, and other media products.

13. It is noteworthy that Himmelweit, Oppenheim, and Vince (1958), writing in the then-dominant public service context of the United Kingdom (Oswell 2002), direct most of their recommendations to broadcasters (the new intermediaries—*in loco parentis* in the process of socialization), since, as Katz (2003) argues, television disintermediated parents; while Schramm, Lyle, and Parker (1961), writing in the commercial context of American (and, now, international) broadcasting, divide theirs more evenly, as today, among broadcasters, parents, schools, and government.

14. Part of this story is that, as outside spaces were construed as increasingly risky for children, home took over as the locus of safety, identity, and leisure. So, supporting Raymond Williams's (1974) identification of the privatization of leisure, historian Hugh Cunningham (1995, 179) concludes that for children, the postwar period saw a "shift from a life focused on the street to one focused on the home . . . [and] this was accompanied by a change in the social organisation of the home. Parents, and in particular fathers, became less remote and authoritarian, less the centre of attention when they were present." One stark illustration: Hillman et al. (1990) found that while in 1971, 80 percent of U.K. seven- and eight-year-old children walked to school on their own, by 1990 this figure had dropped to 9 percent. Within the home, especially for children, the bedroom has become a central locus of media-rich leisure and, hence, of the mediation of everyday life. Thus, while television in the 1950s drew people home voluntarily, by the 1990s children had become trapped at home, with television no longer their preferred activity (Himmelweit, Oppenheim, and Vince 1958), except for a "boring day" when they are not allowed out (Livingstone, Bovill, and Gaskell 1999).

References

Abrams, M. 1959. The teenage consumer. In *LPE (London Express Exchange) papers*. Vol. 5. London: The London Press Exchange Ltd.

Andreasen, M. S. 1994. Patterns of family life and television consumption from 1945 to the 1990's. In *Media, children and the family—Social scientific, psychodynamic and clinical perspectives*, ed. J. Bryant and A. C. Huston, 19-35. Hillsdale, NJ: Lawrence Erlbaum.

Barker, M., and J. Petley. 2001. *Ill effects: The media/violence debate*. 2nd ed. New York: Routledge.

Beck, U. [1986]2005. *Risk society: Towards a new modernity*. London: Sage.

Beck, U., and E. Beck-Gernsheim. 2002. *Individualization*. London: Sage.

Bettelheim, B. 1999. Do children need television? In *Children, television and the new media*, ed. P. Lohr and M. Meyer, 3-7. Luton, UK: University of Luton Press.

Broddason, T. 2006. Youth and new media in the new millennium. *Nordicom Review* 27 (2): 105-18.

Butsch, R. 2000. *The making of American audiences: From stage to television 1750-1990*. Cambridge: Cambridge University Press.

Coontz, S. 1997. *The way we really are: Coming to terms with America's changing families*. New York: Basic Books.

Cunningham, H. 1995. The century of the child. In *Children and childhood in Western society since 1500*, ed. H. Cunningham, 163-85. London and New York: Longman.

Europa. 2007. Media literacy: Do people really understand how to make the most of blogs, search engines or interactive TV? http://europa.eu/rapid/pressReleasesAction.do?reference=IP/07/1970&format=HTML&aged=1&language=EN&guiLanguage=en (accessed July 19, 2008).

Flichy, P. 2002. New media history. In *Handbook of new media: Social shaping and consequences of ICTs*, ed. L. Lievrouw and S. Livingstone, 136-50. London: Sage.

France, A. 2007. *Understanding youth in late modernity*. Maidenhead, UK: Open University Press.

Gadlin, H. 1978. Child discipline and the pursuit of self: An historical interpretation. In *Advances in child development and behavior*, vol. 12, ed. H. W. Reese and L. P. Lipsitt, 231-61. New York: Academic Press.

Giddens, A. 1991. *Modernity and self-identity: Self and society in the late modern age*. Cambridge, UK: Polity.

———. 1993. *The transformation of intimacy: Sexuality, love and eroticism in modern societies*. Cambridge, UK: Polity.

Goodman, I. R. 1983. Television's role in family interaction: A family systems perspective. *Journal of Family Issues* 4 (2): 405-24.

Hill, M., and K. Tisdall. 1997. *Children and society*. London: Longman.

Hillman, M., Whitelegg, J., & Adams, J., 1990. *One false move . . . A study of children's independent mobility*. London: Policy Studies Institute.

Himmelweit, H. T., A. N. Oppenheim, and P. Vince. 1958. *Television and the child. An empirical study of the effect of television on the young*. London: Oxford University Press.

Jenkins, H. 2003. Quentin Tarantino's *Star Wars?* Digital cinema, media convergence, and participatory culture. In *Rethinking media change: The aesthetics of transition*, ed. D. Thorburn and H. Jenkins, 281-312. Cambridge, MA: MIT Press.

Johnsson-Smaragdi, U. 1992. *Learning to watch television: Longitudinal LISREL models replicated*. Lund Research Papers in Media and Communication Studies no. 5. Lund, Sweden: University of Lund.

Katz, E. 2003. Disintermediating the parents: What else is new? In *In the wired homestead: An MIT sourcebook on the Internet and the family*, ed. J. Turow and A. L. Kavanaugh, 45-52. Cambridge, MA: MIT Press.

Katz, E., and M. Gurevitch. 1976. *The secularization of leisure: Culture and communication in Israel*. Cambridge, MA: Harvard University Press.

Kenway, J., and E. Bullen. 2008. Dividing delights: Children, adults and the search for sales. In *International handbook of children, media and culture*, ed. K. Drotner and S. Livingstone, 168-82. London: Sage.

Klapper, J. T. 1960. *The effects of mass communication*. Glencoe, IL: Free Press.

Kline, S. 1993. *Out of the garden: Toys and children's culture in the age of TV marketing*. London: Verso.

Livingstone, S. 1992. The meaning of domestic technologies: A personal construct analysis of familial gender relations. In *Consuming technologies*, ed. R. Silverstone and E. Hirsch. London: Routledge.

———. 2002. *Young people and new media: Childhood and the changing media environment*. London: Sage.

———. 2008. Engaging with media—A matter of literacy? *Communication, Culture and Critique* 1 (1): 51-62.

Livingstone, S., and M. Bober. 2006. Regulating the Internet at home: Contrasting the perspectives of children and parents. In *Digital generations*, ed. D. Buckingham and R. Willett, 93-113. Mahwah, NJ: Lawrence Erlbaum.

Livingstone, S., & Bovill, M. 1999. *Young People New Media*. London: London School of Economics and Political Science.

Livingstone, S., M. Bovill, and M. Gaskell. 1999. European TV kids in a transformed media world: Key findings of the UK study. In *Children, television and the new media*, ed. P. Lohr and M. Meyer. Luton, UK: University of Luton Press.

Luke, C. 1989. *Pedagogy, printing and Protestantism: The discourse of childhood*. Albany: State University of New York Press.

———. 1990. *Constructing the child viewer: A history of the American discourse on television and children, 1950-1980*. New York: Praeger.

MacKenzie, D., and J. Wajcman, eds. 1999. *The social shaping of technology*. 2nd ed. Buckingham, PA: Open University Press.

Millwood Hargrave, A., and S. Livingstone. 2009. *Harm and offence in media content: A review of the empirical literature* (2nd ed.). Bristol, UK: Intellect.

Morley, D. 1986. *Family television: Cultural power and domestic leisure*. London: Comedia.

Nathanson, A. I. 2004. Factual and evaluative approaches to modifying children's responses to violent television. *Journal of Communication* 54 (2): 321-35.

Osgerby, B. 1998. *Youth in Britain since 1945*. Oxford, UK: Blackwell.

Oswell, D. 2002. *Television, childhood and the home: A history of the making of the child television audience in Britain*. Oxford, UK: Oxford University Press.

Pecora, N. 2007. The changing nature of children's television: Fifty years of research. In *Children and television: Fifty years of research*, ed. N. Pecora, J. C. Murray, and E. A. Wartella, 1-40. Mahwah, NJ: Lawrence Erlbaum.

Roberts, D., U. Foehr, and V. Rideout. 2005. *Generation M: Media in the lives of 8-18 year olds*. Menlo Park, CA: Kaiser Family Foundation.

Robinson, J. P., and G. Godbey. 1997. *Time for life: The surprising ways Americans use their time*. 2nd ed. University Park: Pennsylvania State University Press.

Rowland, W. R. 1983. *The politics of TV violence: Policy uses of communication research*. Beverley Hills, CA: Sage.

Scannell, P. 1988. Radio times: The temporal arrangements of broadcasting in the modern world. In *Television and its audience: International research perspectives*, ed. P. Drummond and R. Paterson. London: British Film Institute.

Schramm, W., J. Lyle, and E. B. Parker. 1961. *Television in the lives of our children*. Stanford, CA: Stanford University Press.

Seiter, E. 1993. *Sold separately: Children and parents in consumer culture*. New Brunswick, NJ: Rutgers University Press.

Spigel, L. 1992. *Make room for TV: Television and the family ideal in postwar America*. Chicago: University of Chicago Press.

Valkenburg, P. M., M. Krcmar, A. L. Peeters, and N. M. Marseille. 1999. Developing a scale to assess three different styles of television mediation: "Instructive mediation," "restrictive mediation," and "social coviewing." *Journal of Broadcasting and Electronic Media* 43 (1): 52-66.

Wartella, E., and B. Reeves. 1985. Historical trends in research on children and the media: 1900-1960. *Journal of Communication* 35 (2): 118-33.

Williams, R. 1974. *Television: Technology and cultural form*. London: Fontana.

Ziehe, T. 1994. From living standard to life style. *Young: Nordic Journal of Youth Research* 2 (2): 2-16.

Political Communication —Old and New Media Relationships

This article reflects upon the ways television changed the political landscape and considers how far new media, such as the Internet, are displacing television or reconfiguring the political communications ecology. The analysis explores opportunities and challenges facing media producers, politicians, and citizens. The authors conclude by suggesting that the television-politics relationship that emerged in the 1960s still prevails to some extent in the digital era but faces new pressures that weaken the primacy of the broadcast-centered model of political communication. The authors identify five new features of political communication that present formidable challenges for media policy makers. They suggest that these are best addressed through an imaginative, democratic approach to nurturing the emancipatory potential of the new media ecology by carving out within it a trusted online space where the dispersed energies, self-articulations, and aspirations of citizens can be rehearsed, in public, within a process of ongoing feedback to the various levels and centers of governance.

Keywords: new media; television; politics; democracy; Internet

By
MICHAEL GUREVITCH,
STEPHEN COLEMAN,
and
JAY G. BLUMLER

From the earliest days of television research, the new medium was regarded as having potential to contribute to a more informed, inclusive, and nonpartisan democracy. John Scupham, the BBC's first controller of educational broadcasting, writing in 1967, argued that "radio and television have shifted the emphasis of political controversy in the democratic countries from abuse to argument" (p. 136). Blumler declared in 1970 that television "conveys impressions of the world of politics to individuals whose access to serious coverage of current affairs is otherwise quite limited" and could "promote the development of more effective patterns of citizenship" (p. 100). In his 1972 manifesto for television as a vehicle for participatory democracy, Brian

NOTE: Michael Gurevitch was originally commissioned to write this article and drafted the opening section before his death in March 2008. Jay Blumler and Stephen Coleman took on the task of completing the text.

DOI: 10.1177/0002716209339345

ANNALS, *AAPSS*, 625, September 2009

Groombridge suggested that the medium could "be considered as candidate for a major part in the civilising of our arid communal existence and in the improvement and enlivenment of our democracy, such that more people have the opportunity, the aptitude, the incentive, and the desire to play an active personal part in what is with unconscious irony called 'public life'" (p. 25). These were not merely speculative assessments. Early studies on the effects of televised election coverage (Trenaman and McQuail 1961; Blumler and McQuail 1968) showed quite clearly that through exposure to political broadcasts, voters (including initially less informed ones) acquired significant information about campaign issues and policy proposals.

But as the new medium became settled, ubiquitous, and seemingly invulnerable, it came to seem as if politics in electoral democracies—a game of power, persuasion, mobilizing support for policies and politicians, and aggregating votes—could not take place without or beyond the mediating gaze of television. Thus, television and politics became indeed complementary institutions, existing in a state of mutual dependence. Politics provided the raw materials and television packaged it, subtly reconstructed it, and delivered it to audiences. The rules of the journalistic game precluded any major repackaging of political messages and hence allowed the political sources fairly wide latitude if not full control of their messages. But over time, the rules of the game began to gradually shift. A series of historical events (e.g., the Vietnam War, Watergate) as well as political and technological changes moved television reporters, editors, and executives to adopt more skeptical, less deferential, and often more adversarial stances toward politics and politicians and hence a more actively interventionist role in the presentation of political issues and stories. The balance of power between the two began to shift gradually toward a more even situation.

The late Michael Gurevitch was an emeritus professor at the Phillip Merrill College of Journalism of the University of Maryland, having previously taught and researched at the Open University (England), the Centre for Television Research (University of Leeds), and the Hebrew University of Jerusalem. With James Curran, he coedited a series of influential texts on mass media and society from the 1970s through to the 2000s. With Jay Blumler, he received the 2005 Murray Edelman Distinguished Career Award.

Stephen Coleman is a professor of political communication and codirector of the Centre for Digital Citizenship, Institute for Communications Studies, University of Leeds. New publications include (with Jay G. Blumler) The Internet and Democratic Citizenship: Theory; Practice; Policy (Cambridge University Press 2009); (with Karen Ross), The Media and the Public: Them and Us in Media Discourse (Blackwell 2009); and (with David Morrison and Scott Anthony), Public Trust in the News: A Constructivist Study of the Social Life of News (Reuters Institute for the Study of Journalism 2009).

Jay G. Blumler is an emeritus professor of public communication at the University of Leeds and an emeritus professor of journalism at the University of Maryland. He is a leading, internationally recognized figure in political communication, having published numerous books, including (with Denis McQuail) Television in Politics: Its Uses and Influences (Faber and Faber 1968); (with Elihu Katz) The Uses of Mass Communications: Current Perspectives on Gratifications Research (SAGE Publications 1974); and (with Michael Gurevitch) The Crisis of Public Communication (Routledge 1995). He is a fellow and former president of the International Communication Association. In 2006, he was given a lifetime achievement award by the American Political Science Association.

The changing rules of the game had some significant consequences, both for the political players as well as for the terrain of television's coverage of politics. It thus had several long-range effects on the political processes and their outcomes. First, television moved into the center of the political stage, assuming a "coproducer" role of political messages instead of the earlier journalistically sanctioned "reporter" role, that is, that of transmitting and relating political events to the audience as if from outside the events. Television gradually moved from the role of observer of events and provider of accounts (stories) and emerged as definer and constructor of political reality. Without necessarily breaching journalistic norms, television came to have an impact upon the events it covered.

Second, while television became an integral part of the political process, it ironically contributed to its depoliticization. The accusation that television has shifted the focus of the political discourse from issues to personalities is by now quite familiar. Policy issues and concerns are more often associated with the faces of political leaders rather than with their political, ideological, and philosophical underpinnings. The educational value of election campaigns, which was once regarded as a key benefit of televised politics, was allegedly diminished by this focus on spectacle rather than ideas. It is, perhaps, an inevitable product of the visual character of the medium, in which faces are more easily recognizable by and accessible to mass audiences than abstract arguments about policies. The democratic ideal of conducting election campaigns as platforms for national debates, as an opportunity for societies to discuss their present and future directions (and indeed to examine their past), has been replaced by the familiar notion of the campaign as a horse race or political beauty contest.

Third, television transferred politics to the living room. Since, by definition, politics takes place in the public domain, involving societies in discussions, negotiations, and struggles over public issues and concerns, its natural locus must be in the public arena. Yet, television imported it into the living room and turned it into a parlor game played by small and quasi-intimate circles. The societal aspect of politics was thus diminished and the bonding effects of public debates attenuated. The public/private, outdoor/indoor dualities of the conduct of politics had ironically contradictory consequences. On one hand, by bringing politics into the home, television undoubtedly contributed to the expansion of the audience for politics. It incorporated into the political process individuals and groups in society that in pretelevision times did not regard themselves as participants in the political process, since their exposure to it was at best minimal and marginal. At the same time, the multiplication of television and other media outlets offering diverse contents has allowed viewers to escape from political content into a vast range of diversionary offerings.

Next, while changes in the scope and composition of television audiences require further documentation, the conventional wisdom is that one of the effects of television's forays into politics has been a dilution of the level of partisanship among audience members. The argument hinges on the assumption that changes in the formats of political television, first among them the introduction of televised debates between political leaders, have limited the ability of viewers to exercise selective exposure to political messages. The familiar format of side-by-side presentation of partisan positions, designed, among other things, to display and preserve the medium's claim for balance and impartiality, resulted in "forced exposure" of viewers to both sides (occasionally three or more sides) of political arguments.

Finally, television's entry into the political domain inevitably led to the formation of professional cadres working for the political parties, designed to fashion the parties' messages and the public personae of political actors in ways that are compatible with the medium. Thus, the communicative activities on both sides of the political-media relationship were handed over and conducted by professionals working within and deploying the same set of professional journalistic practices. The professionalization of politics thus constitutes a response and an adaptation to the challenges of professionalized political media.

New Media: Displacement or Reconfiguration?

Does "the end of television" as we know it imply that the intimate relationship between television and politics that has dominated the past half century is fading away? There are some indications that this might indeed be the case.

The most significant change has been the encroachment of the Internet on the terrain hitherto dominated by television. Audiences for television, as well as for other mass media, are on a downward trend. Newspapers are losing readers and the main television outlets are losing viewers. While this is the case for mass media use generally, it is strikingly visible in the figures for audiences relying on television for political news. According to research conducted by the Pew Internet & American Life Project (Pew 2008), the number of Americans citing the Internet as their first source of presidential election campaign news has increased by 23 percent since 2004, while at the same time the number relying on television has declined by 4 percent (see table 1).

The Pew researchers note that "while mainstream news sources still dominate the online news and information gathering by campaign internet users, a majority of them now get political material from blogs, comedy sites, government websites, candidate sites or alternative sites." Moreover, the survey data show that younger people are more heavily represented among new media users, suggesting that the trend will accelerate (Pew 2008).

Rather than seeing these changes as a process of displacement, with new, digital media becoming dominant as analogue, print-broadcast media atrophy, they may be interpreted as evidence of an ecological reconfiguration, recasting roles and relationships within an evolving media landscape. As citizens gain access to inexpensive communication technologies through which they can interact with the media, generate their own content, and create alternative networks of information dissemination, the gate-keeping monopoly once enjoyed by editors and broadcasters is waning. While never merely passive recipients of television's account of political reality, audiences are increasingly becoming

TABLE 1
PRESIDENTIAL CAMPAIGN NEWS: INTERNET
BOOM IN 2008 (IN PERCENTAGES)

First or Second Mention	October 2004	October 2008[a]	2004 to 2008 Change
Television	76	72	−4
Internet	10	33	+23
Newspapers	28	29	+1
Radio	15	21	+6
Magazines	2	3	+1
Other	3	2	−1
Don't know	2	1	−1

SOURCE: Pew (2008).
NOTE: Figures add to more than 100 percent because multiple responses were allowed.
a. Based on combined surveys conducted October 17-20 and October 24-27, 2004.

active participants in public communication, as senders as well as addressees of mass-circulating messages. This profound role change is taking place alongside the continued presence of professional media production aimed at traditional mass audiences. But everywhere, from interactive news Web sites that receive tens of thousands of comments from the public each day to YouTube videos challenging government policy, it is apparent that media producers can no longer expect to operate within an exclusive, professionalized enclave. Media audiences are now able to intervene in political stories with a degree of effectiveness that would have been unthinkable ten or twenty years ago.

Politicians have also become aware of these altered roles and, ever sensitive to shifts in their audiences' media use, have adapted the channels of their message delivery to connect with Internet users wherever they may surf. Already twenty or so years ago, political operatives attempted to reach voters directly by mailing video cassettes containing political messages, thus attempting to supersede the mediation of television. Now they see the Internet as offering a new way of detouring the mass media. In the United States, Barack Obama's presidential campaign relied considerably upon the viral capabilities of social networking sites as a way of overcoming perceived mass-media obstacles. In Britain, Tom Watson, the minister for transformational government, has stated that "the challenge is for elected representatives to follow their customers and electors into this brave new world. . . . As well as blogs, there are many more MPs using Facebook and Yahoo Groups to communicate their ideas and listen to others" (see Tom Watson's blog, http://www.tom-watson.co.uk/?p=1899, March 10, 2008).

As well as destabilizing the traditional roles of analogue political communication, digital technologies have modified the communicative balance of power by reconfiguring "access to people, services, information and technology in ways that substantially alter social, organizational and economic relationships across geographical and time boundaries" (Dutton et al. 2004, 32.). As access broadens to provide an extensive choice of media platforms, channels, and content, and unprecedented opportunities to store and retrieve media content, new patterns of media use are emerging with distinct sociocultural advantages for some groups. For example, the young, the housebound, and diasporic minorities are three groups that have in many cases benefited from the reconfigured social connections that the Internet affords. In the context of political democracy, voters who go online to seek information, interact with campaigns, and share their views with other citizens are likely to feel better informed, more politically efficacious, and more willing to participate in the democratic process (Shah, Kwak, and Holbert 2001; Johnson and Kaye 2003; Kenski and Stroud 2006; Xenos and Moy 2007; Shah et al. 2007).

However, traditional forms of political communication persist. Television remains dominant as the most highly resourced and far-reaching medium of mass communication; it thus continues to be the locus for "media events" (Dayan and Katz 1992) and the main source of political information for most people (Graber 1990; Chaffee and Frank 1996; Sanders and Gavin 2004; Jerit, Barabas, and Bolsen 2006). But the media ecology that surrounds television is being radically reconfigured with major consequences for the norms and practices of political communication. What exactly has changed?

Channel Multiplication; Audience Fragmentation

The mass television audience is in decline. Viewers are faced with more choices than ever before about what to watch, when to watch it, and how to receive it. Until the early 1980s, the British television audience had access to only three terrestrial television channels: BBC1, BBC2, and ITV. The 85 percent of British television viewers who in 2008 had digital sets have access to more than two hundred digital channels, as well as five terrestrials. In the last year of the twentieth century, the five terrestrial channels accounted for 86 percent of the annual share of the television audience. By 2007, their share had fallen to 63 percent. As Britain's public service broadcaster, the BBC's two channels had a combined audience share of 39 percent in 1999; by 2007, it had fallen to 31 percent (BARB, Annual Shares of Individual Viewing, http://www.barb.co.uk/). The collapsing centrality of terrestrial-based television channels coincides with significant changes in the spatial arrangement of domestic viewing (most homes now have several sets) and growing technological convergence between television and other, once separate technologies, such as telephones and computers. Watching television is a much less distinctive cultural activity than it was in the days when families gathered around the box to watch the same programs as most of their neighbors. As Livingstone (2004a, 76) has observed, "The activity of viewing . . . is converging with reading, shopping, voting, playing, researching, writing, chatting. Media are now used anyhow, anyplace, anytime." In the face of intensified competition for public attention and information, political news and analysis that might in the past have reached most people in the course of a week's viewing can be easily missed.

Channel choices and time-shifting options lead not only to fragmentation of the mass audience but to the emergence of distinct issue publics: people who only want to be addressed on their own terms in relation to issues that matter to them. For example, MTV or Sky Sport viewers might not want to hear about crises in the global economy or the causes of international tensions; they can exclude themselves from exposure to issues and forms of address that they find unappealing, disturbing, or bewildering. Television's role as a public sphere is diminished by these easy opt-outs, and democracy suffers from the absence of socially cross-cutting exchanges of experience, knowledge, and comment.

"Publicness" Transformed

Television emerged as a mass medium at a time when cultural boundaries between public and private life were unambiguous. Constituting a new kind of communicative space in which the debates, dramas, and decisions of politics could be played out daily, television brought the vibrancy of the public sphere to the domestic intimacy of millions of private homes. At the same time, it made public hitherto private lifeworlds through documentaries, plays, and dramatized serials that allowed the public to witness its own multidimensionality. Reviewing the political role of television in the late 1970s, Anthony Smith (1979, 4) could say that television confers publicity and influence once enjoyed by parliamentary assemblies:

> The media which have come to dominate mass communication since the 1950s have acquired roles of historic proportions and have even provided the society with a wholly new elite sector. In a sense broadcasting sits astride all other groupings and institutions. A little like the House of Commons of the eighteenth century, it is both barometer of influence and lever of power. It is a yardstick of social visibility and at the same time the essential magnifying glass of prestige.

And while much of that power remains intact, with mass-media agendas still key to the wielding of political influence, there is a sense in which other public spaces are now encroaching upon television's historic management of public visibility. It is no longer only television cameras, studios, and formats that politicians need to focus upon as they seek to promote their messages and control their images. The viral energy of the blogosphere, social network sites, and wikis constitutes a new flow of incessantly circulating publicity in which reputations are enhanced and destroyed, messages debated and discarded, rumors floated and tested. From Senator Trent Lott's incautiously disparaging remarks about the civil rights movement at what he thought was a private gathering, to Senator George Allen's offensive mockery of an Indian opponent at a campaign rally, the slips, gaffes, indelicacies, insults, and errors that were once confined to relative invisibility are now captured and circulated through online media in ways that can disrupt elite agendas and ruin political reputations. The ubiquity of media technologies, from mobile phone cameras and pocket recorders to always-on Internet connections, are eradicating traditional barriers between public and private. As Meyrowitz (1985, 271) has observed, "When actors lose part of their rehearsal time, their performances naturally move toward the extemporaneous." As a consequence, mediated publicity has become a 24/7 presence; from reality TV (in which the private is publicized) to political interviews (in which the impersonal is increasingly personalized), the contours of the public sphere are being reshaped in ways to which political actors must learn to adjust.

Interactivity and Remixing

Television is the quintessential broadcast medium: it transmits messages to a mass audience expected to receive or reject what it is offered. The inherent feedback path of digital media subverts this transmission ethos by allowing message receivers to act upon media content. The digital text is never complete; the fluidity of bits and bytes makes digital communication radically different from broadcasting. In the context of political communication, this has entailed a profound shift in the process of message circulation. Whereas political actors were once concerned to produce polished, finished performances for public consumption, contemporary politicians are compelled to think about interactive audiences and their capacity to question, challenge, redistribute, and modify the messages that they receive. In the era of digital interactivity, the production of political messages and images is much more vulnerable to disruption at the point of reception.

Of course, interactivity is not entirely new. Radio phone-ins have existed for half a century, and even in their high-profile television appearances politicians have encountered critical studio audiences and telephone callers putting them on the spot. Media interactivity has provided a vernacular tone to political debate, allowing lay voices into what was once deemed to be a highly exclusive discourse. Television's recent obsession with interactive content has often been unfocused and seemingly pointless, marred in the United Kingdom by a series of phone-in scandals in which viewers were invited to vote for outcomes over which producers never intended to cede control. Despite this failure by television producers to understand the psychological commitments entailed by interactive communication, it is here to stay. Interactivity is neither an add-on nor a novelty but an innate property of digital media. One cannot credibly establish a Web site, blog, or e-mail list with a view to simply transmitting messages without taking account of the consequent feedback.

The Internet has expanded the range of political sources. On one hand, agenda setting is no longer a politician-journalist duopoly; on the other, the commentariat is no longer an exclusive club. This has led to a radical expansion of the political realm to include aspects of the mundane and the popular, such as celebrity behavior, football management, domestic relationships, and reality TV conflicts. Beyond the subject matter, the style of public interest content has tended to depart from the professional forms that once dominated "high politics." And yet it cannot be ignored by political elites, who are increasingly engaged in efforts to monitor the blogosphere, control the content of wikis, and make their presence felt in unfamiliar environments such as Facebook and YouTube.

As well as the need to respond to the buzz of media interactivity, political actors must consider the possibility that their messages will be modified once they are launched into mediaspace. The digital media environment does not respect the integrity of information; once it has been published online, others are at liberty to remix content, in much the same way as music fans are able to reorder and reconstruct beats, melodies, and lyrics. A good example of such remixing is TheyWorkForYou, a Web site launched in 2004 by independent social hacktivists with the aim of aggregating content from the official *Hansard* reports so that the British Parliament's proceedings could be more comprehensible and accessible to the lay public. The site (http://www.theyworkforyou.com) allows users to track a particular issue or MP, comment on parliamentary proceedings, and register for regular updates on selected themes. This process is known as a "mash-up": a rearrangement of original data with a view to making it more meaningful, usable, or entertaining. For political communicators long used to attaching value to their ownership and control of information, mash-up culture presents a formidable challenge.

The Consequences for Political Communication

Our argument that television remains a significant medium for political communication, but is situated within a reconfigured media ecology, has significant consequences for all of the key actors. It is to the new pressures facing each of these actors that we now turn.

Consequences for the mass media

Producers of political coverage on television, from news broadcasts to election campaign reports and issue analyses, are under intense pressure to compete for the attention of the fragmented audience. Television news viewing has declined significantly in recent years, as have audiences for major political occasions, such as candidate debates and election results. Now that viewers have far more options, there is an increased premium on the production of arresting content. Top political broadcasters are projected as stars. Some journalists respond by simplifying political complexities to expand their audience. They have tried to engage viewers in making and commenting upon political narratives, as well as injecting a more compelling dramaturgical flavor to coverage. Politics is often projected as an arena of gamesmanship, failure, scandal, and gaffes rather than the deliberative discussion of issues.

Faced with an array of bloggers, citizen-journalists, and contributors of user-generated content, professional journalists are increasingly on the defensive

(Lowrey 2006), needing to redefine the nature of their contribution to the political public sphere beyond "simply telling the story." In the crowded contemporary media space they now inhabit, journalists have a unique opportunity to provide authoritative interpretation, free from the most obvious distortions of partisanship; decipher the vast daily swarm of official and partisan political messages with a view to separating information from propaganda; and filter the vast amount of data, news, rumor, and conversation that is now readily accessible, with a view to presenting a broad and balanced account of political events and ideas. But will they be able to seize it?

In addressing audiences that are still larger than those ever reached by Web sites or blogs, professional television journalists have a vital role in reflecting public concerns and speaking to their viewers as a general public rather than as fragmented and segregated audience segments. In short, television still performs a public service function, but this function is struggling to survive in an increasingly market-driven, competitive media environment. Political broadcasters are under pressure to operate across media platforms and engage collaboratively with a broad spectrum of off-line as well as online communities. This pressure takes its toll in terms of working hours required to produce 24/7, cross-platform content, sometimes at the cost of journalistic depth and even accuracy.

Alongside these myriad domestic pressures, television journalists find themselves more exposed than ever before to global issues that impinge upon their coverage of domestic politics. As news budgets diminish, the need to be physically present in more parts of the world increases. As political coverage moves online, there is an added pressure to reach out to international audiences that are able to access content without regard for borders.

Consequences for governments/politicians

Governments and other political actors are forced to deal with more spaces of mediation than ever before. Whereas in the relatively recent past, political communication strategists had a limited range of press, television, and radio bases to cover, they are now involved in multidimensional impression management. This leads to an inevitable loosening of their control over the political agenda, forcing politicians into an increasingly responsive mode rather than the proactive, agenda-setting role they would prefer to adopt. To cover the broad, dynamic, and often unpredictable media environment in which they now operate, political actors are compelled to adopt elaborate cross-media strategies, which may amount to little more than keeping up with the incessant flow of relevant information and hoping to spot embarrassing media content before it damages them.

As political discourse takes a more vernacular, quotidian form, politicians are under pressure to present themselves as personalities with whom citizens would want to interact. The need to construct sincere, authentic personas capable of inspiring trust and generating conversational (parasocial) interaction places new communicative burdens upon political actors who must develop skills in appearing "just like you" and seeming to address "everyone as someone" (Coleman and Moss 2008; Scannell 2000).

At the same time, as citizens increasingly experience interactive relationships with supermarkets, banks, travel companies, and music stores, they express frustration when local councils, members of parliament, and government departments seem incapable of engaging with them online. While governments now deliver numerous services online and provide a wide variety of local, national, and supranational information portals, they tend to offer few interactive features for citizens wanting to provide feedback (Dunleavy et al. 2005). In the interactive era, government has not proved to be a particularly good conversationalist. Politicians speak with increasing frequency about the need for government to listen to and converse with the public, but there are very few examples of good practice; many politicians lack confidence in entering into public discussion beyond the protective walls of the broadcasting studio.

Consequences for citizens

It has never been easy for citizens to become informed and make their voices heard. While the Internet offers an unprecedented opportunity for people to access useful information and engage in civic activities (Bimber 2003; Shah et al. 2005), clear evidence shows that the new media environment is blighted by problems of information overload (Livingstone 2004b; Couldry and Langer 2005) and uncertainty about what to trust (Uslaner 2004; Welch, Hinnant, and Moon 2005; Dutton and Shepherd 2006). There is a need, therefore, for sources of interpretive clarity. While search engines, recommender systems, and wikis are used pragmatically to find, filter, and scrutinize the abundant stores of online information that are now available, these are no substitute for the strong, authoritative signals that television traditionally afforded seekers of political knowledge.

Moreover, while citizens have access to more information and communication resources than ever before, these are not distributed equally. Access differentials reflect patterns of social inequality, with poorer, less educated people least likely to have access to or skills in using the Internet. The growing importance of the online environment could serve to strengthen the voices of the privileged, leaving citizens with limited resources, skills, or confidence reliant upon a narrowing range of mass-media sources providing shallow political information.

Citizens who do have access to the Internet are increasingly energized by the many opportunities for them to ask questions, enter dialogue, raise issues, tell stories, and investigate current affairs; but at the same time, they experience traditional frustrations of political inefficacy. While the Internet offers unparalleled chances to interact with government, elected representatives, and institutions of supranational governance, such as the European Commission, there is meager evidence that their inputs have much impact on policy formation. A disorientating sense of being technologically connected, but politically disconnected, fuels civic disengagement; citizens come to believe that politicians are bound to resist the democratic potentiality of interactive communication technologies (Muhlberger 2003; Kenski and Stroud 2006; Coleman, Morrison, and Svennevig 2008).

Television and Politics—A More
Ambivalent Relationship

In the digital era, the relationship between television and politics has become less clear-cut and more ambivalent. While television remains the principal constructor and coproducer of political messages, the systemic entanglement between journalistic and political elites is threatened by new players in the media game. This "fifth estate" (Dutton 2007) sees itself much more in the position of the eighteenth-century fourth estate: reporting, scrutinizing, and commenting from a critical distance, rather than entering into the portals of institutional power. In contrast, broadcast journalists, having become political insiders capable of shaping agendas, find themselves handicapped by their closeness to power.

At the same time, television's emphasis upon political personalization continues unabated. Political leaders who do not look right on television and do not understand its implicit grammar face major disadvantages. In the new media ecology, political actors are under greater pressure than ever to construct rounded media images, not only on television and in the press, but across a range of outlets. In doing so, however, they have to compete with many others who are in search of public attention, on far more equal terms than previously. In Italy, the radical comedian Beppe Grillo has established the country's most popular blog, attracting far more public comments than those sent to the major political parties. Politicians, parties, and governments cannot expect to attract public attention simply because of the legitimacy of their positions; authority within the new media ecology has to be earned by demonstrating commitments to interactive and networked communication that do not come easily to elite political actors.

While television continues to be the principal conduit between the home and the public sphere, both of these spaces have changed since the heyday of broadcasting. Television remains central to the routines and securities of everyday life (Silverstone 1994), but domestic spaces have become more fragmented, as families disperse within and beyond them. Grand televisual events still bring people together, but the experience of media access is now much more individualized, as particularly younger people spend more time using personalized, hybrid forms of public-privatized media technologies. A negative effect of family breakdown has been the reduction of the interpersonal communication about politics that has traditionally been a key force for socializing political participation. The public sphere, as mediated through television and newer communication technologies, has taken an anti-institutional turn, focusing more earnestly upon forms of informal, communitarian, and networked public presence. In many respects, the digital media networks are more sensitive to this circulatory public sphere than television, with its centralized distance from the grassroots, is capable of being.

And whereas televised coverage of politics diminished partisanship by reducing possibilities for selective exposure, the new media ecology makes it easier to establish partisan patterns of media access by creating more scope for selectivity and more opportunities for group herding and opinion polarization (Sunstein 2001; Mutz 2006; Feldman and Price 2008). The absence of an online equivalent to the public service broadcasting ethos raises profound risks for democracy. Television production might have been industrially top-heavy, unaccountable, and often authoritarian, but it was susceptible to regulation likely to generate some semblance of balanced political coverage.

In the new media ecology, communication strategists need to work harder than ever to cover the expanded media landscape and to adopt new styles in order not to seem contrived, insincere, and heavy-handed. Vast spin operations have turned political marketing from a means of conveying policies and images to a means of determining them. An emphasis upon generating apparently spontaneous discussion is now preferred to didactic declarations about policy. The cultural appeal of the media amateur, posting spontaneously, sporadically, and incompletely contrasts with the clinical efficiency of the party war room. In an age when politicians do not benefit from seeming to be politicians, affected unprofessionalism may well hold the key to successful communication. Explicitly or otherwise, politicians probably remain yet more dependent upon professional campaign and image management and under pressure to find novel ways of presenting themselves within the ever-expanding spaces of the media.

The future of this ambivalent relationship between television and politics, and of political communication more generally, entails normative policy choices. Contrary to the forceful rhetoric of technological determinism, new means of producing, distributing, receiving, and acting upon information do not in themselves shape or reshape the media ecology. Unanticipated and misunderstood, technological innovations not only disrupt settled cultural arrangements but also appear to possess teleological propensities of their own. In the early days of television—and before it, radio and the printing press—many commentators assumed that culture could not withstand their inherent effects. But this is a mistake: technologies are culturally shaped as well as shaping. In these first years of the twenty-first century, policies to shape the new media ecology in a democratic direction are still in their infancy. It is high time for such a policy to be devised, debated, and implemented.

Shaping the New Media Ecology

This emerging complex new media ecology presents several worrying implications for democratic citizenship that warrant policy intervention. An initial concern is that media contain little civically useful political content. Although users have more content to choose from, more channels and platforms from which to receive it, and more opportunities than ever before to comment upon the political events and issues of the day, the overall amount and quality of in-depth, thought-provoking, deliberative, or investigative political news and analysis is atrophying in a media landscape that is increasingly dominated by a focus upon celebrity, rumor, and attack. Politics is presented to the public as a cynical game. Jamieson's (1993,

186) contention that a media focus upon polls and strategy serves to distort the agenda and distract the electorate is supported by subsequent experimental research (Cappella and Jamieson 1997; Moy and Pfau 2000).

Another concern lies in the weakening of public service obligations upon media producers, which has resulted in a marginalization of the citizen role. At the same time, there is a pervasive conception of audience members and new-media users as self-seeking consumers, free-floating individuals, or sensation-seeking hedonists rather than active and responsible members of political communities. Sunstein's (2001, 177) concern about "like-minded people who talk or even live, much of the time, in isolated enclaves" is relevant here, for a fundamental prerequisite of a democratic public sphere is the possibility of encountering others whose positions, perspectives, and values differ from one's own. Without exposure to cross-cutting networks of pluralistic information and opinion, traditionally provided by non-demand-led media formats, it becomes difficult to nurture potentially informed and engaged citizens.

Also worrisome is the gap between the energy and creativity of what Dutton (2007) has called the fifth estate and the powers wielded by the other four estates. In short, the spaces and networks of digital media are at risk of being so disconnected that institutional elites forming policies and making decisions can afford to ignore them. A subterranean universe of blogs, wikis, YouTube videos, and virtual communities cannot compete with the mass media's elite-molded agendas; exclusive access to policy makers; and capacity to frame, measure, and represent public opinion. A paradox of recent media trends has been the increasing incorporation of "the public" into media productions, such as phone-ins, studio debates, online forums, and reality TV, while citizens are left feeling more excluded than ever from influence over the media, government, or public affairs in general (Entman 1989; Bucy and Gregson 2001; Pattie, Seyd, and Whiteley 2003; Syvertsen 2004; Coleman and Ross 2009).

These trends can be reversed, but it will require policy directed toward a more democratic integration of media and politics. Just as it was deemed necessary in the early days of the twentieth century to ask fundamental questions about the potential of broadcasting to enhance, diminish, or reshape citizenship, so in the reconfigured media ecology of the early twenty-first century such questions must be revisited. In doing so, communication scholars can help policy makers to avoid some of the more crass assumptions that misguided the earlier debates. Media effects are not direct and undifferentiated; civic norms cannot be injected into populations through patrician strategies; there cannot and should not be a single public sphere in which the nation would gather "as one man" (Reith 1949, 4); it should not be imagined that media content will be received by patriarchal families, gathered around the domestic set, and journalists should not see themselves as the sole authors of the first draft of history. Broadcasting shaped and was shaped by a set of beliefs about the communication of citizenship that would be likely to distract us from making sense of the new media ecology. Instead, contemporary policy thinking needs to acknowledge a number of significant changes in the complexion of public communication. These include the following:

- *The ubiquity of information and communication technologies, which are no longer monopolized by industrially centralized, professional organizations.* As more people have gained access to media technologies, the capacity to gather information, set agendas, and hold the powerful to account has broadened. But this broadening has not usually been accompanied by opportunities to deliberate collectively about matters of common concern. In short, media production has expanded alongside a fragmentation of public reception.
- *A more diffuse notion of the public.* No longer defined simply in terms of national subjectivity, the public has become more culturally fractured, politically postdeferential, and volatile in its consumption choices. The notion of a singular public sphere, dominated by codified standards of civility, is less realizable than a space of pluralistic interaction within and between diverse social networks. Out of such interactions may come a range of interpretations and enactments of citizenship.
- *Less emphasis upon television as the provision of a public service and more emphasis upon its ability to open up a public space.* Whereas the important role of public service broadcasting has been to develop and promote common knowledge, the expanded role of public communication space is to become an open arena for the production and distribution of potentially universal value.
- *A recasting of the idea of citizenship to take into account the terms of a new relationship between public and private life.* Civic and political roles have percolated into homes, schools, workplaces, shops, and nightclubs. The political no longer relates only to institutions of the state but has come to describe a range of daily encounters with power that give rise to civic—and uncivic—responses. If the media are to promote citizenship in the early twenty-first century, this must embrace much more than occasional moments of voting in elections or being addressed by politicians.
- *An acknowledgement by governments at different levels (local, national, and supranational) that the risks and complexities of governance cannot be managed without drawing upon the experience, expertise, and networked linkages of the represented public.* While this is widely recognized by smart governments and politicians, mechanisms capable of capturing, filtering, summarizing, and acting upon public knowledge remain crude and inefficient, resulting in a pervasive sense that government consultations and "listening" exercises cannot be trusted.

These new features of political communication present formidable challenges for media policy makers. Thus far, governments, regulators, and mass-media executives acknowledge that the media ecology is changing but cling to long-standing paradigms and models to explain and regulate it. The broadcast ethos still prevails in most policy thinking, with many-to-many interactivity, social networking, and user-generated content regarded as a secondary tier of public communication. This approach pays too much attention to technological changes that seem to be revolutionizing the media, while neglecting the cultural and political reconfigurations that are much more far-reaching.

New technologies are most certainly implicated in the changes we have described, but they do not determine the direction and do not possess teleological propensities. In short, the Internet is not "good" or "bad" for democracy. But from a normative perspective, which regards communication media as always having an emancipatory, democratic potential, the pressing requirement is to base policy upon theoretical and empirical knowledge.

Our approach to the current policy challenge, which we have outlined and revised over the past decade (Blumler and Coleman 2001; Coleman and Blumler

2008), is to nurture the emancipatory potential of the new media ecology by carving out within it a trusted online space where the dispersed energies, self-articulations, and aspirations of citizens can be rehearsed, in public, within a process of ongoing feedback to the various levels and centers of governance. The civic commons, as we have called it, would be an enduring structure that would serve as a protected space of civic interaction, in all of the pluralistic senses that this is now understood. It would be a space in which individuals and groups could campaign to set legislative agendas, parliamentary and council committees could consult with citizens online, government departments and agencies could be held to account by service users, and the most pressing and sensitive questions of the day could be opened up to well-moderated and consequential public deliberation. The civic commons, as we understand it, would be a space of agonistic politics as well as consensus-seeking, of rational discourse as well as many other ways of expressing views and values, and of institutional as well as grassroots citizenship. Creating an online civic commons would involve the establishment of an entirely new kind of public agency, funded by government but independent from it in its everyday work, charged with forging fresh links between communication and politics and connecting the voice of the people more meaningfully to the daily activities of democratic institutions.[1] Within such a space, television and politics will continue to be mutually dependent. But this complementarity will converge increasingly with an array of other information and communication technologies that reconfigure access to the institutions, events, and debates that once took place exclusively on the other side of the screen.

Note

1. The terms and shape of this institutional arrangement are outlined more fully in Coleman and Blumler (2008).

References

Bimber, B. 2003. *Information and American democracy: Technology in the evolution of political power*. New York: Cambridge University Press.

Blumler, J. G. 1970. The Effects of Political Television in *The Effects of Television*, ed. J. D. Halloran. London: Panther.

Blumler, J. G., and S. Coleman. 2001. *Realising democracy online: A civic commons in cyberspace*. London: Institute of Public Policy Research.

Blumler, J. G. and McQuail, D. 1968. *Television in politics: Its uses and influence*. London: Faber and Faber.

Bucy, E., and A. Gregson. 2001. Media participation: A legitimizing mechanism of mass democracy. *New Media & Society* 3 (3): 357-80.

Cappella, J., and K. H. Jamieson. 1997. *Spiral of cynicism: The press and the public good*. Oxford: Oxford University Press.

Chaffee, S., and S. Frank. 1996. How Americans get political information: print versus broadcast news. *The Annals of the American Academy of Political and Social Science* 546:48-58.

Coleman, S., and J. G. Blumler. 2008. *The Internet and democratic citizenship: Theory; practice; policy*. Cambridge: Cambridge University Press.

Coleman, S., and G. Moss. 2008. Governing at a distance—Politicians in the blogosphere. *Information Polity* 13 (1/2): 7-20.

Coleman, S., D. Morrison, and M. Svennevig. 2008. New media and political efficacy. *International Journal of Communication* 2: 771-791.

Coleman, S., and K. Ross. 2009. *Them and us: How the media frame the public*. Oxford, UK: Blackwell.

Couldry, N., and A. Langer. 2005. Media consumption and public connection: Toward a typology of the dispersed citizen. *Communication Review* 8 (2): 237-57.

Dayan, D., and E. Katz. 1992. *Media events: The live broadcasting of history*. Cambridge, MA: Harvard University Press.

Dunleavy, P., Margetts, H., Bartholomeou, P., Bastow, S., Escher, T., Pearce, O., Tinkler, J. and Broughton, H. 2007. *Government on the internet: progress in delivering information and services online*. London: National Audit Office.

Dutton, W. 2007. Through the network (of networks)—The fifth estate. Inaugural lecture, University of Oxford Examination Halls, October 15.

Dutton, W., S. E. Gillett, L. W. McKnight, and M. Peltu. 2004. Bridging broadband Internet divides: Reconfiguring access to enhance communicative power. *Journal of Information Technology* 19:28-38.

Dutton, W., and A. Shepherd. 2006. Trust in the Internet as an experience technology. *Information, Communication & Society* 9 (4): 433-51.

Entman, R. 1989. *Democracy without citizens: Media and the decay of American politics*. New York: Oxford University Press.

Feldman, L. and Price, V. 2008. Confusion or Enlightenment? How Exposure to Disagreement Moderates the Effects of Political Discussion and Media Use on Candidate Knowledge. *Communication Research*, 35 (1):61-87

Graber, D. 1990. Seeing is remembering: How visuals contribute to learning from television news. *Journal of Communication* 40 (3): 134-56.

Groombridge, B. 1972. *Television and the people: a programme for democratic participation*. Penguin: Harmondsworth.

Jamieson, K. H. 1993. *Dirty politics: Deception, distraction and democracy*. Oxford: Oxford University Press.

Jerit, J., J. Barabas, and T. Bolsen. 2006. Citizens, knowledge, and the information environment. *American Journal of Political Science* 50 (2): 266-82.

Johnson, T., and B. Kaye. 2003. A boost or bust for democracy? How the Web influenced political attitudes and behaviors in the 1996 and 2000 presidential elections. *Harvard International Journal of Press Politics* 8 (3): 9-34.

Kenski, K., and N. Stroud. 2006. Connections between Internet use and political efficacy, knowledge, and participation. *Journal of Broadcasting and Electronic Media* 50 (2): 173-92.

Livingstone, S. 2004a. The challenge of changing audiences. *European Journal of Communication* 19 (1): 75-86.

———. 2004b. Media literacy and the challenge of new information and communication technologies. *Communication Review* 7 (1): 3-14.

Lowrey, W. 2006. Mapping the journalism-blogging relationship. *Journalism* 7 (4): 477-500.

Meyrowitz, J. 1985. *No sense of place: The impact of electronic media on social behavior*. New York: Oxford University Press.

Moy, P., and M. Pfau. 2000. *Malice toward all? The media and public confidence in democratic institutions*. Westport, CT: Greenwood.

Muhlberger, P. 2003. Political values, political attitudes, and attitude polarization in Internet political discussion: Political transformation or politics as usual? *Communications* 28 (2): 107-34.

Mutz, D. C. 2006. *Hearing the other side: Deliberative versus participatory democracy*. NY: Cambridge University Press.

Pattie, C., P. Seyd, and P. Whiteley. 2003. Civic attitudes and engagement in modern Britain. *Parliamentary Affairs* 56 (4): 616–33.

Pew Research Center for People and the Press. 2008. Internet now major source of campaign news: Continuing partisan divide in cable TV news audiences. October 31. http://pewresearch.org/pubs/1017/internet-now-major-source-of-campaign-news.

Reith, J. 1949. *Into the wind*. London: Hodder and Stoughton.

Sanders, D., and N. Gavin. 2004. Television news, economic perceptions and political preferences in Britain, 1997-2001. *Journal of Politics* 66 (4): 1245-66.

Scannell, P. 2000. For anyone-as-someone structures. *Media, Culture & Society* 22 (1): 5-24.

Scupham, J. 1967. *Broadcasting and the community london; New Thinker's Library*. London: C.A. Watts.

Shah, D., J. Cho, W. Eveland, and N. Kwak. 2005. Information and expression in a digital age: Modeling Internet effects on civic participation. *Communication Research* 32 (5): 531-65.

Shah, D., N. Kwak, and L. Holbert. 2001. Connecting and disconnecting with civic life: Patterns of internet use and the production of social capital. *Political Communication* 18:141-62.

Shah, D., D. McLeod, L. Friedland, and M. Nelson. 2007. The politics of consumption/the consumption of politics. *The Annals of the American Academy of Political and Social Science* 611 (1): 6-15.

Silverstone, R. 1994. *Television and everyday life*. London: Routledge.

Smith, A. 1979. *Television and political life: Studies in six European countries*. London: Macmillan.

Sunstein, C. 2001. *Republic.com*. Princeton, NJ: Princeton University Press.

Syvertsen, T. 2004. Citizens, audiences, customers and players: A conceptual discussion of the relationship between broadcasters and their publics. *European Journal of Cultural Studies* 7 (3): 363-80.

Trenaman, J. and McQuail, D. 1961. *Television and the political image*. London: Methuen.

Uslaner, E. 2004. Trust, civic engagement and the Internet. *Political Communication* 21 (2): 223-42.

Welch, E., C. Hinnant, and M. Moon. 2005. Linking citizen satisfaction with e-government and trust in government. *Journal of Public Administration Research and Theory* 15 (3): 371-91.

Xenos, M., and P. Moy. 2007. Direct and differential effects of the Internet on political and civic engagement. *Journal of Communication* 57 (4): 704-18.

Television News and the Nation: The End?

By
MENAHEM BLONDHEIM
and
TAMAR LIEBES

The golden age of television news gave a large majority of otherwise diverse Americans a unified, seamless, and clear-cut image of their nation, its central players, and its agenda. Carefully scheduled, edited, sequenced, and branded, heard and seen simultaneously across America, it provided a pretense of order to the chaos that is news. The permanence and stability of the nation, as expressed in a complex way by TV news, provided Americans with an all-important sense of existential security experienced on an unarticulated emotional level. Today, a disjointed news environment is crushing the nature of network news as a transitional object. Television news no longer reassures viewers by connecting them to a surmountable world out there but carries them on a loop from themselves to themselves.

Keywords: television; news; news technologies; telegraph; transitional object; nationalism

In 1900, people the world over got their news from the printed editions of their local newspaper. A hundred years later, they get it from a plethora of sources spanning 24/7 global television news networks and a myriad of specialized news outlets. But in between, for a full generation, classical television dominated the news

Menahem Blondheim teaches in the department of History and the department of Communication and Journalism at the Hebrew University of Jerusalem. He earned his BA from the Hebrew University and his MA and PhD degrees from Harvard University. He has published books and articles in the fields of history of communication and communication in history, American and Jewish communications, and communication technologies old and new.

Tamar Liebes is a professor of media and journalism and holds the Carl and Matilda Newhouse Chair in Communication at the Hebrew University of Jerusalem. Her books include American Dreams, Hebrew Subtitles: Globalization at the Receiving End *(Hapmpton Press 2004);* Reporting the Arab-Israeli Conflict: How Hegemony Works *(Routledge 1997);* The Export of Meaning: Cross Cultural Readings of Dallas, *with Elihu Katz (Polity Press 1992); and two edited volumes:* Media, Ritual, and Identity *(with J. Curran, Routledge 1998) and* Canonic Texts in Media Research *(with E. Katz, J. D. Peters, and A. Orloff, Polity Press 2002).*

DOI: 10.1177/0002716209338574

experience of billions. Nowhere was the dominance of television as obvious as in the United States. By 1960, observed Ted White, "it was possible for the first time to answer an inquiring foreign visitor as to what Americans do in the evenings . . . they watch television" (White 1961, 336). News became a centerpiece of that daily diet; so that by 1970, if an inquiring foreign visitor were to ask whence Americans get their news, a majority would answer—they watch it on television (Comstock 1991, 81-82; Schudson 1995, 181). By now, that short experience seems outlandish enough to raise wonderment but also significant enough to justify a look at its nature and texture and, further afield, at its possible significance and impact.

We believe that the classic era of television news can be best understood by tracing where it came from and what it disappeared into. In doing so, we review the parallel development of media technologies, institutions, and practices, on one hand, and processes of social and cultural change, on the other. In this bifocal look at television and society, we place special emphasis on people's need for identity and ontological security.

We propose that the golden age of television news reflected and affected a unique era in the social history of the twentieth century—an era in which the nation was the focal point of social belonging. Television news—carefully scheduled, edited, sequenced, and branded; heard and seen simultaneously across America—could provide a pretense of order to the chaos that is news. With one anchor, one accent, one look, one message at a time, and one viewpoint of "the way things are," the evening news gave a large majority of otherwise diverse Americans a unified, seamless, and clear-cut image of their nation, its central players, and its agenda.

People's sense of the reliability and the permanence of their social and physical environment, as Anthony Giddens suggests, is the foundation of trust and therefore the basis for ontological security, experienced on an unarticulated emotional rather than cognitive level (Giddens 1984). The permanence and stability of the nation, as expressed in a complex way by TV news, provided Americans with the all-important sense of existential security.

Precursors of National News

America in the nineteenth century was a society of island communities in a "search for order." "Weak communications," posits historian Robert Wiebe, "severely restricted the interaction among these islands and dispersed the power to form opinion and enact public policy" (Wiebe 1967, xiii). The main medium of information and opinion of the time was the newspaper, and the source of most of the news published in American newspapers before the mid-nineteenth century was other American newspapers. This singular condition was of course a function of transmission rather than of news gathering. Although each news item still had to be culled from real life to be made public, it was made known throughout the country via the circulation of the newspaper first reporting it. Since colonial times, postal policy was to allow editors to exchange their publications post-free.

By incoming mail, they received news accounts that papers in other regions had first collected and reported. Editors then cut and pasted these bits of news in their own sheet, alongside the news they collected firsthand (Kielbowicz 1989; John 1995).

This process of journalistic surveillance produced scattered bits of information and opinion from various places and sources, each reflecting its own specific concerns. Only in editorials would publishers try to correlate the pieces to fit a coherent pattern. This pattern emphasized the local but also provided glimpses of other island communities and of what was shared with them, together with an emerging awareness of a common nationality uniting them.

This changed with the telegraph. Once it spread over the United States, newspapers could enter the business of reporting distant news events themselves. Far beyond its ability to speed bilateral exchanges across space, the telegraph provided a new dimension of communication—broadcasting. By closing its circuits, a message sent from any station on the telegraph network could be "scattered broadcast" over the country instantaneously, in a single writing (Blondheim 1994). The news wire service was first to discover this potential. Employing the telegraph as a one-way means of transmission, it could have its report reach all points on the telegraph network simultaneously and thus could "impress the whole nation . . . with the same idea at the same time" (A Journalist 1855, 365). The telegraph's new broadcast mode had the power to centralize, even nationalize, information. By applying the telegraph's news broadcast mode, explained the editor of the *New York Express* in 1846, "the Union will be solidified at the expense of the State sovereignties." He predicted that

> we shall become more and more one people, thinking more alike, acting more alike, and having [a common] impulse. Washington is near to us now as our up-town wards. We can almost hear through the Telegraph, members of Congress as they speak.The country now will be excited from its different capitals. Man will immediately respond to man. An excitement will thus be general, and cease to be local. Whether good or ill is to come from all this, we cannot foresee.[1]

But this revolutionary prospect had its limitations. Unlike subsequent broadcast technologies, this kind of news broadcast would remain a two-step process: while in each station along the national network of telegraph wires the news message would be received simultaneously, it was the local newspaper that would then take over and bring the broadcast news before the large public. In the process, national news would be embedded in local news and be presented from a local perspective.

"Processes of communication are the basis of the coherence of societies and cultures," averred scholar Karl Deutsch. Therefore, he suggested, "even where we have one people . . . the range and effectiveness of social communication within it may tell us how effectively it has become integrated and how far it has advanced, in this respect, toward becoming a nation" (Deutsch 1953, 65). To judge from nineteenth-century newspapers, the process did not advance very far, even with the telegraph and wire service. The outbreak of a bloody Civil War a decade after the discovery of national news broadcast by telegraph would demonstrate that.[2]

If the wire service represented a national perspective tucked into local journalism, national magazines that emerged in the latter part of the nineteenth century were in themselves creatures of the nation. However, their infrequent appearance made them not much of news media—they were more a model of how common content could be attuned to all Americans.[3]

The Voice of National News

Ironically, it was the smallest of the small media of its times that would ultimately link vast populations to an imagined center via news. Radio developed gradually in the 1920s from a hackers-holiday of chat and performance to a system linking an increasingly dense scattering of receivers. From high, space-binding transmission towers, it began to provide common content: the beginning of broadcast news. At first, wire service reports were read out loud as filler for the thinly populated schedule. Americans could find the same words in their newspapers (Barnouw 1966, 138).

But there was a difference between the embedding of national news reports in newspaper space and radio's programming stretched over time. National news, as incorporated in the newspaper mosaic, was an element to be focused according to the reader's choice (Williams 1975). Furthermore, its mere presence beside the dizzying variety of items, some local, some from other localities, some "federal," and some international, precluded a sense of hierarchy, let alone dominance. The spatial arrangement of the newspaper underscored the discrete nature of each item and the possible independence of items and sections from each other.

Radio's time-ordered nature, however, dictated full attention to any item: none could be skipped, and first things would have to be first. The first and last would be remembered best—a key endowment when, unlike the newspaper, one could not return to the fleeting, evanescent words. Thus, when it was the oracular radio talking, it talked exclusively, reflected a broadcaster's hierarchy, and could dominate the attention of one and many simultaneously. People could, and did, listen together; when they were listening, they knew many others, over a vast expanse, were doing precisely the same thing in the same time (Scannell 1996).[4]

Thus, the voice of the nation was heard in the early news bulletins over the air. But in time, the Associated Press (AP) bulletins read by radio announcers expanded into a new kind of endogenous radio news; nonetheless, the heritage of the national focus remained. As the Second World War neared, radio's voices with a persona—Kaltenborn, Murrow, Shirer, Trout, Wells—began expanding the news. And an impending international crisis led to a dramatic reinforcement of its national focus. To be more exact, the developments in Europe and Japan focused attention on America as a nation within a framework of contending nations. Thus, when CBS introduced *World News Roundup*, featuring shortwave pickups from all continents, it gathered a storm of threats to the future of the nation. When the war came, and people needed more trust and assurance than ever, radio became the voice of the nation. Its fears and hopes banked on the words, but no less on the tone, of Morrow in the Blitz, Shirer in the Reichstag.

Their voices conveyed the same kind of unifying assurance that the "fresh, natural and true" voice of singer Vera Lynn gave Englishmen—"irrespective of what it might actually say."[5] Like Vera Lynn, the voices of American newsmen radiated a nationwide message of consolation and hope, then celebration. They were agents of the nation and through serving it became symbols of its unity of purpose, its resolve, and its mood. As the war drew to an end, Lynn's American counterpart, Kate Smith, would demonstrate this same power to solidify and express national unity of purpose by voice. Her dramatic eighteen-hour appeal for contributions to rebuild the nation's military-industrial complex was carried live by radio. Her voice—consoling, exciting, carrying hope—made a whole nation stir and give (Merton 1946).

Television News: The Face of the Nation

In this historical context, television broadcast took shape. The nation's engrossment with national news conveyed by the reigning medium—radio—impacted TV architects' idea of news by the new medium. They tried to emulate radio news' intimacy and sociability, adding a face to it. In fact, the early television news arrangements called for the network to provide the "news sources and voices"; they just "needed help with pictures." They got those by commissioning film producers to take care of the visuals (Barnouw 1990, 101).

This is not to say that news was a primary programming feature in the mind of TV entrepreneurs. Television identified sports and entertainment as what might be called today its "killer applications." But regulatory pressures and public uproar over allegations of corruption surrounding the ostensibly fair play of quizzes made television lords nurture more responsible, public-oriented features. News topped their list.

As television news developed, it became apparent that arranging for the integrated product of news reports, voices, and pictures would be a formidable organizational and financial undertaking. Therefore, only a few bureaus with permanent personnel were maintained beyond headquarters. Inevitably, they were located at the centers that generated "federal" news—such as New York and Washington, D.C.—the White House in particular (Bennet 1996). In images such as Vice President Richard Nixon's Checkers speech, with his wife Pat in the background, or John F. Kennedy with his kids in the Oval Office, the president was treated as personalizing the nation. In this case, personalization may have shaded over to anthropomorphism. "At times," notes Leon Sigal, the press portrays the president as if he were the embodiment of the government, if not of the whole country. It has written of "Reaganomics" as if President Reagan had repealed the laws of supply and demand [and] personally tamed inflation. . . . As people become surrogates for institutions in the minds of journalists, it is reflected in the news-gathering practices and press coverage. (Sigal 1986, 14)

The same logic that led TV producers to focus on the White House guided the dispatching of mobile crews for live broadcasts out of the studio. The momentous operation and great costs involved dictated that this would happen only on rare, great events in the life of the nation, events that would focus identification from coast to coast. Whether McArthur's Chicago parade or the McCarthy hearings, television news covered the national, and the national became news. The concentration of media attention on the powers that be and the rituals they stage made the nation the talk of the nation, at every office water fountain (Dayan and Katz 1992, chaps. 2-3).

Media convey a sense of community, which in the age of the newspapers was reinforced by the social and geographic surroundings. With television, the sense of belonging extended to the more abstract social space beyond the local. If previously the newspapers helped individuals routinize their lives and respond to local challenges, now media expanded the circle of disorder and threat. The increased range of danger that media portended also gave it the added responsibility of allaying fears and ensuring normalcy. This was achieved by routinizing news—which could potentially break any minute—and assigning it to a particular hour, giving a sense that things are not chaotic: that all is under control and within the limits of the manageable. There will be another newscast tomorrow, "same time, same place"; hence, there will be a tomorrow.

The style of news presentation by radio reinforced this sense of order out of chaos, with two variants. In the class-ridden, top-bottom U.K. society, security could be underscored by the formal "anonymous, authoritative (ruling class) voice," indicating an apparatus out there that was in charge and taking care (Williams 1975). This anonymity would be compromised by personal identification of presenters only as a security measure under the wartime threat of invasion and capture of the station. As long as the name was connected to the voice as a PIN to the user name, the content was bona fide and the realm was in the right hands. In British television, the notion of authority speaking to the people (the integrity of its control ensured by the institutions of public broadcast) was reinforced by the corporate nature of the newscast. It was underscored in the early days of television by ensuring that the viewers saw the presenter being handed his text, or arranging these texts at the end of the news bulletin, sometimes with the news writers visible behind him (Scannell in Silverstone 1994, 1-23).

In America, where bureaucracy and government institutions were traditionally suspect, and where accordingly broadcast was private-sector-driven, authority was founded on the personal. There, the same effect was achieved with "less emphasis on a script and more on personal presentation." It assumed the form of "studied informality": the effect of a group of men telling you things they happened to know (Williams 1975). As the Camel News Caravan's John Cameron Swayze had it at the end of his fifteen-minute news broadcasts of the 1950s, "That's the news, folks. Glad we could get together" (Barnouw 1990, 103; cf. Comstock 1991, 86). In America, tremendous importance was assigned to selecting the anchor (Epstein 1973), since on the persona he radiated would lie the trust and security of a nation that trusts God and individuals but not institutions.

A further characteristic of television news that can be seen in the same light is the narrative closure of each item in the parade of stories constituting the news program's lineup. In America, closure and coherence give a sense of controlled development, while elsewhere, such as in Italy, each item can be much more open, giving different perspectives on the issue, even at the price of inconclusiveness (Hallin and Mancini 1984). This would fit the difference in the nature of that which is "national" in either society. While in Italy nationalism unites, leaving ideology divergent, in the United States, a republic of nationalities, shared ideology is what unites. Thus, in the latter, radical ideological differences are threatening, and a coherent shared narrative is necessary for a feeling of cohesion and security (Arieli 1964).

Television News as a Transitional Object

We propose that the television newscast, as shaped by technology and institutions, cultural trends, and social development, transformed news into a "transitional object." Here we are building on Roger Silverstone's general proposition, emerging from critical theories of modernity and psychoanalytical perspectives on identity-building within the social process (Silverstone 1994). Silverstone's approach hinges on Anthony Giddens's argument that trust is a fundamental ingredient of modern people's workaday experience, enabling them to contain existential anxiety and to interact socially and ideologically with others. In modernity, primary personal and communal ties became less significant in shaping identity and security. Mediated portraits of society and culture take their place, shaping what Giddens (1991) calls "distant trust."

According to object relations theory, as expounded by Winnicott (2005), the individual's self-identity is acquired through interaction with the social world, as represented mainly by the media. For the process of integration to succeed, and yield security, there needs to be a fit between distinct visions of the world outside: an internal vision and external indicators of its "real" nature. Becoming a social subject requires a "transitional space" in which the subjective and the real meet; the individual can experiment in adjusting his or her internal expectations to external manifestations of the world in the quest for security. This general process can be symbolized by the child's use of a blanket or doll as real objects distinct from his or her mother, but substituting for her.

Silverstone (1994) proposes using this developmental module of positioning the individual vis-à-vis the real world as a parable for the use of television by grownups, who are bereft of primary social attachments. For them, television is the ultimate transitional object—located in the security of the individual's castle but yielding to signals from a monumental external broadcast antenna, talking about the dangerous world out there with the confidence and assuredness of familiar, engaging faces and voices (Ellis 1982). It represents a delicate balance between alerting people to real dangers lurking at a distance (like storms or terrorists) or imminent in time but, at the same time, signaling that things are under control and manageable. Like yesterday's potential threats, the new ones will ultimately also be contained.

Television's rhetoric, blending stark reality and promised comfort, is achieved not only by this mix of messages but also in the overall texture of television programming, underscoring regularity, authority, and continuity. While Silverstone (1994) refers to news as a mere element of the overall confidence-building nature of television, we think the entire dynamic can be focused on the televised news broadcast. Its regular and central place in the daily schedule, its fixed format, its familiar anchors and reporters and the real-world characters they routinely interact with—even Ahmadinajad becomes domesticated—provide security, even if illusionary. Like the pied piper of Hamlin, the anchor parades the events of the day in a queue and under the control of his rich voice, bland accent, and appealing personality. The same kind of control is experienced in the overall format of the newscast that packages the day into less than a dozen items. Each is formatted in a traditional narrative structure: an introductory exposition, a story, and commonly a personal summation, moving in an hierarchical order from top headlines to human interest. Most significant, perhaps, the news becomes a parade of visual glimpses of harsh reality in the real world, controlled by the trusted processing environment of the studio, with the anchor zooming in and out of them.[6]

In recasting our historical description of the development of television news through Silverstone's (1994) suggestion, the key point is the emergence of the nation as the social entity to which the individual becomes connected via television news. As Giddens (1991) suggests, in the new postwar world, the community can no longer provide security and identity. In a modernizing world generally, and in America's impersonal desert of faceless suburbs and urban jungles in particular, the nation is personalized in the image of a CBS, a Walter Cronkite, and a newscast logo. They provide the sense of belonging and of safe haven, in the abstract, constructed world of the nation, built on distant and impersonal symbols and mechanisms—one's credit card, air ticket, and so on. These symbols exist only in mediation—they are parasocial—and only a simile of real social relations (Horton and Wohl 1956). But according to Silverstone, they become tokens of primary social relations. They themselves serve as the basis for sharedness in real social relations—an icon for your neighbor in the aisle seat of a Delta flight.

True enough, national TV's entire content product can serve as such a prosthetic. Soap operas perhaps are the most obvious ingredient with overall development, side plots, and the regularity of familiar figures fending their way through life, in pace with the overall social clock. But this operates only on a person-to-person level, and moreover, it is packaged and explicitly identified as fantasy. No one can really think of an episode of *Dallas* as reality or a shared meaningful agenda. "No one in real life is really like that," to quote one of Herta Herzog's interviewees (Herzog [1942-1943] 2003). By comparison, national news can stand for reality.

Thus, most generally, there appears to have been a perfect fit between the trio of sociopolitical conditions of a world of contending nations, a society focused economically and politically on its national center, and a particular set of broadcast technologies. Networked radio and television news could reach the nation in its entirety, but not beyond it; its regulatory constraints, economic rationale, and technological capacities all led to a focus on an imagined center of the culture within the real boundaries of the nation—an orientation to the most broadly shared within the national confines.

Historically, the rise of national news in America paralleled the rise of the imperial presidency, from Roosevelt to Reagan. This congruence could have led to a parallel surge of conformism and rebellion. With a single, coherent, forceful picture of the day and the nation, the anchor and the president, the correct ideology and the right necktie width, one could either try to blend in or opt out, discovering how distant one really was from it all. Only a coherent picture of national political culture could give rise to alternative political countercultures: hippie curls and silver-rimmed spectacles rejecting crew-cuts and black, square frames.

The Loss of Teddy Bear: Post-national News

This American story of tight congruence between news programs and the nation would be paralleled, albeit with variations in the nature of broadcast systems, throughout Western nations, then in developing countries (Katz and Wedell 1974). By the fin de siècle, the world and television were in the process of radical change. Globalization from without, and fragmentation from within, shattered the nation as the ultimate unit of social organization. Rather than a cold war between states, the world came to experience a rash of heated conflicts within state boundaries, between factions, cultures, and religions. Economic forces both affected and reflected this new alignment, juxtaposing the global and the local and, in effect, crowding out the national. Media would move to the forefront of this geopolitical and sociocultural pattern. National networks, and particularly their news operations, were pushed to the margins of a new media ecology focused on the parallel poles of the ecumenical and the microparticular (Blondheim 2008).

CNN charted the path toward the global, broadcasting news round the clock, with breaking news taking over the rudimentary schedule as it happened. The audience of these new global players, broadcasting in the lingua franca of the times, was inevitably humankind. The Internet's spread and universality represented another aspect of globalization, but as a supermedium, it also unleashed communicative potentials in the opposite direction. It could maintain the universal, but also the subgroup-specific, and all the way to interpersonal and small group communications, which could now be redefined in entirely new ways such as chat communities.[7] But further, these trends could also liberate people from news altogether. National anchors are no longer an essential part of people's media diet.

Via both these trajectories, the nature of news as a transitional object is being irrevocably transformed. The evening news in its heyday had achieved a delicate balance between threat and trust. It not only exposed the drama and danger of events, with all the potential anxiety they arouse, but also supplied a remedy: the sense of closure and control provided by the news format and its regularity, the sheltered viewing experience, the sense of personal rapport with anchors and familiar correspondents (with all their spontaneity and reserve). These latter features had managed to balance interest and anxiety; they bred trust and a sense of credibility, competence, control, and comfort. Speculation was compensated for by certainty, the uniqueness of events by the fixity of interpretative patterns. We call this *editing*—the icon of the continuous fine-tuning of the open and the closed.

Like any genre that is recognizable only as it is being displaced, the contemporary news environment allows us to characterize classic television news and make out its unique nature. Only in hindsight can we appreciate its remarkable social and psychological endowment and its social functions.

The new news environment is crushing the nature of network news as a transitional object, on all the levels that had sustained it. Consider "place" as a place to begin: the TV set has migrated from the living room to bedrooms (Freidson 1953; Livingstone 2007), while the news is migrating from television to the office PC and to the cell phone everywhere. This reshuffle pulled the rug from under a significant element of the interface between the security and normalcy of the living room and the dangerous world outside (Ellis 2000; Gerbner et al. 1979). On the time dimension, TV news has migrated from the evening newscast to TV news magazines and variety shows, merging the news with other aspects of the world—disruptive and threatening to the individual. It would go all the way to quasi-pornographic, prurient curiosity, not exactly the sanctified context of an educated citizenry.

Then, with the proliferation of rapid satellite transmission and mobile shooting crews—ultimately media-distributed camcorders—news can come from anywhere, anytime, and be framed on the fly by anyone, without regard to conventional news and editorial standards. This can signal to viewers that anything can be expected to happen, anytime: preplanned events no longer constitute landmarks in the democratic process (note the coverage of demonstrations stealing the show from conventions, or at least sharing a split-screen with them [Danner 2000]). In fact, breaking news often steals the show from the news programs themselves. The slow, orderly pace of the latter simply cannot keep up with the urgency now given by newsrooms to world and local events exploding on viewers in real time (Katz and Liebes 2007).

The mode of news presentation itself underscores these developments. What had previously signaled familiarity and order—professional deliberation, advance preparation, and tight packaging—is giving way to spontaneous improvisation. News stories are now navigated while developing, providing no clear picture of the details and conclusion of the story, let alone its moral. Most news is now live, its details being brought breathlessly as they occur. The back stage of news gathering now emerges with the pathetically bewildered façade of the anchor behind an orderly desk.

Even the news net, which had traditionally fed the front of the news operation, is showing signs of breakdown: amateur reporters, passers-by with cameras and 3G cell phones, can hijack the news reporting process from the preconceived spread of the newsgathering apparatus. Candid camera—the reality of human interest vignettes—is crowding traditional reportage off the screen. Just as the former well-planned news net focused on the national—central places, institutions, people—the new virtual (inter)net is everywhere, diffusing the focus on the national. We are moving from General Schwartzkopf's daily press conference with the most manipulatively prepared visuals of a war that perhaps never happened (Gerbner 1992; Baudrillard 1991) to embedded correspondents a decade later, giving moment-by-moment portraits of genuinely authentic fragments that do not cohere, with the reporter as frontispiece rather than backstage collator and analyst (Katz 1992).

In between, nothing can underscore the collapse of news as a buffer of confidence and order better than television's performance on September 11, 2001. Suddenly, the networks and CNN, just like the members of their audience, were taken by terrorized shock and awe. All were mesmerized by the larger-than-life images. Anchors and tavern sitters were simultaneously and spontaneously saying, "Oh my God," as the drama unfolded. With government in hiding, the awestruck public turned to the old, trusted, news networks only to find them as shocked, if not as speechless, as they. Viewers and broadcasters had to wait for hours for the initial dust to clear, then days and months for the mystery of "who did it" and "why" to be properly addressed (Blondheim and Liebes 2002, 2003). But initially, rather than order, security, structure, context, and meaning, what live television yielded was further bewilderment. Control was no longer there: the tube of plenty went empty.

With the model of classical television bowing out, perhaps even the unifying Tower of Babel yielding once again to multilingual breakdown, the quest for order, and for a source of ontological security, only intensifies. We are beyond our mandate here, separated by a new media age from the classical age of television.

Understandably, with no trust, no meaning, no order, no control, and no uses and gratifications, vulnerable individuals in a threatening world seem to be zooming out, rather than tuning in, to the dated stories of national televised news. On the supply side, as Paddy Scannell (1996) has suggested, classical TV news had constructed the viewer as a member of the polity, a citizen. By contrast, the new TV—particularly "on-demand"—is constructing the viewer as a private consumer while undermining television's public role.

On the level of belonging, once the nation lost its hold, the trajectory of withdrawal seems to be taking us even further away—as the units of social affiliations shrink, and the virtual social affiliations remain marginal, leaving people to themselves, to "bowling alone". People are at least as separated as they are united by the unbinding media of sites, chats, instant messaging, and microblogging. Save for vestiges of the public broadcasting tradition, television is responding to the chaos out there by offering an escapist paradise in the form of a narcissist bubble connecting the viewer to no one but himself or herself. It features self-improvement and makeover—fitness, spiritual salvation, better looks, better cooking, and so on. Television no longer reassures viewers by connecting them to a surmountable world out there but carries them on a loop from themselves to themselves.

The news experience seems to be following this pattern. The constant breathless bombardment of news fragments that do not cohere and make no sense represents a breakdown of the illusion of a safe and manageable world outside. The essence of classic television news—the routinization of the unexpected, the "excitement governed by order," works no longer (Tuchman 1973). News knowledge as provided by classic television has been replaced by scattered news bites, served and corrected on the fly, not necessarily related to anything meaningful outside. In other words, with the end of television, we may be experiencing the end of news.

Notes

1. Quoted in the *Philadelphia Dollar Newspaper*, June 17, 1846.

2. The war could also be seen as a reaction to the process of nationalization. After all, according to Lewis Mumford, there was a "paradox of communication"—the greater the contact between social elements, the greater the friction. Close communications may underscore difference, not commonality. Thus, a civil war would break out once dramatic technological and organizational steps had been taken toward national unity (Mumford 1963, 239-41; Blondheim 2004).

3. Only with the turn of the century would newspapers targeting mass and highly heterogeneous urban markets, such as Hearst's *New York Journal* and Pulitzer's *New York World*, assume a truly national outlook.

4. Most important, when radio talked one listened, and the auditory experience is significantly different from the visual. Sound penetrates, brings the external stimulus into the individual for processing (symbolically, but also as a physical reality). This is in sharp contrast to both newspaper and television, although the visuality of either is quite different. The visual task of reading requires deciphering and reintegrating the visual cues, creating a barrier of active cognitive work between the message and the receiver. In television, reception is as effortless as in radio, but rather than absorbing the message within, viewers are drawn to the visual stimulus outside them. They export themselves, so to speak, to the visual source (Dresner 2005; Halberstam 2000).

5. In 1941, the BBC introduced her in a program titled "a letter from home in words and music" to the troops fighting for the nation in Europe. Although Lynn had used other people's words and had not gone through the experiences she was describing, her power lay in her capacity to convey sincerity (Scannell 1996, 66-67).

6. According to Fiske, news is characterized by "strategies of containment" that attempt to control "reality." It plays out as a "constant struggle between these strategies and the disruptive forces that are characteristic of both 'the reality' that news refers to and the social differences amongst its various audiences." Accordingly, in his view, "Controlling anarchy works through the processes of selection and categorization (paradigmatically) and combination and narrativization (syntagmatically)" (Fiske 1987, 282-83).

7. These trends provide an old-new focus on local news, on network TV and on news addressed to particular nonlocal groups on cyberspace.

References

Arieli, Yehoshua. 1964. *Individualism and nationalism in American ideology*. Cambridge, MA: Harvard University Press.

Barnouw, Erik. 1966. *A tower in Babel: A history of broadcasting in the United States to 1933*. New York: Oxford University Press.

———. 1990. *Tube of plenty: The evolution of American television*. Oxford, UK: Oxford University Press.

Baudrillard, Jean. 1991. *La Guerre du Golfe n' a pas eu Lieu*. Paris: Galilée.

Bennet, Lance. 1996. An introduction to journalism norms and representations of politics. *Political Communication* 13:373-84.

Blondheim, Menahem. 1994. *News over the wires: The telegraph and the flow of public information in America, 1844-1897*. Cambridge, MA: Harvard University Press.

———. 2004. "Slender bridges" of misunderstanding: The social legacy of transatlantic cables. In *Atlantic communications: Political, social and cultural perspectives on media technology in American and German history*, ed. Norbert Finzsch and Ursula Lehmkuhl, 153-70. Oxford, UK: Berg.

———. 2008. Narrating the history of media technologies: Prospects and pitfalls. In *Narrating media history*, ed. Michael Bailey. London: Routledge.

Blondheim, Menahem, and Tamar Liebes. 2002. Live television's disaster marathon of September 11 and its subversive potential. *Prometheus* 20 (3): 271-76.

———. 2003. From disaster marathon to media event: Live television's performance on September 11, 2001 and September 11, 2002. In *Crisis communications: Lessons from September 11*, ed. A. Michael Noll, 185-98. Lanham, MD: Rowman & Littlefield.

Comstock, George. 1991. *Television in America*. Newbury Park, CA: Sage.

Danner, Mark. 2000. The shame of political TV. *New York Review of Books*, September 21.

Dayan, Daniel, and Elihu Katz. 1992. *Media events: The live broadcasting of history*. Cambridge, MA: Harvard University Press.

Deutsch, Karl W. 1953. *Nationalism and social communication*. New York: Wiley.

Dresner, Eli. 2005. The topology of auditory and visual perception, linguistic communication, and interactive written discourse. *Language@Internet* 2: 1-32.

Ellis, John. 1982. *Visible fictions: Cinema, television, video*. London: Routledge.

———. 2000. *Seeing things: Television in the age of uncertainty*. London: I. B. Tauris.

Epstein, Edward Jay. 1973. *News from nowhere*. New York: Random House.

Fiske, John. 1987. News reading, news readers. Chap. 15 of *Television culture*, 181-308. London: Methuen.

Freidson, Eliot. 1953. The relation of the social situation of contact to the media in mass communication. *Public Opinion Quarterly* 17 (2): 230-38.

Gerbner, George. 1992. *The triumph of the image: The media war in the Persian Gulf–A global perspective*. Boulder, CO: Westview.

Gerbner, George, Larry Gross, Nancy Signorielli, Michael Morgan, and Marilyn Jackson-Beeck. 1979. The demonstration of power. *Journal of Communication* 29:177-96.

Giddens, A. 1984. *The constitution of society*. Cambridge, UK: Polity.

———. 1991. *Modernity and self-identity: Self and society in the late modern age*. Cambridge, UK: Polity.

Halberstam, David. 2000. *The powers that be*. Urbana: University of Illinois Press.

Hallin, Daniel C. and Paolo Mancini. 1984. Speaking on the president: Political structure in American and Italian news. *Theory & Society* 13:829-50.

Herzog, Herta. [1942-1943] 2003. On borrowed experience. In *Canonic texts in media research*, ed. Elihu Katz, Tamar Liebes, and John Peters. Cambridge, UK: Polity.

Horton, D., and R. R. Wohl. 1956. Mass communication and para-social interaction. *Psychiatry* 19:215-29.

A Journalist [Isaac C. Pray]. 1855. *Memoirs of James Gordon Bennett and his times*. New York: Stringer and Townsend.

John, Ricard R. 1995. *Spreading the news: The American postal system from Franklin to Morse*. Cambridge, MA: Harvard University Press.

Katz, Elihu. 1992. The end of journalism? Notes on watching the war. *Journal of Communication* 42:3.

Katz, Eihu, and Tamar Liebes. 2007. "No more peace!" How disaster, terror and war upstaged media events. *International Journal of Communication* 1: 157-166.

Katz, Elihu, and E. G. Wedell. 1974. *Broadcasting in the third world*. Cambridge, MA: Harvard University Press.

Kielbowicz, Richard B. 1989. *News in the mail: The press, post office, and public, 1700-1860s*. New York: Greenwood.

Livingstone, Sonia. 2007. From family television to bedroom culture: Young people's media at home. In *Media studies: Key issues and debates*, ed. E. Devereux, 302-21. Thousand Oaks, CA: Sage.

Merton, Robert K. 1946. *Mass persuasion*. New York: Harper & Row.

Mumford, Lewis. 1963. *Techniques and civilization*. New York: Harcourt, Brace and World.

Scannell, Paddy. 1996. *Radio, television and modern life: A phenomenological approach*. Oxford, UK: Blackwell.

Schudson, Michael. 1995. *The power of news*. Cambridge, MA: Harvard University Press.

Sigal, Leon. 1986. Who? Sources that make the news. In *Reading the news*, ed. R. K. Manoff and M. Schudson. New York: Pantheon Books.

Silverstone, Roger. 1994. Television, ontology and the transitional object. Chap. 1 in *Television and everyday life*, 1-23. London: Routledge.

Tuchman, Gay. 1973. Making news by doing work: Routinizing the unexpected. *American Journal of Sociology* 79 (1): 110-31.

White, Theodore H. 1961. *The making of the president, 1960*. New York: Atheneum House.

Wiebe, Robert H. 1967. *The search for order, 1877-1920*. New York: Hill & Wang.

Williams, Raymond. 1975. *Television: Technology and cultural form*. New York: Schocken.

Winnicott, Donald W. 2005. *Playing and reality*. London: Routledge.

End of Television and Foreign Policy

By
MONROE E. PRICE

The transformation of television has altered the capacity of the state to control the agenda for making war, convening peace, and otherwise exercising its foreign policy options. In the age of the state gatekeeper, there was at least the illusion (and often the reality) that the government could substantially control the flow of images within its borders. With transformations in television systems, national systems of broadcast regulation have declined, replaced by transnational flows of information where local gatekeepers are not so salient. The rise of satellites with regional footprints and the spread of the Internet give governments the ability to reach over the heads of the state and speak directly to populations. Both receiving and sending states will have foreign policies about the meaning of the right to receive and impart information and the extent to which satellite signals can be regulated or channeled.

Keywords: diplomacy; public diplomacy; CNN effect; international broadcasting; free flow of information

Should a specific kind of foreign policy be (more or less) identified with the classic era in broadcast television? If such a media-influenced foreign policy existed, has its content and approach been modified or altered because of transformations in communications technologies and distribution systems? Two questions when thinking about foreign policy and the media are (1) Do modern technological developments cause foreign policy to be

Monroe E. Price is director of the Center for Global Communication Studies (CGCS) at the Annenberg School for Communication, University of Pennsylvania; and a professor of law at the Benjamin N. Cardozo School of Law at Yeshiva University. He also serves as director of the Stanhope Centre for Communications Policy Research in London and chair of the Center for Media and Communication Studies at the Central European University in Budapest. He served as dean of Cardozo School of Law from 1982 to 1991. Among his many books are Media and Sovereignty: The Global Information Revolution and Its Challenge to State Power *(MIT Press 2002);* Television, the Public Sphere and National Identity *(Oxford University Press 1995); and a treatise on cable television.*

DOI: 10.1177/0002716209338701

increasingly affected by media concerns? and (2) Is there what might be called a foreign policy of media structures, namely, an interest by one state (or the international community) in the mode by which media are developed through an interdependent set of nations? The answer to both questions is yes, and the issues are interconnected.

Think of the cold war—or elements of it—mapped against the 1950s and 1960s structure of radio and television broadcasting. A claim might be that the cold war was only possible in a period of (almost) hermetically sealed borders with strong and centralized spheres of influence. In this telling, the effectiveness of the Berlin Wall depended on the very conditions that yielded to the increased information permeability of borders by media, the images of freedom projected through transborder media. International broadcasting (the Voice of America, Radio Free Europe/Radio Liberty, and the BBC World Service among others), relying on short-wave facilities, helped to crack information monopolies, but the dam broke with the rise of satellite and the increase in spillover broadcasts from neighboring states. In parallel, one might argue, the system of scarce broadcasting with heavy licensing or state-connected public broadcasting systems in Western Europe and the United States allowed for the reinforcement of a national consensus against the Soviet threat.

A second, more general, claim, easier to substantiate, would be that any intelligent foreign policy involved in relations with publics abroad (and maintaining support at home) would have a necessary relationship with changing structures of the media (for a general introduction, see Nye 2004). National identities—and interactions between states—are consequences, in part, of media and communications systems. The concept of an effective national identity, associated with a state, presupposes a kind of information system that produces it. That information system may have, as part of its composition, narratives about the place of the state in the world. As information systems alter, indeed alter substantially, it might be assumed that there are knock-on effects for national identities and for the states with which such identities are politically central. Television is only a small part of an information system or set of systems that are used to produce national identities. But even so, reorganizations in the mode of making, distributing, and controlling television images yield consequences for those fashioning attitudes toward the greater world.

To understand how the "end of television" in its classic sense may have implications for diplomacy and public diplomacy, a few initial words about these terms are in order. The historic element of foreign policy is the diplomatic interaction between officials of two or more states; "public diplomacy" seeks to bypass the state and reach directly to audiences. How the balance between the two has changed with altered television technology is implicated in the "CNN effect." The term was first used during the Gulf War of 1990. With the rise of CNN and its twenty-four-hour style of reporting, it was argued, leaders learned more from television than from their own officials about what was going on in the battlefield (and in the diplomatic sphere). Leaders could conduct diplomacy in real time, and in the fishbowl of a global news service, they could directly reach past official and autocratic gatekeepers to broad civil publics. Steven Livingston (1997) has listed three potential shifts because of this phenomenon: media as (1) an enhanced agenda setter (where the media trump the agenda-setting effort of the government), (2) an impediment to policy making (where the existence of the media effect narrows or forecloses options open to the government), and (3) an accelerant to policy decision making (where the impact of media coverage forces the government to take an action it might otherwise not have been inclined to).

The case most often cited for the "CNN effect" relates to events in 1992 to 1993 in Somalia. Graphic pictures of starving children led to the humanitarian effort of President George H. W. Bush, who sent in American military personnel; almost a year later, similarly graphic pictures of a gang desecrating the body of an American and dragging it through the streets led President Bill Clinton to announce that the United States would be leaving Somalia. Television brought the Americans in, and television forced the Americans out.

There has been much controversy over the extent of the CNN effect and its transformation of the diplomatic sphere. Several conclusions can be drawn. First, most of those who seek to shape multiple foreign policies or react to them have internalized the phenomenon of global news services and have adjusted their behavior. What was most striking about the supposed impact of media in the early 1990s was the novelty of the new opportunities it presented. Like militaries seeking to cope with new weaponry, diplomats had to adjust to an altered media world. Once they had done so, once they could more consciously calibrate the consequence of various appearances on global news services, the transformative impact of the new technology was lessened. Second, the impact of the changes have now extended far beyond CNN: Al-Jazeera and multiple other broadcasters now compete for the attention of international publics, with the resulting impact that this reach could have on foreign policy. While the internalization of the changed media environment works toward reducing the CNN effect, the continued expansion of global broadcasters works toward increasing it.

The CNN phenomenon tended to locate the broadcaster as the independent variable and the leaders, governments, and publics as the dependent variables. We now see a broader interplay between leaders, governments, and publics than was identified in connection with the CNN effect, but the examination of a foreign policy of the media sphere demonstrates how almost all aspects are interdependent. James Hoge (1994) has argued that the impact of the media is greatest during a humanitarian crisis, when domestic communities mobilize to press their officials to take action. Hoge sees a special impact as well where a broadcast shows, to a government's domestic audience, a sustained set of images that, through its tragic and dramatic force, undermines the narrative of success that officials have proclaimed. Here such a broadcast narrative can impede or accelerate government action or alter the agenda. The issue can be put differently. The ubiquity of media and their capacity to provide unfiltered access to harsh global events increases emotional impact (and an emotional impact not constructed or controlled by the government or its gatekeepers). This is not to say that foreign policy has always been based entirely on reason and conducted in an environment wholly immunized from public opinion. But at certain times, and subject to the varying skills of international players, media can foreshorten time for reflection and raise spectacularly the way the stakes are perceived and governments are measured.

As significant, perhaps, is the impact that changed broadcasting technology and structure have had on public diplomacy. There are elements of the conduct of foreign policy where public opinion plays little if any role. But the proportion of foreign policy initiatives that involve influencing the public (to influence leaders) seems to have increased. There is a new imperative for reaching out to publics, changing hearts and minds, and engaging in soft power. New technologies enable and, as a result of competition, virtually require that states have a strategy to deal with foreign audiences (Dizard 2004).

For decades, states have invested in persistent and large-scale "international broadcasting" efforts to subsidize radio (and later television) that would alter the flow of ideas in a target society. The Voice of America and Deutsche Welle emerged during World War II; Radio Free Europe/Radio Liberty and the BBC World Service were established during the cold war. But the process of developing government-subsidized efforts for radio and television that reach a global audience has altered greatly with technological and political change.

The strongest of these international services, like the U.S.-funded Voice of America, Radio Free Europe/Radio Liberty (established as "surrogate radios" in the cold war, ostensibly to provide information-deprived populations with access to news and information about their own society), and the BBC World Service, financed by the United Kingdom's Foreign and Commonwealth Office, had extensive ambitions that were tied to foreign policy goals (sometimes only the goal of greater access to information, but sometimes more). In the early-twenty-first century, the U.S. foreign policy question was which of these services to maintain and at what level or, put differently, whether, given scarce resources, international broadcasting efforts to reach, inform, and persuade should be redirected from the former Soviet Union toward target publics elsewhere, such as in the Middle East.

Subsidy on a large scale is used to determine what languages, what technologies, and what groups to persuade. In the 1990s, Serbia invested in a satellite service to reach its diaspora and gain moral and financial support for its position; Hungary, after its transition, created Duna TV to reach ethnic Hungarians in Transylvania (Romania). In 1996, Qatar, in a novel use of funds, established Al-Jazeera and altered the media face of the Middle East. Other governments in the region, including Saudi Arabia, saw to it that their satellite presence was bolstered. Western governments, seeking to reach the "hearts and minds" of Arabic youth across borders, have responded in kind: the BBC, France 24, Deutsche Welle, and Russia TV today have launched or expanded their Arabic-language television offerings; and the United States limps along with al Hurra, its entry into the competition among Arabic satellite channels for the privilege of defining "news" and presenting a stronger image of the United States (Heil 2007). Even independent satellite services are tied to government-related interests. Beginning with the post-Soviet transition, Western nations have subsidized (or invested in) the development of an indigenous media in transitioning societies as part of the process of democratization. Without being too reductionist, the United States has emphasized the development of "free and independent media" as an integral part of this process, while the United Kingdom has preferred to focus on strengthening public service broadcasters. In some transitional contexts, this odd Great Powers contestation has led to temporary stalemates. It is not clear that there is a formula that works.

Shifts in broadcasting technologies and distribution systems have had limited impact on these elements of foreign policy, the foreign policy of broadcasting structures, and the transformations of international broadcasting. Undoubtedly, institutions like the BBC World Service and the Voice of America will change substantially because of the Internet and satellite, but the existing relationships, the confidence in the existing method of reaching audiences, and institutional inertia have meant less change than might have been expected. For some target societies, the "end of TV" in the classic sense of broadcasting has not yet occurred.

Yet another way to look at the structure of broadcasting and foreign policy is through the lens of the global debate over information flows and development. The 1970s and 1980s involved competing policies (with the United States often in opposition to many other states) over the proper information system to support political, economic, and social growth. Notions of "modernization" (Lerner 1958; McClelland 1961; Rogers 1962; Schramm 1964) competed as a basis for policy debates with ideas of eliminating "dependence" (emphasizing decolonialization and liberation) (Baran 1957; Dos Santos 1970; Frank 1969; Galtung 1971). Anthony Giddens (1990) argued for the important role that media culture plays in the development of world markets, the cohesion of the nation-state, the perception of military blocs, and the capacity to industrialize.

In this global debate, "the free flow of information" became an aspect of foreign policy for some countries in the West, particularly the United States. As Ulla Carlsson (2003) has written, the concept of the free flow of information captured U.S. attitudes after World War II. Under the U.S. position, national frontiers should not be allowed to hinder the flow of information between countries. Prior to World War II, the media and entertainment corporations in the United States had only limited access to media markets in the extensive territories under the control of colonial powers such as Great Britain. After the war, "The U.S. saw before them a world without colonial ties, a world that lay open for an expansive economy in the U.S. The information sector was a key factor in paving the way for economic expansion" (p. 6).

In the 1970s, advocates of "free flow" found increasing resistance at UNESCO and the United Nations Assembly, especially from nonaligned and developing countries that had a very different set of starting points in terms of shaping their own national identities in the fresh era of independence. A report from a UN symposium at the time noted,

> Since information in the world shows a disequilibrium favouring some and ignoring others, it is the duty of non-aligned countries and other developing countries to change this situation and obtain the de-colonization of information and initiate a new international order in information. (Carlsson 2003, 11)

All of this set the stage for the appointment of the International Commission for the Study of Communication Problems, known as the MacBride Commission, following the 1976 UNESCO General Conference. It is impossible to summarize adequately the findings and the consequent debate over the MacBride Commission, but it encapsulated a "foreign policy" of media structuring. For the commission, Cees Hamelink defined a new international information order as an international exchange of information in which states develop their cultural system in an autonomous way, have sovereign control of resources, and fully and effectively participate as independent members of the international community (Hamelink 1979). The MacBride Commission and the proceedings following its submission became a lightning rod for voices in the United States, Great Britain, and elsewhere that sought to implement global processes that reflected the principles of free flow of information. So sharp was the discord over these questions, so committed was U.S. foreign policy, that the government withdrew from UNESCO, not returning for nineteen years until 2003.

The end of TV is marked by the decline of state control over information space. As that occurs, voluntary negotiations between states (or between states and media conglomerates) concerning the flow of certain categories of information (for example, hate speech, pornography, and information related to national security) increase—as do new means for states to reinstate their authority. Historically, states have had a tacit agreement that the media of one state would not persistently permeate the boundaries of another. The International Telecommunication Union was, in a sense, created to help police the allocation of spectrum so that, for the most part, radio (and then television) signals would be contained within national boundaries. Short-wave efforts designed at first to reach subjects around a colonial world were an exception to this general rule. While there were accepted and less accepted violations of the general principle, it was only with the arrival of the satellite (and to a lesser extent cable) that the general understanding disintegrated. Even then, the UN and other organizations attempted to transfer to the satellite regime the state-protective elements of terrestrial radio and television.

The 1982 UN resolution concerning direct television broadcasting sought to encourage consultation between broadcasting states and receiving states (UN General Assembly 1982). The Television without Frontiers Directive of 1989 (and the subsequent revisions of 1997 and 2007), governing members of the European Union, is an example of a more successful operative effort to establish a regime that mediates information crossing the relevant boundaries. Article 22 requires bilateral consultations where a member state hosts programs that significantly impair the moral development of children in a receiving member state, thus imposing a limit (though only an extremely narrow one) on the circumstances in which one member state can allow signals to flow, without objection, into the territory of another (Craufurd Smith 1997).

In addition to bilateral and multilateral negotiations between states, other unofficial (and often much less transparent) forms of negotiation between states and between states and broadcasting entities or distributors limit or affect the impact of transborder information flow.

This hidden "foreign policy" of the media reflects changes in media technologies. New competitors are much more dependent on agreements with states or with gatekeeper broadcast entities within states than is realized. Domestic structures are the pillars upon which global media systems are built. The television signals of CNN or BBC do not simply waft through the air, encountering no controllable gatekeeper before they invade the collective local consciousness. Today, to understand the actions of News Corporation or MTV, or the competition between CNN and BBC World, we must look at the domestic structures in the receiving countries, structures upon which dependence often still exists. We must see how shifts in those pillars are used to temper the entry of the global players. Indeed, "law," in the sense of officially developed norms that control behavior, may be less often the result of unilaterally declared statute or regulation than of negotiation.

These negotiations take place in the midst of two transitions: the transformation of scope and scale among the producers of channel services and programming who seek to distribute signals transnationally and the transformation of the structure of receiving mechanisms that exist as gatekeepers and filters within every country. For music video channels to gain entry into certain markets, or to gain shelf space on cable or in a bouquet of channels carried by a direct-to-home provider, the channel must negotiate the program content with the provider. There is usually no explicit legal standard at the base of such negotiations: channels may promise that they will confine themselves to entertainment and not carry news, not as a result of formal law but as an informal condition for entry. Another example is to be found in negotiations between international broadcasters and local transmission facilities. Formal or informal arrangements between states and large-scale international news organizations will become more frequent, implicating contractual ties with governments to operate terrestrial transmitters, to broadcast via the national system, or merely to gather information. Increasingly, states seek to regulate who has access to transponders or uplink facilities.

An increasing number of such negotiations protects information space. Some of the most well-known examples are between the receiving state and the large multinational private broadcasting firms. In 1995, India agreed, in an arrangement that soon fell apart, to permit CNN to broadcast on a favored Doordarshan frequency if CNN agreed that the Indian broadcasting host would provide most of the news about its own domestic affairs (Page and Crawley 2001). China agreed to more extensive entry for Star-TV but, in apparent exchange, Star-TV's parent, News Corporation, agreed that the BBC would not be carried. It is extremely likely that MTV, the popular global music television service, negotiates to ensure that it is cognizant of and, to the necessary extent, abides by local custom and preference in its choice of music, music videos, and hosts. More confident post-Soviet Republics negotiated with Russia to admit Russian-language programming under approved circumstances. Similarly, a meeting of information ministers of the Gulf Cooperation Council (GCC) served, even before the war in Afghanistan, as the arena to mediate disputes between Qatar, the home of outspoken satellite broadcaster Al-Jazeera, and the government of Bahrain, which considered Al-Jazeera's broadcasts deleterious and violative of the public order (BBC 1999).

Other efforts have focused not on the broadcaster itself but on the distribution channel. One example is the story of MED-TV, the satellite service established in 1994 in the United Kingdom, which targeted Kurdish populations worldwide but particularly in Turkey, Iran, and Iraq. Turkey contended that MED-TV was a "political organization" that supported the PKK, widely characterized as a terrorist organization, and attempted to suppress MED-TV unilaterally by policing the purchase and mounting of satellite dishes within Turkey's borders. Failing at this, Turkey was required to employ a bilateral strategy to stifle the MED-TV channel: officials mounted a campaign to pressure the British government to withdraw MED-TV's license and sought, in other European capitals, to deny MED-TV leasing rights on government-controlled transponders on Eutelsat.

International human rights norms, such as Article 19 of the Universal Declaration of Human Rights, which outlines the right to receive and impart information, can be said to be part of an international "foreign policy" of media structures. States have used Article 19 to press for a greater range of domestic voices, especially in societies that are thought to be authoritarian or oppressive of domestic minorities. The general proscription against hate speech and bilateral agreements to adjust media use in the interest of peace is another example. In the ill-fated Oslo Accords, part of the Middle East Peace Process, Israel and the Palestinian Authority mutually sought a media sphere that was more conducive to sustained amity. Increasingly, regional efforts, such as the Arab Satellite Broadcasting Charter adopted in February 2008, try (often in vain) to control the implications of new technologies for multilateral relations. The power of images will create novel ways, in the future, for foreign policy goals and the uses of media to intertwine.

Conclusion

From the perspective of foreign policies, there are implications of transformations in television systems. The major change is the seeming decline of national systems of broadcast regulation and the rise of transnational flows of information where local gatekeepers are not so salient. In the age of the state gatekeeper, there was at least the illusion (and often more) that the government could substantially control the flow of images within its borders. No foreign government's policy could reach local audiences in a massive and effective way. States could play with this system around the edges, through international broadcasting, cultural exchanges, and other devices. But the system was maintained, almost by common understanding among the powers.

The rise of satellites with regional footprints, the forest of dishes in major cities where diasporic groups live, and the spread of the Internet and Internet cafes give governments the ability, if they are clever enough (which few may actually be), to reach over the heads of the state and speak directly to populations. This process may have limits that are not yet well understood, as states intent on control regulate the use of dishes or the carrying of signals on transponders. States will have foreign policies about the meaning of the right to receive and impart information and the extent to which satellite signals can be regulated or channeled.

Finally, the transformation of television has—at least to the extent the CNN effect is alive—altered the capacity of the state to control the agenda for making war, convening peace, and otherwise exercising its foreign policy options. As broadcasters become more abundant, more diverse, and more partisan, the locus and substance of debate on global issues shifts. Oddly, states may opt for greater commercialization to counter this danger of lack of control or seek other means to restore systems to the status quo ante.

References

Baran, Paul A. 1957. *The political economy of growth*. New York: Monthly Review Press.

BBC Summary of World Broadcasts. 1999. GCC information ministers voice concern at activities of Al-Jazeera TV. October 15. *Al-Ra'y*, Amman [in Arabic], October 10, 1999. [Al-Jazeera has also generated complaints from Algerian, Moroccan, Saudi Arabian, Kuwaiti, and Egyptian governments.]

Carlsson, Ulla. 2003. The rise and fall of NWICO—And then? Paper presented at EURICOM Colloquium on Information Society: Visions and Governance. http://www.bfsf.it/wsis/cosa%20dietro%20al%20 nuovo%200rdine.pdf.

Craufurd Smith, Rachel. 1997. *Broadcasting law and fundamental rights*. Oxford, UK: Clarendon.

Dizard, W., Jr. 2004. *Inventing public diplomacy: The story of the U.S. Information Agency*. Boulder, CO: Lynne Rienner.

Dos Santos, Theotonio. 1970. The structure of dependence. *American Economic Review* 60 (2): 231-36.

Frank, Andre G. 1969. *Capitalism and underdevelopment in Latin America*. New York: Monthly Review Press.

Galtung, Johan. 1971. *Members of two worlds; a development study of three villages in western Sicily*. New York: Columbia University Press.

Giddens, Anthony. 1990. *The consequences of modernity*. Cambridge, UK: Polity.

Hamelink, C. 1979. *The new international economic order and the new international information order*. Mauve Paper 34. Paris: UNESCO, International Commission for the Study of Communication Problems.

Heil, Alan L., Jr. 2007. Rate of Arabic language TV start-ups shows no sign of abating. *Arab Media and Society*. http://www.arabmediasociety.com/?article=180.

Hoge, James F., Jr. 1994. Media pervasiveness. *Foreign Affairs* 73 (4): 136-44.

Lerner, Daniel. 1958. *The passing of traditional society: Modernizing the Middle East*. New York: Free Press.

Livingston, Steven. 1997. Beyond the "CNN effect": The media-foreign policy dynamic. In *Politics and the press: The news media and their influences*, ed. P. Norris, 291-318. Boulder, CO: Lynne Rienner.

McClelland, David. 1961. *The achieving society*. Princeton, NJ: Van Nostrand.

Nye, Joseph S. 2004. *Soft power: The means to success in world politics*. New York: Public Affairs.

Page, David, and William Crawley. 2001. *Satellites over South Asia: Broadcasting, culture, and the public interest*. New Delhi, India: Sage.

Rogers, Everett M. 1962. *Diffusion of innovations*. New York: Free Press.

Schramm, Wilber. 1964. *Mass media and national development*. Stanford, CA: Stanford University.

UN General Assembly Resolution. 1982. Principles governing the use by states of artificial earth satellites for international direct television broadcasting. A/RES/37/92. Adopted at 100th plenary meeting, December 10. http://www.un.org/documents/ga/res/37/a37r092.htm.

Television and the Transformation of Sport

By
GARRY WHANNEL

Sport played a significant part in the growth of television, especially during its emergence as a dominant global medium between 1960 and 1980. In turn, television, together with commercial sponsorship, transformed sport, bringing it significant new income and prompting changes in rules, presentation, and cultural form. Increasingly, from the 1970s, it was not the regular weekly sport that commanded the largest audiences but, rather, the occasional major events, such as the Olympic Games and football's World Cup. In the past two decades, deregulation and digitalization have expanded the number of channels, but this fragmentation, combined with the growth of the Internet, has meant that the era in which shared domestic leisure was dominated by viewing of the major channels is closing. Yet, sport provides an exception, an instance when around the world millions share a live and unpredictable viewing experience.

Keywords: sport; Olympic Games; football; mega-events

If we live in an era of fragmentation, time shift, and video-on-demand in which television viewing has ceased to be a shared collective and communal experience, major televised sporting events are the exception. These events continue to have a compelling audience appeal, and technological innovation has allowed sports broadcasting itself to undergo a continual renewal of its appeal. Indeed, the televisual experience of live sport is, for many, superior to the experience obtained by viewing in person. There is, however, a paradox between television's constant technological recomposition of sport

Garry Whannel is a professor of media cultures at the University of Bedfordshire in the United Kingdom. He has been writing on media and sport for thirty years, and his published work includes Culture, Politics and Sport *(Routledge 2008),* Media Sport Stars, Masculinities and Moralities *(Routledge 2001),* Fields in Vision *(Routledge 1992), and* Blowing the Whistle *(Pluto 1983). His current research interests include celebrity culture and the vortextuality process, journalism, politics and the Olympic Games, the growth of commercial sponsorship, and the roots of political humor.*

DOI: 10.1177/0002716209339144

and the liveness and uncertainty of the protelevisual event. On one hand, television demonstrates its absolute mastery of the image in increasingly elaborate ways, while, on the other, it trades on the total unpredictability that only sport can offer. Major sport events are media events and not just television events. Televised around the world, they can dominate sports pages of newspapers or serve as the subject of special supplements and daily updates. They can appear on magazine covers, in advertising, and even in apparent sport-free zones such as supermarkets. They are promoted in special displays urging women to provide sufficient viewing-oriented snack food and alcohol for their menfolk. Major sport events can be the occasion for carnivalesque behavior—face painting, singing and chanting, partying, and the wearing of eccentric costume and headgear. In 2008, even though England failed to qualify for the European Nations Championships, cars were seen in the United Kingdom flying the flags of Portugal, Italy, France, Spain, Greece, and other nations. Much of this carnivalesque behavior is concentrated around public venues that provide giant television screens. So it is not just that these events are television events—it is that the event itself becomes a new dispersed form of spectacle taking place not merely at the stadiums but all over Europe.

Of the various ways in which television has impacted upon social and cultural patterns, it can be argued that the impact on sport has been particularly dramatic. Television transformed sport into a set of commodified global spectacles, producing huge audiences and massive new sources of income. Sport in turn provided television with an endless supply of major spectacular events and an enduring form of pleasurable and popular viewing. This transformation had a number of dimensions. By bringing live pictures to the home, television brought immediacy and uncertainty from the public domain to the domestic sphere. Television turned sport events into, in the words of Scannell and Cardiff, "shared rituals of national corporate life"(1977, 4). Technological innovation eventually enabled a naturalistic perfection that enhanced the value and appeal of televised events. By extending the live network globally, television enabled the transmission of events from any part of the globe and their dissemination and consumption to much of the world. By manipulation of time and space, the television version became in some ways superior to the experience of live spectatorship. Now that deregulation, digitalization, and the multichannel environment have fragmented the mass audience, major television sport events are one of the few televisual forms that can still assemble exceptionally large television audiences. Indeed, the widespread availability of television sport in cafés and bars around the world enables this communal viewing audience in both domestic and public space.

Along with technological and aesthetic transformation came an economic transformation. By making television sport attractive to sponsors and advertisers, new forms of revenue for sport were established and grew rapidly from the 1960s. The new cultural visibility of sport, in turn, stimulated a rapid growth in sport-branded merchandising. The governing bodies of sport became desperate to offer television what it wanted in order to secure these revenues. These processes led to the undermining of nineteenth-century benevolent paternalist and voluntary sport governance by new entrepreneurial sport agencies and forced sport governing bodies to transform themselves to accommodate the primacy of television, commercialization, and commodification. Television has undermined the embedded localism of sport, enabling the emergence of global fan bases for the market leaders—the New York Yankees, the Dallas Cowboys, Real Madrid, and Manchester United. The close-up-centered basis of television helped transform sport performers into stars and celebrities. Television created the dispersed audience for major events, de-centering the host city and country; fostering a disembodiment of spectacular sport; and contributing to the emergence of three distinct cultures—major televised elite sport spectacle, nontelevised professional sport, and participatory amateur sport.

Sport and the Media before Television

Although sport has a long history, and spectator sport has been in existence at least since ancient Greece, modern professionalized sport first emerged in the late nineteenth century, during the same period that saw the emergence of mass media, brand-based advertising, and retail chain stores. The development of organized spectator sport during the late eighteenth and early nineteenth centuries had been accompanied by interest from literary figures and social commentators.[1] New sport magazines and guides began to appear in the mid-nineteenth century.[2] The first newspaper sports department was started in 1883 at the *New York World*, and the first newspaper sports section appeared in the *New York Journal* in 1895 (McChesney 1989, 53). The launch of the *Daily Mail* in 1896 ushered in the era of the mass circulation popular press, and from the first issue, the new *Daily Mail* devoted at least 10 percent of its space to sport (Mason 1988, 49). In the 1920s, the Associated Press established a sports department with a staff of twelve (McChesney 1989, 56). The first public cinema performance in Britain was also in 1896, and there were between four and five thousand cinemas by 1914. Cinema newsreels brought movement and hence sporting action to the audience for the first time. The first regular topical coverage was by the Biograph Company, a U.S. firm with a base in the United Kingdom. Among other events, they covered the Derby and the Boat Race. The Pathé organization was set up in 1908, and its first newsreel featured a sculling contest (Aldgate 1979, 17-19).

Consequently, when radio was launched in the 1920s, sport was already established as an element of news and of entertainment. In Britain, a radio service was launched in 1922 when six radio and electrical companies combined to form the BBC, which, four years later, was transformed into a public corporation. Pressure from the Newspaper Proprietors Association prevented the new company from offering proper news and sport, but when the BBC became a public corporation in 1927, these restrictions ceased and live commentaries of sport events such as Grand National, the Boat Race, The Inter-varsity Sports, Rugby Union, Amateur Golf, and Wimbledon became part of the radio repertoire (see Whannel 1992). As the first domestic medium, radio enabled the establishment of new shared national rituals—the Christmas message, Cup Final Day, the Boat Race, and the Last Night of the Proms. In the United States, baseball, boxing, and American football were broadcast to large audiences. The percentage of U.K. radio households rose from 10 percent in 1924 to 71 percent in 1938. By 1929, one-third of American households had radio. The radio broadcast of the 1927 Dempsey versus Tunney fight was reported to have generated $90,000 of radio sales in one New York store alone (McChesney 1989, 59).

From Birth to Maturity

The emergence of television in the 1930s enabled a combination of the immediacy and uncertainty of live sport, the domestic context of radio, and the drama and spectacle of newsreel. By bringing live pictures to the home, it brought sport from the public domain to the domestic sphere. Television was launched in Britain in 1936 and relayed a range of sport events before 1939, when the television experiment was suspended with the outbreak of war. But in this period, reception was restricted to the London area, and the high price of receivers meant the audience never rose above twenty thousand. In the United States, television sport began in 1939, with NBC televising baseball and American football. In Germany, television technology was used to relay live pictures of the 1936 Berlin Olympics, and later other sporting events, to cinema screens.

The relaunch of television in Britain in 1946 was part of postwar reconstruction, boosting the electrics industry, but its popularity was slow to grow. The London Olympic Games in 1948 were the first to be broadcast on television. In 1950 there were only 5 million television sets in the world, and only Great Britain, the United States, and the USSR had established television systems. Television was launched in Australia in 1956, the year of the Melbourne Olympics. By 1970, live color pictures could be beamed around the world, and there were 250 million sets in 130 countries (Green 1972).

Still in its infancy, television captured some early sporting moments that have become mythologized—the first sub-four-minute mile by Roger Bannister in 1954 and the 1953 Football Cup Final in which veteran England winger Stanley Matthews finally gained the winners medal (see Whannel 2002a, 2005b, 2006). In the United States, televised boxing became popular during the 1950s, but American football and baseball had to wait for higher-quality zoom lenses. Neither the cameras nor the sets were able to deliver the spectacle of sport adequately, and it was not until the 1970s that television sport came to maturity. Between 1954 and 1970, the television landscape was limited. U.S. broadcasting was dominated by the three major networks: NBC, CBS, and ABC. The United Kingdom acquired a second, commercial channel only in 1955, while the BBC was able to launch a second channel in 1964. It was not until 1982 that the fourth channel, Channel 4, was established. During the key period of growth from 1954 to 1970, production conventions and key program forms were established. Among the landmark programs were *Sportsview* (BBC 1954), *Grandstand* (BBC

1958), *Wide World of Sport* (ABC 1961), *Match of the Day* (BBC 1964), *World of Sport* (ITV 1965), and *Monday Night Football* (ABC 1970). Following a deal between the NFL and the AFL, the Super Bowl, which rapidly became the biggest single sport event on television in United States, was launched in 1967. The most popular sport events, such as the FA Cup Final, Wimbledon tennis, and the Super Bowl, were able to win large audiences and establish themselves as shared national rituals.

The requirements of sport broadcasting were a significant stimulant to technological innovation. In the early 1950s, the Eurovision network of permanent landlines was established across Europe (Ross 1961, 128-39). Its existence helped the establishment of football's European Cup, now the Champions League. The first communication satellite, Telstar, launched in 1962, bridged the Atlantic; in 1964, the Tokyo Olympics were broadcast live to thirty-nine countries; and the 1968 Olympics were the first to be seen in color in Britain. Immediacy is now technically universal—given the financial will, any event can be flashed around the world.

The blurred and grainy quality of early television pictures drove a desire for greater verisimilitude. New CPS Emitron cameras introduced in 1948 had better pictures and a greater focal range and depth of field, useful for outside broadcasts (Ross 1961, 75-76). Also in 1948, a new parabolic reflector, improving capture of crowd sounds, was introduced (Briggs 1979, 869). New camera suspensions were developed to reduce vibration effects on moving cameras mounted in vehicles.[3] Zoom lenses were introduced and new mobile cameras were developed in the fifties.[4] Most important, color was gradually introduced to the United Kingdom in the late sixties. Technological innovation helped to sell sets; sport was a particularly important element in the advertising of television sets. Access to live events; the offer of "the best seat in the house"; and the enhanced quality of viewing promised by replay, slow motion, color, and live pictures from around the world were all used to promote the medium. Indeed, in the case of sport, by manipulation of time and space, the television version became in some ways superior to the experience of live spectatorship. Action replay and slow-motion replay were introduced during the 1960s. Multiple camera positions became common. Lightweight cameras enabled new shot angles.

During the 1980s and 1990s, television as a medium was further transformed by deregulation and by a second wave of technological innovation. Videos, DVDs, computers, and computer games provided alternative screen-based entertainment. Video recording and digital time-shift devices freed viewers from the structure of the television schedule. Cable, satellite, and above all digitalization have established a multichannel environment. Convergence of hitherto distinct technological platforms—television, computers, and mobile phones—is transforming our concept of the screen and its functions. The audience is fragmented but has a far greater range of means of responding to and interacting with the screen. Many traditional television program formats came to seem staid and static in the era of Internet chat.

Sport broadcasting, however, continued to use technological means of renewal of its aesthetic excitement. Teletrack made it possible to trace the path of a moving ball. Such devices, used in golf, snooker, tennis, and cricket, enabled a more precise analysis of controversial decisions and dramatic incidents. By the 1990s, digital rotation of still images further aided analysis of controversial decisions. These resources, applied to sports as diverse as cricket and American football, have greatly enhanced the ability of television to dissect and analyze sporting moments. Technological developments enabled a seamless combination of studio and location material and live and recorded material. The presentation was enhanced by expert opinion and analysis and instant statistics. It is partly by means of such innovation that television sport has continually renewed its presentational style and ability to produce engaging viewing experiences.

The prime instance of major sport events that win audiences around the world are the football World Cup and the Olympic Games. Megaevents such as the Olympic Games are not best understood simply as empty spectacles, products of what the Frankfurt School dubbed "the affirmative culture." Neither can they effectively be analyzed as, in Boorstin's (1961) term, "pseudo-events." It is not useful to view them as part of, in Guy Debord's (1977) term, "the society of the spectacle."[5] The problem with these three approaches is that they tend to drain events of content and context and to treat them as merely formal phenomena. The Olympic Games are perhaps more usefully conceptualized as megaevents and as media events.[6] Like other media events, in the terms of Dayan and Katz (1992), major sport events "interrupt the rhythm and focus of people's lives," create an "upsurge of fellow feeling, an epidemic of communitas"(p. 204). They connect center and periphery and produce cathartic experiences for viewers.

It is important here to distinguish between two different forms of television sport. The majority of sport on television, watched by small audiences, is in regular routinized slots, often well outside peak viewing times, sometimes in the middle of the night, or on dedicated sport channels that often have tiny audiences but generate much subscription revenue. The exceptions occur at times of major events, which have their own regularity but not one that fits neatly into television's own weekly scheduled routines. Sport appears in peak time, on major channels. Schedules are disrupted to accommodate it. The event features prominently across media. Public interest becomes manifest, in a variety of forms. Audiences can be exceptionally large. These major events take on a "vortextual" character. I developed the concept of vortextuality while analyzing the media frenzy around the wedding of David Beckham and Victoria Adams, the death of Princess Diana, and the verdict announcement in the Michael Jackson trial, but it is also applicable to major sport events. The context for the effect was established by the combined impact of the erosion of the public-private distinction, the declining powers of regulation and censorship, and the growth of celebrity culture, combined with the expansion of the media and the increase in the speed of circulation. The media feed off each other in a process of self-referentiality and intertextuality, but in the era of electronic and digital information exchange, this process is very rapid. Some major events dominate the headlines, and, temporarily, it is difficult for columnists and commentators to discuss anything else, even if they have no abiding interest. The media agenda is compressed, and other topics either disappear or have to be connected to the vortextual event. In the middle of a vortextual moment, cartoons, radio phone-ins, celebrity columnists, news magazines, cultural commentators, and letter pages are all drawn in (see Whannel 2002b). The development of a vortextual effect during a major sport event provides momentum for the building of television audiences.

Television Sport and Commercialization

Along with the technological and aesthetic transformation came an economic transformation. Television brought a new source of revenue in rights payments, and by making television sport attractive to sponsors and advertisers, additional new forms of revenue for sport were established and grew rapidly from the 1960s. The launch of BBC 2 in 1964 led to an increase in the amount of sport on TV and gave the BBC the means to increase the range of sports and provided space for Sunday cricket and extended coverage of cricket, tennis, and golf (Bough 1980, 118-35). At the start of the 1960s, in the United Kingdom, the television fees for rugby, cricket, show jumping athletics, and tennis were typically between £1,000 and £2,000 per day.[7] Television fees rose as the audience increased, and competition between channels developed. The television rights for the baseball World Series, which cost $6 million for 1951 to 1956, rose to $15 million in the period from 1957 to 1962. American football rights cost $4.5 million per year from 1961 to 1964, when CBS signed a new two-year contract for $14 million, which pushed NBC into signing a five-year deal to cover the new AFL, which cost them $42 million (Rader 1984). The age of competitive bidding was about to enter a period of dramatic growth.

The presence of cameras proved a huge attraction for potential sponsors of sporting events. Although sport sponsorship goes back at least to 1861, when Spiers and Pond sponsored a cricket tour, it was of no great significance until the mid-1960s. In 1957, the only sponsored event on British television was the Whitbread Gold Cup (Wilson 1988, 157). The banning of cigarette advertising on television in Britain in 1965 and in the United States in 1970 triggered a growth in direct sport sponsorship, led by the tobacco companies. While not all sponsorship was from cigarette firms, it was firms like Rothmans, John Player, and Benson and Hedges that led the way. Sport sponsorship in Britain grew from less than £1 million in 1966 to £16 million by 1976 and £100 million by 1983 (Howell 1983, 9-10). As sponsorship proved its worth as a device for marketing and for establishing a corporate image, tobacco and alcohol sponsors were joined in increasing numbers by financial institutions. In 1981, when Cornhill's banners at test match cricket appeared 7,459 times on television, the awareness level (the number of people who mentioned Cornhill when asked to name all the insurance firms they could remember) shot up to 17 percent compared with 2 percent in 1977 (*The Economist*, May 22, 1982). Of the top ten sponsored sports in 1982, all had been among the eleven most televised sports the previous year.[8] That television coverage was attracting sponsorship could hardly have been clearer.

The close-up-centered basis of television helped transform sport performers into stars and celebrities. Televised sport made top performers recognizable stars, enhancing their earning potential from endorsements and advertising. Muhammad Ali and footballer George Best were two of the first television-era stars, as well known for their faces as for their performances. In 1978, half of England footballer Kevin Keegan's £250,000 earnings came from advertising, endorsements, and other promotional activities (*Sunday Times*, October 15, 1978, and November 16, 1980). In the late seventies, tennis player Bjorn Borg's promotional contracts brought him well over $500,000 a year (Kramer 1979, 271). New quasi-sports events such as *Superstars*, called *trash sports* by their critics and *synthetic sports* by their proponents, grew out of the desire to exploit the fame of sport celebrities. In the mid-1980s, tennis stars such as Ivan Lendl and Martina Navratilova and many top American baseball and basketball stars were making more than £1 million annually. By the late 1980s, only one-tenth of Boris Becker's multimillion-dollar tennis income came directly from playing (Wilson 1988, 55). By the 1990s, top U.S. stars earnings from playing and other sources were soaring well above $10 million annually. In 2007, English soccer star David Beckham signed a contract worth $1 million a week to play in Los Angeles.

The power of traditional governing bodies was challenged by sport agents. In the 1950s, Jack Kramer's professional tennis circuit had been successful in luring top tennis stars away from the amateur game. In the 1960s, Mark McCormack built his sporting empire, the International Management Group (IMG), by representing the business interests of three top golfers. By 1983, IMG had twelve subsidiary companies and fifteen offices around the world, with gross revenues exceeding $200 million (McCormack 1984, 161). In the 1970s, West Nally had introduced a new level of capitalist rationalization in its handling of sponsorship promotion and advertising contracts for the international governing bodies of football and athletics, only to be replaced in this role during the early 1980s by a company founded by Adidas boss Horst Dassler (see Whannel 1992). Meanwhile, McCormack's Television World International had become the world's leading independent sports producer with around two hundred hours of sports programming annually. McCormack's organizations acquired a significant power to define the organizational form of sports such as tennis and golf.

The governing bodies of sport became desperate to offer television what it wanted to secure these revenues. These processes led to the undermining of nineteenth-century benevolent paternalist and voluntarist sport governance by new entrepreneurial sport agencies and forced sport governing bodies to transform themselves to accommodate the primacy of the new televised elite events. New associations were formed in attempts to get airtime, often without long-term success.[9] Sport governing bodies were increasingly prone to changing the rules and the format to attract television and sponsors. The opening of tennis to professionals in 1968, the establishment of the Super Bowl in 1967, and the rapid growth of one-day limited overs cricket from the mid-1960s were early examples. Track and field began moves toward professionalism in 1981, and the English Football League finally agreed to live football in 1983, in exchange for which television allowed shirt advertisements—thus greatly increasing the sponsorship potential of major clubs.

The new cultural visibility of sport in turn stimulated a rapid growth in branded merchandising. In the post-Fordist era of the hollowed-out corporation, major companies increasingly saw their main product as the brand rather than the commodity itself. The brand, properly managed, can promote and sell a range of commodities. Sporting brands possess desirable attributes and associations—youth, fitness, high performance, and success. Television was key to the brand promotion of the leaders in their sports.

Globalizing Processes

Sport has been at the forefront of globalizing processes in that many of the earliest forms of international organization were sport-based. International governing institutions were established for the Olympic Games (1894), track and field (1912), tennis (1913), and football (1930). Yet, sporting cultures also have resistances to globalizing processes—the major North American sports (American football, baseball, basketball, and ice hockey) have much less popularity in the rest of the world. The United States resists the appeal of soccer. Cricket has not extended itself significantly beyond the old British Empire countries. However, track and field, golf, tennis, and motor sport have all been transformed by the forces of globalizing processes.

Television undermined the embedded localism of sport, enabling the emergence of global fan bases for the market leaders. American football, Australian rules, basketball, soccer, cricket, baseball, and even sumo sought to broaden their audience by internationalizing their market strategies, with mixed successes. The growing global visibility of major sport was of considerable appeal to advertisers. The marketing of the 1982 World Cup and the 1984 Olympic Games proved that selling sponsorship in limited product categories with exclusive rights would become a major new source of revenue for sport. The 1984 Olympic Games made more than $100 million from sponsorship, ten times that made in previous games.

In the United States, only the McDonald's logo (recognized by 100 percent of respondents) is more recognizable than the Olympic rings (recognized by 99 percent). Almost half of people interviewed in the United States, Singapore, Portugal, and West Germany thought the presence of the Olympic rings on a product indicated its good quality (Wilson 1988, 28). The staging of soccer's World Cup in the United States in 1994 made little sporting sense but extensive commercial sense as another attempt to persuade the U.S. public to buy into the world's most popular sport. Subsequent World Cup venue choices have been driven by the desire to develop new markets for the game and its merchandising (Japan/South Korea in 2002, South Africa in 2010, and possibly Australia in 2018). Television created the dispersed audience for major events, decentering the host country, fostering a disembodiment of spectacle. The World Cup is watched around the world, even in the United States, particularly among Hispanic audiences, and more than ever, the sense of location is fragmented. Did the World Cup take place in the stadium or in the bars, parks, clubs, and beaches and in front of giant communal screens around the world?

After 1988, it was clear that the Olympic Games had moved from an era of political protests, boycotts, and economic problems into an era of economic success and city image-building. The International Olympic Committee (IOC) had taken control of the television and sponsorship negotiations.[10] It seems likely that for the 2012 games the rest of the world will provide more than 50 percent of the TV revenue for the first time (see Whannel 2005a). The Olympic Games have become a deterritorialized television event, in which location is no longer the focus. NBC's keenness to sign a deal for the 2012 Olympic Games two years before the choice of site suggests that the choice of site is no longer seen as a crucial element in determining the value of the rights.[11] Fear over the rise of the Internet, and doubts about the stability of revenues, meant that the major U.S. networks were keen to secure television rights for future Olympic Games, and the IOC was keen to arrange such a deal. In June 2003, NBC agreed to pay more than $2 billion for the Winter Olympics of 2010 and the Summer Games of 2012 (see Whannel 2005a).

The Impact of Television Sport

So what, in the second half of the twentieth century, has been the impact of television on sport? There are two aspects to this question: first, the impact upon the institutions, rituals, and practices of organized sport; and second, the impact upon spectators, the television audience, and social practices more generally. Clearly, television has transformed sport beyond recognition. The major events, sports, and organizations now command extremely high revenues. This income has enabled sport to be organized on a more elaborate and spectator basis. Top sport performers have become major global celebrities with matching earning power.

The new revenue sources challenged and then usurped the traditional authority of sport governing bodies. The original sport governing bodies for cricket, horse-racing, and golf were products of the society of eighteenth-century gentlemen. The next wave of sport governance grafted onto this world the nineteenth-century bourgeois snobberies and insecurities, creating the concept of "amateurism" as a means of excluding, discouraging, or marginalizing the lower orders. In the two decades before the First World War, this mode of governance was copied around the world and extended to the new international governing bodies.

These bodies reigned without major challenge until the rise of television. The new revenues available from television advertising endorsement and sponsorship placed amateurism under growing strain. Governing bodies that refused to compromise found themselves under threat of losing their power to new entrepreneurially oriented organizations. Traditionalists fought a long, losing battle against modernizers. By the mid-1980s, amateurism was all but dead, and most governing bodies had been forced to come to terms with the new world of sport agents, sponsorship brokers, and television deals. Sport was reshaped to meet the needs of television and the promotional industry.

Major sports events have been transformed into the focal point of intense commercial activity, in which the commodified spectacle generates huge cash flows. Sport is still multifaceted, but among other functions, it has certainly become a branch of the advertising and promotion industry as a result of television. The impact of this economic transformation has produced new tensions for sport organization to manage—increasing the pressure for success, the use of performance-enhancing drugs, forms of cheating and gamesmanship, corruption, and betting coups.

In the process of commercialization, a gap was opened between the elite spectator sports and the rest, consigned to a nontelevised obscurity. Although more sport is on television than ever, the range of sports is narrower; football dominates the television sport schedules in much of the world. Given the importance of demographic profile to the selling of advertising, sports with an upmarket profile, or a generalized appeal, such as American college football, tennis, and golf, have tended to be given more prominence than sports with a largely working-class or blue-collar appeal, such as NASCAR motor racing or greyhound racing. On pay-per-view television in much of the world, football is the one sport that can attract subscriptions. Within the major sports, the small elite level grabbed the bulk of the resources, with the traditional redistributive role of governing bodies challenged by the desire of the elite to retain as much as possible of the revenue. The broad base of spectator sport has suffered as a result, although one unexpected consequence has been the resurgence of communalist and collectivist responses to economic crisis—many lower-division football clubs in England are now run by nonprofit football trusts.

These processes of spectacularization have tended to separate the practices of spectatorship and participation. Watching and taking part in sport now seem like two very distinct forms of social practice, and few of the most popular active leisure activities—walking, running, swimming, cycling, gym-based workouts, keeping fit, yoga, and martial arts classes—have any real correspondence to elite spectator sport. Of course, these forms of participation have also been affected by the imagery and iconography of sport. Since the 1970s, the sporting goods business has grown enormously, but it has also become part of the lexicon of fashion. The fine details of brand and styling have built the humble running shoe into the global trainer industry. The forms (such as the track suit) and institutions (such as Gap) of leisure clothing have grown out of the fitness chic of the 1980s. The massive cultural visibility of major sport stars, their connotative power and symbolic value, and the absorption of sporting costume within the lexicon of the fashion industry could not have occurred without television.

The experience of spectatorship has been transformed. Walter Benjamin (1970) famously argued that in the age of mechanical reproduction, the unique aura of the work of art would be eroded. Benjamin's essay, which seems to me brilliant but wrong about art, may in fact be more applicable to top-level sport. The experience of live spectatorship, before television, had an aura of uniqueness, of authenticity. Only those at the stadium could experience the event, and the event was staged for those spectators. Once television began showing live events in their entirety, this uniqueness eroded. It was possible to experience the event without being physically present. At first, the spectators could feel, smugly, that being there was special. But then television improved the technical facility of its coverage. Suddenly the live experience seemed to be missing something. Live spectatorship, with a distanced view and lacking replay, could seem to be missing an element. No longer was the spectacle staged simply for those who were there; now it was, increasingly, stage-managed for the television viewer.

Of course there are gains here—a new, more relaxed social space, less pressurized and intense than the stadium, brings its own pleasures of communal viewing and shared cultural experience, albeit one heavily masculine in its ritual character. Indeed, sporting serves far more to demarcate than to unite the genders. In gender terms, television sport is one of the more unevenly skewed audiences, with a typical percentage of around 60 to 70 percent men.

In the television-driven transformation of sport, embedded specificities of class and locality have been eroded. At the same time, television has fostered other modes of collective identity. It has brought the drama of uncertainty and spectacle of major occasion into the domestic sphere. It has been one of the cultural forms constructing, albeit in temporary and often partial forms, a sense of shared national experience. The many Olympic victories of the United States, the one (1966) victory and many football failures of England, and the rather smaller number of Olympic successes by the United Kingdom have been inscribed into history as emblematic television moments, although, in varying degrees, their audiences have often been predominantly male.

However, despite the substantial reconstruction of sport as a managed, regulated, and promoted spectacle serving the purposes of corporate advertising, it still has a unique power to grip, enthrall, and enhance with its unscripted capacity for uncertainty. The best major events build toward a climax; in the process, audiences around the world become gripped but also increasingly aware of the communal nature of the experience. To watch a major football game in a bar is to be conscious that in Buenos Aires, São Paulo, Tokyo, Athens, Seville, and Naples, indeed everywhere, fellow fans are doing the same thing at the same moment. In this instance, it is not so much, as Dayan and Katz (1992, 211) suggest, that media events shift the locus of ceremoniality from the stadium to the living room, but, rather, that stadium and living room, café and bar, center and periphery, domestic and public space, venue and audience are temporarily united and distinctions blurred. If anything suggests the continuing resonance and relevance of television as a global medium, this does. The live broadcast of major sporting events became in the 1970s one of television's most successful program forms. In a future in which people compose their own viewing schedules from a large range of instantly downloadable sources, major live sport may just be the last bastion of the experience of simultaneous communal viewing.

Notes

1. William Hazlitt wrote an essay, "The Fight," in *The New Monthly Magazine* in February 1822 (Shipley 1989). Dickens portrayed boxing as "a more scientific, humane and democratic method for men to settle their differences than the duel" (Kidd 1987, 253). See also Marlow (1982).

2. See Mason (1988, 48). For more details and sources on the early sporting press, see the footnotes to Whannel (2002b).

3. Bridgewater, T.H. Televising the boat race, *BBC Quarterly* 5, no. 2 (1950): 107-115.

4. *BBC Annual Report 1955/56* (London: BBC, 1956), 33; and T. H. Bridgewater, "TV outside broadcasts," *BBC Quarterly* 5, no. 3 (1950): 179-92.

5. Adorno and Horkheimer (1979); Boorstin (1961); Debord (1977).

6. See Roche (2000); Dayan and Katz (1992).

7. Based on information in file T14/492/493 Grandstand-General 1959-60, in the BBC Written Archives.

8. *Sportscan* (monitoring report on television sport), 1982.

9. Examples include the American Basketball Association (1967), the World Hockey Association (1972), World Team Tennis (1973), and the United States Football League (1983).

10. See Larson and Park (1993).

11. For relevant studies of the power of U.S. TV, see Spence (1988), Wilson (1988), McPhail and Jackson (1989), O'Neil (1989), and Real (1989a, 1989b); and for studies of sport and the media, see Moragas, Rivenburgh, and Larson (1996) and Rowe (1996, 1999).

References

Adorno, Theo, and Max Horkheimer. 1979. *Dialectic of enlightenment*. London: Verso.

Aldgate, Anthony. 1979. *Cinema and history: British newsreels and the Spanish Civil War*. London: Scolar.

Benjamin, Walter. 1970. *Illuminations*. London: Jonathon Cape.

Boorstin, Daniel. 1961. *The image*. Harmondsworth, UK: Penguin.

Bough, Frank. 1980. *Cue Frank*. London: MacDonald Futura.

Briggs, Asa. 1979. *Sound and vision*. London: Oxford University Press.

Cardiff, David, and Paddy Scannell. 1977. *The social foundations of British broadcasting*. Milton Keynes, UK: Open University Press.

Dayan, D., and E. Katz. 1992. *Media events: The live broadcasting of history*. Cambridge, MA: Harvard University Press.

Debord, Guy. 1977. *Society of the spectacle*. London: Practical Paradise.

Green, Timothy. 1972. *The universal eye*. London: Bodley Head.

Howell, Denis. 1983. *Howell Report on sponsorship*. London: CCPR.

Kidd, Bruce. 1987. Sports and masculinity. In *Beyond patriarchy: Essays by men on pleasure, power and change*, ed. M. Kaufman, 250-61. Toronto, Canada: Oxford University Press.

Kramer, Jack. 1979. *The game: My forty years in tennis*. London: Andre Deutsch.

Larson, James, and Heung-Soo Park. 1993. *Global television and the politics of the Seoul Olympics*. Boulder, CO: Westview.

Marlow, James. 1982. Popular culture, pugilism and Pickwick. *Journal of Popular Culture* 15 (4): 16-30.

Mason, Tony. 1988. *Sport in Britain*. London: Faber and Faber.

McChesney, Robert W. 1989. Media made sport: A history of sports coverage in the USA. In *Media sports and society*, ed. L. Wenner. London: Sage.

McCormack, Mark. 1984. *What they don't teach you at Harvard Business School*. London: Collins.

McPhail, Tom, and Roger Jackson, eds. 1989. *The Olympic movement and the mass media*. Calgary, Canada: Hurford Enterprises.

Moragas, Miquel de, Nancy K. Rivenburgh, and James F. Larson, eds. 1996. *Television in the Olympics*. London: John Libbey.

O'Neil, Terry. 1989. *The game behind the game: High stakes, high pressure in TV sports*. New York: Harper & Row.

Rader, Benjamin G. 1984. *In its own image: How TV has transformed sports*. New York: Free Press.

Real, Michael. 1989a. Super Bowl versus World Cup soccer: A cultural-structural comparison. *Media sports and society*, ed. L. Wenner. London: Sage.

———. 1989b. *Super media*. London: Sage.

Roche, Maurice. 2000. *Mega-events and modernity: Olympics and expos in the growth of global culture*. London: Routledge.

Ross, Gordon. 1961. *TV jubilee*. London: W H Allan.

Rowe, David. 1996. The global love-match: Sport and television. *Media, Culture & Society* 18 (4): 565-82.

———. 1999. *Sport, culture and the media*. Milton Keynes, PA: Open University press.

Shipley, Stan. 1989. Boxing. In *Sport in Britain: A social history*, ed. T. Mason. Cambridge: Cambridge University Press.

Spence, Jim. 1988. *Up close and personal*. New York: Atheneum.

Whannel, Garry. 1992. *Fields in vision: Television sport and cultural transformation*. London: Routledge.

———. 2002a. From pig's bladders to Ferraris: Media discourses of masculinity and morality in obituaries of Stanley Matthews. *Culture, Sport, Society* 5 (3): 73-94.

———. 2002b. *Media sport stars, masculinities and moralities*. London: Routledge.

———. 2005a. The five rings and the small screen: Television, sponsorship and new media in the Olympic movement. In *Global Olympics: Historical and sociological studies of the modern games*, ed. Kevin Young and Kevin Wamsley. Boston: Elsevier.

———. 2005b. Pregnant with anticipation: The pre-history of television sport and the politics of recycling and preservation. *International Journal of Cultural Studies* 8 (4): 405-26.

———. 2006. The four minute mythology: Documenting drama on film and television. *Sport in History* 26 (2): 263-27.

Wilson, Neil. 1988. *The sports business*. London: Piatkus.

The Dialectic of Time and Television

By
PADDY SCANNELL

The article reviews the key question of the effects of television as proposed by Elihu Katz in his introduction and the various responses to it in the contributions to this volume. It argues that the question is a proper concern of sociology, engaged as it is with the politics of the present and immediate, short-term effects. The question of long-term effects, however, is beyond the scope of a social science methodology concerned with the impact of the new. Long-term effects only show up with the passing of time and are the concern of historical studies. As television begins to have a history, it begins to be possible to examine its historical record to try to tease out its long-term impact on the world—so far!

Keywords: short term; long term; television; effects; history

I

For nothing is more important, nothing comes closer to the crux of social reality than this living, intimate, infinitely repeated opposition between the instant of time and that time which flows only slowly. Whether it is a question of the past or of the present, a clear awareness of this plurality of social time is indispensable to the communal methodology of the human sciences. (Braudel 1980, 26)

In the late 1950s, French historian Fernand Braudel drew a distinction between two different orders of time: the short and the long term. The former he called *histoire événementielle* and the latter the *longue durée*. The short term is the time of everyday life, the life and times of the present, full of noise and bustle, movement

Paddy Scannell is a professor in the Department of Communication Studies at the University of Michigan, which he joined in fall 2006. Before that, he worked at The Polytechnic (which later became the University of Westminster). He is a founding editor of Media Culture & Society *and author (with David Cardiff) of* A Social History of British Broadcasting, 1923-1939 *(Blackwell 1991),* Radio, Television and Modern Life *(Blackwell 1996), and* Media and Communication *(Sage 2007).*

DOI: 10.1177/0002716209339153

and activity. The long term is the past, receding back, further and further, into remote, inaccessible prehistoric time. In sharp contrast with the noisy, changing present, it becomes increasingly silent, unchanging, motionless, and fathomless. How are the two connected? It is rather like the surface and depths of the sea. The surface, endlessly ruffled by wind and weather, is in perpetual, restless motion. But beneath it lies the deep, and the more you descend into it, the more you encounter its dark and motionless silence. Braudel thought the *longue durée* was the proper object of historical enquiry. He dismissively compared *histoire événementielle* with a candle flame whose "delusive smoke, fills the minds of contemporaries" but that quickly flickers and dies, leaving no lasting trace (Braudel 1980, 27). For Braudel, as for many intellectuals of the past century, the eventful time of everyday life was the sphere of illusion, deception, and ideology. The historian's proper concern was with the unchanging, underlying, structural determinants of the everyday, for these were what shaped and defined it. This "structuralist turn" was by no means confined to historians at the time. In France and elsewhere, structuralism was becoming the new big idea in the humanities and social sciences of the 1960s and 1970s.

Braudel's era was a long time ago, and the tide has gone out on the moment of structuralism. But the distinction Braudel drew helps us understand the question addressed by this collection of essays on "the end" of television and clarifies its central problematic—the question of "effects." Accepting as valid the distinction between the short and the long term is not a matter of preferring one to the other. Rather, it is a question of how the two are inextricably interconnected. The endless interplay between past and present, properly understood, is the dialectic of history: the play of the past as it acts upon the present and of the present as it acts upon the past in order to bring on the future. History is indeed "made" in the present (where else?) but is not visible as such to those who dwell in it, the generations of the living in any present time. History only appears *as* history as it exits from the restless, noisy present and enters the silent and unchanging past. The present, in which we live, is indeed the time and place of action, in which decisions are made and courses of action committed to with fateful consequences for a future made possible only by what is done in the here and now. But we, who are caught up in the present, can never foresee, in spite of our best efforts, the actual long-term consequences of what we do. These *only* become apparent with the wisdom of hindsight, which is the effect of the passing of time from the present into the past. The owl of Minerva takes flight at dusk.

Academic engagement with media has always been concerned with the shock of the new; successive generations have grappled with the impact of new media in their times. In the United States in the 1930s and 1940s, the then very new medium of radio provoked high anxiety. It could stimulate widespread panic (Cantril, Gaudet, and Herzog 1941); persuade the masses to part with their money (Merton [1946] 2004); and was, as someone put it at a conference attended by Paul Lazarsfeld, "as powerful as the atomic bomb" (Lazarsfeld and Merton [1948] 2004). Forty years ago, when the new medium of television became the focus of study for an emergent "media studies," it too was seen as a powerful "ideological state apparatus." Nowadays, radio and television are thought of by those who pursue today's "new media" as "old" or "traditional" compared with shiny new things like the Internet, cell phones, iPods, Facebook, YouTube, and so forth. In all three moments, academic engagement with the new media of the day has been absorbed in and by the politics of the present, which always attends to significant events in the contemporary world and to upcoming phenomena as they emerge in the here and now.

The recurring, unavoidable question of the present concerns the effect, the impact of the new; and whether we are talking about radio, television, or the Internet, that question has two parts: what is the new thing doing to us, and what are we doing with it? In the sociology of mass communication, the so-called effects tradition, the initial question addressed was radio's impact on the masses. That it had a direct and powerful effect seemed self-evident in the light of the first notorious "media event"—Orson Welles's spoof Halloween radio play based on *War of the Worlds* by H. G. Wells. If, as was estimated, a million or so listeners were seriously frightened by the broadcast on October 31, 1938, its effect was obvious. The question to investigate concerned what made some listeners susceptible and others not to the power of the new medium. The study of media effects is necessarily concerned with the short term, with the immediate impact of broadcast output on its audiences. It must treat this as a matter for empirical investigation by trying to find out how real people, one way or another, respond to media and how they use them. Media studies and the sociology of mass communication confront the politics of the present, the play of *histoire événementielle* (of "media events") while being themselves caught up in the historical process whose lineaments they struggle to perceive.

But how can this be done? How do we know that a short-term effect is anything more than that? And if a short-term effect is no more than that, then indeed it has, as Braudel thought, no lasting significance. The question of the long term *has* to be posed as the solution to the study of the short term if its research is to have any claim to any long-lasting relevance and significance. But how is the long term available for study? The new, by definition, has no history as it enters into the life of the present. Its newness is its strangeness. What *is* it? Who can say? The long-term effects of new media can only be a matter of conjecture, for all of us caught up in the immediate present and its politics, for their long-term effects are yet to come. The only prophet media studies has produced thus far is Marshall McLuhan, who quickly became famous for his divinations of the new electronic era and was equally quickly assigned to oblivion (Meyrowitz 2003). By the 1980s, McLuhan had become, as Anthony Giddens (1991) put it, "the forgotten prophet of the electronic global village." Not until the 1990s, years after his death, was McLuhan hailed as the one true prophet of the Internet, the one who had foreseen, decades ahead of his time, the full potential impact of the emerging global telecommunications infrastructure that underpins the world we inhabit today.

McLuhan remains a quirky, isolated figure in the history of media and communication studies; his attempts to read the future could only be confirmed retrospectively as the future entered into the present and moved on to become the past. Long-term effects, which arise in the present, only become visible as such in the journey into the darkness and silence of the *longue durée*. In this transitional passage of time, the essence of history is disclosed, for it contains the dialectic of long-term temporal continuity and short-term temporal change. How then does this process work—more exactly, *when* does the present become the past? What is the transitional order of time in which the long term begins to appear out of the short-term present? The answer to this question is in one way or another in many of the contributions to this collective effort at understanding the effect of television. Let us call it *generational* time, the time of generations, in which the fundamental historical work of regeneration (of change and renewal from one generation to the next) is enacted.

A Kenyan friend once told me that the Kikuyu perform a ceremony every twenty-five years or so in which the elders hand over their authority to the younger generation, who take over and become the elders. Here we see the wise acknowledgement of generational time and the work of regeneration made ritually explicit. But for modern societies, which have uncoupled the present from the past, generational time is invisible from the short-term perspective of 24/7 time, a perpetual here and now without a past or future. The question of effects belongs to the present. It is perhaps *the* question that confronts the living: What will be the effects and consequences of our actions? Will their outcomes be as we hoped? Will they be good? Will they last? Or not? Long-term answers to the questions of the present only become apparent in the past. Thus, it is observable, with the wisdom of hindsight, that it took a generation of work in the sociology of mass communication to answer its initial question and hypothesis concerning the direct effect of powerful media on powerless, vulnerable individuals. This was the "original position" of the field as it got going in the 1930s. Gradually, incrementally, it began to be turned around. By the mid-1950s, when *Personal Influence* was eventually published, the media were found to have, at best, an indirect effect on individuals who were more immediately responsive to the personal influence of other people in the interpersonal networks of everyday life (Katz and Lazarsfeld 1955). Over a span of twenty years or so, we see the regenerative working through of generational time and societal change. America in the mid-1950s was a very different place from America in the mid-1930s. Social science, always situated in and confronting the present, imperceptibly adjusts and readjusts to change taking place at the time. That change, within sociology, only becomes apparent as the discipline itself begins to have a history, thereby becoming historical in the working through of its own institutional time.

II

These general considerations are implicated in the particular question of television addressed by our collective efforts. We can note, for a start, that "television" has been part of the world long enough to have accumulated a history—not a very long one, of course, but increasingly evident and mappable as several of our contributors show. The time span under discussion is not much more than sixty years, although, as William Uricchio, Menahem Blondheim, and Tamar Liebes all pertinently remind us, television has a longer back story that reaches well into the nineteenth century. Television as we know it is a social, political, and cultural phenomenon of the postwar world, and the 1950s is commonly taken as the point of departure for our varied narratives of television, since in the 1950s people began to have time for television. Television, like radio, is a time-based medium. Time is what it consumes (eats up). John Robinson's study of time budgets (what people do with time) is a fundamental contribution to understanding the basic temporal considerations that underpin the supply and demand sides of television (Robinson and Martin, 2009 [this issue]). On the supply side, the industry needs to have basic information about who is available for viewing at any time and who is not (and why) to adjust programming to correspond with potential usage. On the demand side, what viewers find when they turn on the TV set had better be broadly attuned to their moods and requirements, which are always in part determined by time of day and the day itself within the temporal rhythms of the week and the seasons. Thus, Saturday afternoon in the fall is college football time in America and soccer time everywhere else, when everyone turns on in the expectation of watching the game. But the times of television presuppose that people in large numbers do, in fact, have time for it; those social and economic conditions only became generally available in North America and Britain in the 1950s, in Northern Europe in the 1960s, in Southern Europe and elsewhere in the 1970s, and today most evidently in India and China. The preconditions that give the possibility of TV ownership do not yet exist in large parts of Africa.

The starting point for thinking about television must be the TV set, whose purchase presupposes a marginal surplus of disposable income and time on the part of purchasers. Those general economic conditions only became prevalent in the advanced economies of North America and Europe after the Second World War. The TV set in the 1950s is one significant index of an emerging economy of abundance and a culture of everyday life to which it gives rise (Scannell 2008). It is a new kind of domestic appliance whose utility is inseparable from the things that accompany it, all of which presuppose the wired household as the condition of their usage. The use of television has "free time" as its essential precondition, time freed *from* other things, time *for* watching television. But without all the other time- and labor-saving appliances in the home—vacuum cleaners, cookers, fridges, freezers, dish and clothes wash-and-dry machines—television is no use for there is no time for it. A major new study of "discretionary time" takes it as a fundamental measure of individual freedom. We may be materially rich and yet still "time-poor" if we have to work long hours to sustain our material lifestyle or if our time is taken up by housework, child care, and so on. In their remarkable survey of time pressures on individuals and households in Australia, Europe, and the United States today, Robert Goodin and his colleagues calibrate how much control people have over their time and how much they could have under alternative welfare, gender, or household arrangements (Goodin et al. 2008). The availability of a significant amount of free time, time at the personal disposal of individuals, is the precondition of a society oriented toward leisure. It is not for nothing that television became, as Robinson's (2009, this issue) data show, the major leisure-time activity for the majority of Americans in the 1950s and remains so to this day.

The entry of the TV set into everyday life back in the 1950s has been wonderfully examined by Lynn Spigel (1992). It was from the start a source of pleasure and anxiety. It was a new way of relaxing and of sharing "family time," but was it good for children or not? Sonia Livingstone (2009, this issue) shows how that question became an academic object of inquiry in the 1950s and has remained an important issue ever since. Worries about the young point to a more general anxiety that watching television is a waste of time for grown-ups, too, who, like their children, could (and should) be spending their time on better things. Robert Putnam blames television for the decline in social capital. People, in his view, are shirking their civic responsibilities. They ought to spend more time involved in their communities and less time involved in watching television (Putnam 2000). In this widespread, commonsense (and misleading) view, watching TV is a solitary, passive, indoors thing in contrast with outdoors social and communal activity.

What we get to watch when we turn on the set are mainly talking heads—the faces of people as they face us and address us directly (in news and studio-based talk shows of various kinds) and as they interact with each other on camera. What we get to see, Paul Frosh (2009, this issue) argues, is determined in part by the form of the technology. TV is good for showing faces, but not much more. It is not a richly visual experience, like the movies, or, rather, not when it got going back in the 1950s. Frosh reminds us how the TV set has changed over the years. In its beginning it was a bulky box with a squarish screen that lit up to produce low-definition moving images in various shades of gray. Today, the bulky box has been displaced by larger, flat, rectangular screens with the same aspect ratio as wide-screen cinema and a high-definition moving image in full color. But the functions of the technology remain unchanged: it is a device for the display of audiovisual material live and in real time or recorded (or both), and we still face it as it faces us.

In Frosh's essay, and many others, television confronts us as technology. Almost all contributors note the impact of changing technologies *on* television as well as the changing technologies *of* television. The question of technology is at the heart of any effort to think about TV, although some of us feel moved to add disclaimers that in dealing with the question, we are not guilty of the sin of technological determinism. As Robert Heilbroner has argued, however, technologies in general do make history: they arise in definite historical moments as sought-for solutions to general social problems and thereby enter into the historical process, the material life of the societies that produced them (Heilbroner 1994). Machines make a difference—of course they do. Would any of us willingly forgo the new postwar electric utilities that freed us from domestic toil (washing clothes by hand) and time-consuming daily activities (lighting coal fires; going on foot each day to different shops for different things and carrying them back) and in so doing freed up time for other things that television conveniently filled? What is much harder to say with any precision is just what difference they make, what the real and particular effects of television might be and at what level of analysis.

One general effect of television has been the transformation of visibility. Television shows us things. How it does so and with what consequences is the theme of several contributions to this collection. Joshua Meyrowitz has influentially and persuasively argued that television transforms the social geographies of everyday life in private and in public (Meyrowitz 1985). He returns to this theme for this collection, reviewing the "televations" of television: the ways in which, by making visible what hitherto was unseen and private, television elevates the experience of watching and transforms the status of certain classes of people in the eyes of others (parents and men, for instance, in the eyes of women and children) (Meyrowitz 2009, this issue). The impact of television on public life is most evident in politics, where the management of visibility has become, as Meyrowitz shows, a matter of increasing concern for political leaders since the 1950s.

For Daniel Dayan (2009, this issue), classic television (the television that speaks from the center to the periphery of a given nation-state) produces a focused attentiveness to an output simultaneously viewed by millions and thus characterized by "sharedness"—the shared experience of events as defined and distributed by the center. The work of focusing collective attentions is what he means by *monstration*. But the "solid" media of the center are now surrounded by newer, "liquid" digital media: the media at the margins, on the periphery, that are linked to each other in complex networks no longer constrained by ideas, interests, opinions, and events generated and defined from sociocultural and political centers. If television of the center demonstrates, peripheral media re-monstrate, he argues. *Re-monstration* means to show again, a second showing that serves as a reproach and critique of what is first shown through the monstrations of the television of the center. Such is the function of the blogosphere. A similar argument for the evolving impact of television on politics is proposed in the article by Michael Gurevitch, Jay Blumler, and Stephen Coleman. They concur with Meyrowitz that classic television had far-reaching consequences for the management and conduct of politics and political performances on and off camera. The primary definers of political reality continue to be the politicians, subject to the intense scrutiny of traditional media (the news reporters of print, radio, and television). This symbiotic relationship has increasingly been challenged by the emergence of new media and new publics. The Internet is a different public sphere to that constituted by traditional news and comment. The blogosphere is an ever-ready vociferous and critical chorus and commentary not only on the politics of the center but the media of the center as well.

The medium theory approach, as defined by Meyrowitz here (and in Meyrowitz 1994), assumes that the form of the technology has a determinate effect on its content and the uses to which it can be put. One use of television is for monitoring the environment, a technology of surveillance, as Meyrowitz shows. *Broadcast* television is a technology of communication. As such, it exists in relation to other, similar technologies: to those that precede it (the telegraph, telephone, and wireless telephony or radio, as Blondheim and Leibes [2009, this issue] remind us) and to those that come later. Technologies can become obsolete. The typewriter (a technology of the late nineteenth century) was made redundant a century later by the word processor and, more recently, audio and videocassette recordings have been replaced by CDs and DVDs. Is broadcast television becoming redundant? Has it passed its prime?

Such questions began to be posed in the 1990s when it seemed as if (1) the end of channel scarcity brought about by satellite and cable services and (2) the rise of the Internet might combine to render broadcast television superfluous. The first era of television was one in which a small number of content providers delivered a daily program schedule throughout the country in which they were situated. This "national-popular" television began to fade in the 1980s and was arguably eclipsed in the following decade by new "on-demand" TV services. Lotz provides an authoritative account of American television from the 1950s to the present that clearly shows the transition from the network era to the postnetwork present and how change was effected and affected by technological innovation within and outside the industry itself (see Lotz 2007). Uricchio offers a more critical interpretation of national popular television as an ideological state apparatus but confirms the general trajectory and force of Lotz's account. But what was the essence of broadcast television, and how is it different from later televisions?

The early radio and television industries had a dual function; they provided a program content that they produced (or commissioned) and delivered into the households of the owners of receiving sets. This dual process of production and transmission had two crucial characteristics: it was live and it was broadcast (as distinct from narrowcast). Instant live connectivity is the crucial feature of all the new electronic technologies that started with wired telegraphy and developed into wired and then wireless telephony (called the wireless in Britain, radio in America) and lastly television. In all these technologies, distant people and places are connected to each other in the immediate, living, enunciatory now—the now of the speech act, the now of the event. Wired technologies afforded point-to-point connection between two places and two signal transmitter receivers or speakers. Wireless technologies afforded an indiscriminate broadcast scatter. Anyone within range of reception and with an adequate receiver had access to what was transmitted. The scatter of wireless was initially problematic in its pre-broadcast usage for point-to-point contact between the fighting fronts and HQ in the rear during the war of 1914 to 1918. Transmissions were encrypted to avoid giving vital information to an eavesdropping enemy. *Broad*cast transmission was discovered after the war as a by-product of the technology and a way of creating a market for the sale of radio sets. Broadcasting, first on radio, then on television, created a new kind of general public whose general interests were served by the provision of a range of varied program content on the same channel, a mixed supply of news and entertainment for a large audience whose members all watched the same thing at the same time. This formation was, in large part, an effect of the constraints *and* the affordances of the technology in its early stages.

Two key technological innovations were developed to overcome some of the constraints of early television. First, and crucially, recording technologies complemented and relieved the initial pressures of continuous live-to-air transmission. Then new delivery systems were developed that overcame the twin problems of spectrum scarcity and its regulation and control by governments for purposes other than broadcasting. From the 1970s onward, satellite and cable services began to put an end to channel scarcity; today, viewers in Europe and North America have access to hundreds of channels from around the world.

These developments were intrinsic to the technology from the start. Electronic media in principle overcome the time-space constraints of older transport and communication systems that Harold Innis had encountered in his historical studies of the Canadian economy. This was McLuhan's key insight, one that was taken up and explored by an emerging theory of postmodernity in the last two decades of the twentieth century as rapid innovation in telecommunications overcame time-space constraints on information flows to produce the global connectivity of a common world forever caught up in an immediate never-ending now (Harvey 1989; Giddens 1991). The 1980s, the pivotal decade in which "new" televisions begin to appear alongside "old" television, was one of those moments that appeared to the living as if they were dwelling in new times. The New Times of the 1980s were marked, so it seemed to the British Left, by a shift in the capitalist mode of production, from scarcity to plenty, which they characterized as the change from Fordism to post-Fordism (Hall and Jacques 1989). In Fordism (the classic mode of mass-production developed by the auto industry in 1920s America), supply dominates demand. You could have any color Ford you liked, so the old joke went, as long as it was black. In the 1980s, this suddenly seemed to have changed, and an accelerating and increasingly diverse post-Fordist consumer culture at last confirmed what Raymond Williams had remarked on thirty years earlier—namely, the end of the masses and mass culture (Williams [1958] 1962). In the late twentieth century, the balance tipped from the supply side to the demand side, and consumer power seemed increasingly assertive. On-demand television is but one instance of the full transition to an economy of abundance, characterized by seemingly unlimited choice and diversity in the material culture of the late twentieth century, which began in postwar Northern Europe and America in the 1950s.

For most of the twentieth century, the culture of the masses was supplied by the culture industries. The supply side seemed dominant, powerful, and in control of the definition of culture, while there was no demand side to speak of. Rather, the early-twentieth-century consumers of mass culture appeared, to contemporary critics, as isolated, vulnerable individuals, victims of a fraud perpetrated on them from above by the culture industries (Adorno and Horkheimer [1946] 1986). By the late twentieth century, all this had changed as new technologies enabled individuals increasingly to pick and mix and variously put together their own social and cultural identities. On-demand television, part of a general shift in supply-demand relations at the time, emerged in the 1990s as an effect of two related technological developments: new distribution systems (cable and satellite) and new time-shifting technologies that began with videocassette recording in the 1980s, now displaced by digital recording technologies (DVD and TiVo). In Britain, BSkyB marketed its on-demand services under the slogan, "Say goodbye to the schedules." Liberated from the constraints of the broadcast schedules, individuals could create their own timetable and watch what they wanted when they wanted it.

These developments provoked alarm in the "old" television industry—the networks in the United States, the public service broadcasters in Europe. The British Broadcasting Corporation is often taken as the original model of public service broadcasting (PSB). David Morrison traces the fading of its moral and cultural authority in Britain from the 1950s through the 1980s, a decline that was part of a wider erosion of power hitherto confidently exercised by the British political and religious establishment. This moral decline was certainly blamed on television in the 1960s by religious conservatives such as Mary Whitehouse, a schoolteacher, who proved to be, for a time, a formidable lobbyist and thorn in the flesh of senior BBC management, accusing it of religious blasphemy, promoting sexual promiscuity, and corrupting the young. Was television the cause or more simply the conduit of social change in the 1960s and 1970s? Morrison points out that the so-called fragmentation of national audiences from the 1980s onward was not an effect of technology; rather, the technology gave expression to already existing diversity and difference in society and allowed it new channels of recognition. But this, he argues, was at the expense of a moral and cultural unity and coherence that the old elites had held in place.

Peter Lunt's (2009, this issue) paper picks up where Morrison leaves off. Lunt accepts as fact the erosion, by the end of the past century, of the cultural and moral authority of a top-down public service tradition. He sees, however, the emergence of a new ethic of the personal: a concern with the quality of one's own life and what is good for one's self and those with whom one lives—parents, partners, children—an ethics of personal and interpersonal care. And this he finds in the despised category of reality television, which he discusses in relation to an American and British example of the genre. Experts appear in reality TV shows, but less as authoritative and prescriptive voices (as in the older PSB dispensation) and more as life-support systems providing practical therapy for people with problems. Is it, Lunt wonders, negatively, yet another soft form of social regulation and control or, more positively, a sign of the politics of recognition and the care of the self?

Reality TV points to the increasing diversity and individualization of everyday life today in which people tailor their own cultural preferences and pick and mix their own viewing schedules. Does this not imply the end of broadcast television and its fixed schedules? Who needs it anymore? And what of the irresistible rise of the Internet? More time spent in the online world means less time in the offline world of television and other things. We are still very much caught up in the unavoidable business of working through and working out the implications of these innovations that are still part of the politics of present times. The Internet has, as yet, no history, for it has yet to recede into the past. It is impossible to say at this point in time whether Facebook and YouTube, for instance, are passing fads or long-term uses and gratifications furnished by the virtual world. But one thing that innovations do, as McLuhan noted, is to shed light on the uses and gratifications of existing things. Television, when it was new, both impacted on cinema-going and illuminated, by its difference, something of the essence of cinema and the cinematic experience. Today's old television is illuminated by new screen-based technologies of communication and the new postnetwork televisions of the 1990s. The new televisions of the late twentieth century do not displace the functions of the older television of the mid-twentieth century, but complement them. Taken together, they are formally indicative of long-term historical processes working through the twentieth century and in particular of the transition from modernity to postmodernity, the structural transformation of the world that emerged from the ruin and catastrophe of the Second World War.

III

The historian's task, Braudel thought, was to be concerned with the silent, imperceptible movement of slow time, while the sociologist attended to the noise of history in the making, the life and times of the present. The study of television, and of media in general, requires that we attend to both, but it is only now that the historical study of television is becoming possible, for only now do we begin to see its recession into the past and the working through of generational time in its output. Press's narrative, from the 1950s to the present, of changing relations between women and men, of new attitudes to sex and gender, shows this most clearly. The generation that grew up in and was radicalized by the 1960s (in reaction to their parent culture of the 1950s) in time became the parent generation to children born in the 1980s. The relationship between older and younger generations, parents and children, mothers and daughters—the politics of re-generation—is vividly apparent in the tensions between second-wave feminism of the 1970s and third-wave feminism or postfeminism of the 1990s. And this is seamlessly displayed in television's fictional output, which is naturally and rightly treated by critical feminist television studies as a key historical resource for the exploration of changing social relations within and between the sexes (Douglas 1994; Lotz 2006). Such work has only recently become possible. All the programs discussed by Press (2009, this issue) were produced in and for their own time with no thought for a future in which they would become the past. Only as the programs of today disappear from the schedules do they enter into the past, becoming part of the historical record through recording technologies that preserve them as such. Season by season, year by year, today's output begins to settle as sedimentary time strata silently bedding down, layer by layer, on the ocean floor of the *longue durée*. Only as these sedimentary deposits build up can we begin to see the long-term effects of the politics of the present. Television shows of the 1990s take for granted what women of an earlier generation had to fight for. They also forget that what they are able to presume is the gift of the politics of the present in the past.

What then does the emerging historical record that is television tell us about itself and about history? First, the emerging record is the totality of output; everything—news, documentaries, reality shows, quiz programs, sports, and so on. None of these genres have any privileged status over the others. It is not that, say, a documentary program of the 1960s will necessarily be more historical (tell us more, be more revealing of that time) than a soap opera. John Ellis (2009, this issue) finds evidence of an emerging performative requirement for sincere self-presentation from actors on television across a range of genres in fictional and nonfictional settings: whether it is news, a game show, a documentary, a police series, or a soap opera, he argues that actors (real and fictional) must prove themselves, in their speech and body language, to be the genuine article. His discussion of the first commercial game show on British television makes it clear that no one, including the show's host, Hughie Green, quite knew how to do it—how to perform "being oneself" on television. It is not a coincidence that a new sociology of interpersonal relations emerged in the 1950s at the same time as television became part of everyone's everyday life in the United States. *The Presentation of Self in Everyday Life* by Erving Goffman ([1959] 1971) might have been written as a self-help guide for people new to television. One thing that all of us know today is how to perform being a person on TV, since all of us have spent our time since earliest childhood watching and closely scrutinizing other people's self-enactments on television. The historical record that is now emerging thus furnishes evidence of social change in the very pores of history, makes available for study hitherto invisible things—micro-histories of looks and gestures (Bremer and Roodenberg 1993), of conversation and silence (Burke 1993), and of talk in all its varieties including those created by broadcasting itself: the commentary, the interview, or the panel discussion (Hutchby 2006; Montgomery 2007; Tolson 2006).

Future generations will treat radio and television as prime historical sources of the twentieth century and after. Historians will study this or that televised record at, say, French, Danish, or Japanese television archives to learn something of the historical past of their own countries. But television was not primarily a national thing from the start, even though at first it seemed to be. What all of us have written about is "television"—not British, American, Israeli, or any other national televisions as if they were unique, but as instances of television in the singular, tacitly understood as the universal phenomenon that it is. Technologies are not like languages. When I am in France, Denmark, or Japan, I encounter difficulties because I do not know the languages of these countries. But I do not have similar difficulties with the material environment in these countries or wherever I am in the world. A TV set, a car, a fridge, a washing machine is the same—works in the same way, does the same things—all over the world and, indeed, necessarily so if there is to be a common world in which all of us can be and act, no matter where we are. Thus, the essence of television is to be found not so much in the television industries of different countries and their linguistically encoded outputs, but in the universal form of the technology and its communicative constraints and affordances. The technology, of course, is not some static thing. Nor is it imposed on history from above by the invisible hand of God or the market.

It is never a transcendent supervening necessity but is historical through and through. The history of television-as-technology is, on one hand, as Frosh (2009) has pointed out, the history of innovation in the design of receiving sets; on the other hand, there has been continuous industry-driven innovation in distribution technologies, recording equipment, and television camera design (three crucial and neglected aspects of media studies), and these have had immediate, sought-for, and lasting effects on the scope and scale of program making.

Two areas of television production have consistently taken the lead in techno-logical innovation: news and sport. Both operate in the here and now and depend on and exploit the live immediacy of television. Both are, in different ways, con-cerned with worldly events, and it is through televised news and sport, as much as anything, that all of us now know and understand that we are living in a com-mon world in which all our lives are interconnected. Garry Whannel (2009, this issue) shows how sport has been transformed by television into what it is today: a truly global phenomenon, with key events in premier sports drawing huge worldwide audiences. And this transformation—from local and amateur to global and professional—was brought about by sought-for innovations in transmission, distribution, and coverage that combined to improve, in seen but unnoticed ways, the experience of sporting events for audiences not present at the event itself.

News was powerfully driven in similar ways by the imperatives of immediacy, and the hidden history of its technological development into the global thing that it is today has much in common with that of innovations in sports transmission and coverage. In both cases it has become increasingly evident that television does not function as an observer and presenter of live events (a mere onlooker with no effect on what is happening) but has become part of the structure of the events themselves, impacting on the ways in which they are managed by those ultimately responsible for them: the national and international governing bodies of various sports and military and political leaders in times of war. The "CNN effect" became something that the American military and political authorities had to take into account in the Gulf War of 1991, adjusting their strategy accord-ingly. This is but one recent instance of the impact of broadcast news on politics and diplomacy, as Monroe Price (2009, this issue) makes clear.

IV

When Elizabeth Eisenstein tried to assess the historical impact of the printed book, she looked back over a time span of five hundred years (Eisenstein 1979; see Baron, Lindquist, and Shevlin [2007] for a review of the impact on scholar-ship of Eisenstein's pioneering study). As we struggle to evaluate the effect of television on the world so far, we are working with a span of seventy years at most. As our collective efforts show, the outputs of television, in all their diversity, have only recently entered into the historical record, thereby becoming historical and retrievable and analyzable as such. We can now begin to look at television of the past fifty or more years, not only country by country but on a comparative transnational basis to see what the output discloses about the world-historical character of social and cultural life, the politics of everyday life routinely in play in day-to-day output. Television is now revealed, through the whole range of its content, as a prime historical record and a prime historical agent of the late twentieth century. The study of television output begins to disclose the play of the historical process, the work in the present of generational renewal, continuity, and change. It can do so only insofar as the output of television, in all its parts and as a whole, can be taken and trusted as a true and reliable record of what was going on in the world at the time. We have yet to begin to engage with the crucial methodological issues at stake in such an assumption since so far most of the output of television has been treated as part of the present, not the past.

The subtitle of *Media Events* was "The Live Broadcasting of History" (Dayan and Katz 1992). Most discussion of this canonic text has focused on its ceremonial aspects—the ritual character of media events situated within the framework of Durkheimian sociology. Less attention has been paid to the historical character of events—Braudel's *histoire événementielle*. But the connection between events and history is fundamental—no events, no history. The uneventful life is unhistorical—there is nothing to be said of it. In the fall of 2008 an event took place that today's media are hailing as historic: the election of Barack Obama as the next president of the United States. Election night, November 4, 2008, was and will be remembered as a classic "media event," an unforgettable instance of "the live broadcasting of history." The meaning and significance of this historic moment lies in the future and is, at present, beyond conjecture despite the news channels' attempts. How the Obama presidency will impact American and world history will and can only become apparent several generations from now. Today we talk and hope, but we cannot really say.

To focus on media events is indeed to attend to the live broadcasting of history, history in the making, in the vivid immediacy of the here and now. It does not, however, yield insights into the historicalness of media *as such*. That question requires a different way of thinking about media effects in which the focus shifts from the historical life of human beings to the historical life of humanly made things. What connects the question of the impact of printing with the impact of television? It is surely to do with the effect of newly invented things, the things that constitute the material culture of the material world, in which, as Madonna succinctly reminded us, you know that we all live. If we ask what print, radio, and television have in common, we might say two things about them—they are tech-nologies of dissemination and record. They broadcast (disseminate, scatter) human knowledge and understanding in the widest sense. They also preserve, for the record, the historically produced and situated knowledge and understandings that they contain. If one definition of the unhistorical is the uneventful, its other definition is the unrecorded. History begins with events but only becomes his-torical as it is recorded. We read books and watch television for their contents, whose meaning and significance have a never-ending fascination that we end-lessly discuss in and out of academia. But questions of the impact of printing or of television require an entirely different focus on the materiality of the things that provide the contents they disclose and the ways we engage with them.

Our collective thinking about television has considered it as such and in relation to other electronic technologies of communication, with similar and different affordances, that come before and after it. Material things cannot be thought of in isolation from the other things with which they coexist and with which they combine to endow the everyday world in which we live. When Raymond Williams tried, in the early 1970s, to consider the material culture of which television was a then very new component part, he looked back fifty years to the emergent consumer culture of the interwar period. He identified the radio set and the small family car as significant indices of a new way of life characterized by what he called "mobile privatization." In *Television: Technology and Cultural Form* (1974), Williams tried to hold together two distinct ways of thinking about television: as technology *and* as cultural form. When he addressed, in the opening chapters, the question of television-as-technology, he did so within a long-term framework—television as the terminus ad quem of innovations in electronic technologies going back a hundred years or more. When he addressed television as a cultural form in the following chapters, he tried to capture the forms of television in the present and in terms of their industry-defined genres (news, documentaries, and so on), their distribution and reception as a continuing flow. He then proceeded to the question of the impact and effect of television under both aspects, as a distinctive technology of communication with distinctive applications and uses developed by the television industry. What he crucially tried to retrieve in considering both was a proper balance between structure and agency, between determinate structures and a human intentionality inscribed in them.

Williams reminds us that in the history of the development of electronic media of communication, it was always the technology that preceded its cultural forms—its applications and uses. It is simply ingenuous to think of television today as an "old" technology. It would be so only if it had not, since its inception, undergone continuing innovation and change both as a technology and in its applied usage. Of course it is not what it was six decades ago, and our task, in this collection, has been to distinguish between the short and the long term and to try and read the past in the present, the present in the past, in the thus far short life of television. I think we can assume that five hundred years from now there will be television, just as now we have lived through five hundred years of printing. Television is as basic as the book, which it has no more destroyed than the Internet is likely to destroy it, or the book for that matter. The challenge, which we have tried to address, is to think of television not to the exclusion of other technologies with which it coexists but as a central component of a globally connected, communicatively joined-up world that is today routinely disclosed to all of us as such through worldwide television output. As for its impact and effect—while this is experienced and responded to in the present, it only begins to become apparent in the past. This basic historical truth is what television as a technology and cultural form most basically discloses.

References

Adorno, T., and M. Horkheimer. [1946]1986. *Dialectic of enlightenment*. London: Verso.

Baron, S. A., E. N. Lindquist, and E. E. Shevlin. 2007. *Agent of change; print culture studies after Elizabeth L. Eisenstein*. Amherst: University of Massachusetts Press.

Blondheim, Menahem, and Tamar Liebes. 2009. "Television newsand the nation: The end?" *Annals of the American Academcy of Political and Social Science*, 625:182-195.

Braudel, F. 1980. *On history*. London, UK: Weidenfeld and Nicolson.

Bremer, J., and H. Roodenberg. 1993. *A cultural history of gesture*. Cambridge, UK: Polity.

Burke, P. 1993. *The art of conversation*. Cambridge, UK: Polity.

Cantril, H., H. Gaudet, and H. Herzog. 1940. *The invasion from Mars: A study in the psychology of panic*. Princeton, NJ: Princeton University Press.

Dayan, Daniel. 2009. "Sharing and showing: Television as monstration." *Annals of the American Academy of Political and Social Science*, 625:19-31.

Dayan, D., and E. Katz. 1992. *Media events*. Cambridge, MA: Harvard University Press.

Douglas, S. 1994. *Where the girls are: Growing up female with the mass media*. New York: Times Books.

Eisenstein, E. 1979. *The printing press as an agent of change: Communications and cultural transformations in early modern Europe*. 2 vols. Cambridge: Cambridge University Press.

Ellis, John. 2009. "The performance on television of sincerely felt emotion." *Annals of the American Academy of Political and Social Science*, 625:103-115.

Frosh, Paul. 2009. "The face of television." *Annals of the American Academy of Political and Social Science*, 625:87-102.

Giddens, A. 1991. *The consequences of modernity*. Cambridge, UK: Polity.

Goffman, E. [1959] 1971. *The presentation of self in everyday life*. Harmondsworth, UK: Pelican.

Goodin, R., Rice, M., Parpo, A., and Eriksson, L. 2008. *Discretionary time*. Cambridge: Cambridge University Press.

Hall, S., and M. Jacques. 1989. *New times*. London: Lawrence and Wishart.

Harvey, D. 1989. *The condition of postmodernity*. Oxford, UK: Blackwell.

Heilbroner, R. L. 1994. Do machines make history? In *Does technology drive history? The dilemmas of technological determinism*, ed. M. R. Smith and L. Marx. Cambridge, MA: MIT Press.

Hutchby, I. 2006. *Media talk: Conversation analysis and the study of broadcasting*. Milton Keynes, PA: Open University Press.

Innis, H. 1962. *The fur trade in Canada*. Toronto: University of Toronto Press.

Katz, E., and P. Lazarsfeld. 1955. *Personal influence. The part played by people in the flow of mass communications*. Glencoe, IL: Free Press.

Lazarsfeld, P., and R. K. Merton. 1948/2004. Mass communication, popular taste and organized social action. In *Mass communication and American social thought*, ed. J. D. Peters and P. Simonson, 230-41. Lanham, MD: Rowman & Littlefield.

Livingstone, Sonia. 2009. "Half a century of television in the lives of our children." *Annals of the American Academy of Political and Social Science*, 625:151-163.

Lotz, A. 2006. *Redesigning women: Television after the network era*. Urbana-Champagne: University of Illinois Press.

Lunt, Peter. 2009. "Television, public participation, and public service: From value consensus to the politics of identity." *Annals of the American Academy of Political and Social Science*, 625:128-138.

———. 2007. *The television will be revolutionized*. New York: New York University Press.

Merton, R. K. [1946] 2004. *Mass persuasion*. Edited and with an Introduction by P. Simonson. New York: Howard Fertig.

Meyrowitz, J. 1985. *No sense of place: The impact of electronic media on social behavior*. New York: Oxford University Press.

———. 1994. Medium theory. In *Communication theory today*, ed. D. Crowley and D. Mitchell. Cambridge, UK: Polity.

———. 2003. Canonic anti-text: Marshall McLuhan's *Understanding media*. In *Canonic texts in media research*, ed. E. Katz , J. D. Paters, T. Liebes and A. Orloff. Cambridge, UK: Polity.

————. 2009. "We liked to watch: Television as progenitor of the surveillance society." *Annals of the American Academy of Political and Social Science*, 625:32-48.

Montgomery, M. 2007. *The discourse of broadcast news*. London: Routledge.

Press, Andrea. 2009. "The end of television: Gender and family in television's golden age and beyond." *Annals of the American Academy of Political and Social Science*, 625:139-150.

Price, Monroe E. 2009. "End of television and foreign policy." *Annals of the American Academy of Political and Social Science*, 625:196-204.

Putnam, R. D. 2000. *Bowling alone: The collapse and revival of American community*. New York: Simon & Schuster.

Robinson, John P and Steven Martin. 2009. "Of time and television." *Annals of the American Academy of Political and Social Science*, 625:74-86.

Scannell, Paddy. 2008. The question of technology. In *Narrating media history*, ed. M. Bailey. London: Routledge.

Spigel, L. 1992. *Make room for TV: Television and the family ideal in post-war America*. Chicago: University of Chicago Press.

Tolson, A. 2006. *Media talk*. Edinburgh, UK: Edinburgh University Press.

Whannel, Garry. 2009. "Television and the transformation of sport." *Annals of the American Academy of Political and Social Science*, 625:205-218.

Williams, R. [1958] 1962. *Culture and society*. Harmondsworth, UK: Pelican.

————. 1974. *Television: Technology and cultural form*. London: Fontana.

SAGE Journals Online
SAGE's Online Journal Delivery Platform

SAGE Journals Online allows users to search over 500 journals in business, humanities, social sciences, and science, technology and medicine and their related backfiles to retrieve peer-reviewed articles crucial to their research.

Features and functionality of the **SAGE Journals Online** platform include the following:

- Quick Search and Advanced Search (includes Fielded Boolean Search)
- Browse articles by title or by discipline using TopicMap
- My Tools feature, including Alerts, Saved Citations, Saved Searches, My Favorite Journals, and Manage My Account
- OnlineFirst (forthcoming articles published ahead of print)
- OpenURL 1.0 linking to articles
- Toll-free inter-journal linking to full text of cited articles in non-subscribed articles on the HighWire platform
- COUNTER-2 and SUSHI compliant usage statistics

- Enhanced PDF display (new, easier to navigate interface)
- Streaming video (coming soon on select titles)
- Spell Check feature in search (coming soon)
- Podcasting (select titles)
- PDA downloading (select titles, Palm devices only)
- Related articles in Google Scholar
- "Free/free to you" icons in content box
- Multilanguage abstracts (select titles)
- "Email this article to a friend"

Web 2.0 Features
- RSS feeds
- Social bookmarking

QUICK SEARCH

ADVANCED SEARCH

Visit http://online.sagepub.com to browse the SAGE Journals Online platform.

Winner of the PSP Award for Excellence for Best Platform

"HighWire Press pioneered the role of digital facilitator a decade ago to help publishers in developing their digital archives using intuitive and smart design. It has not been resting on its laurels but keeps introducing new features. Some of these grace the *SAGE Journals Online* collection."

—Péter Jacsó, *Reference Reviews*, Thomson Gale

SSAGE journals online